D1165918

IN THE JURY BOX

WITH CONTRIBUTIONS BY:

James J. Alfini
Robert M. Bray
Richard Christie
Robert Colman
Shari Seidman Diamond
Amiram Elwork
Barbara Emrich
Irwin A. Horowitz
Martin F. Kaplan
Saul M. Kassin
Norbert L. Kerr
Robert J. MacCoun

Lynn E. Miller
G. Thomas Munsterman
Martha A. Myers
Charlan Nemeth
Audrey M. Noble
Michael J. Saks
Bruce D. Sales
Jay Schulman
Phillip Shaver
David U. Strawn
Lawrence S. Wrightsman
Han Zeisel

IN THE
JURY
BOX
Controversies In
The Courtroom

EDITORS
Lawrence S. Wrightsman
Saul M. Kassin
Cynthia E. Willis

SAGE PUBLICATIONS
The Publishers of Professional Social Science
Newbury Park   Beverly Hills   London   New Delhi

For information address:

SAGE Publications, Inc.
2111 West Hillcrest Drive
Newbury Park, California 91320

SAGE Publications Inc.
275 South Beverly Drive
Beverly Hills
California 90212

SAGE Publications Ltd.
28 Banner Street
London EC1Y 8QE
England

SAGE PUBLICATIONS India Pvt. Ltd.
M-32 Market
Greater Kailash I
New Delhi 110 048 India

Printed in the United States of America

Library of Congress Cataloging-in-Publication Data

In the jury box.

(Controversies in the courtroom ; v. 1)
Bibliography: p.
1. Jury—United States.   2. Psychology, Forensic.
I. Wrightsman, Lawrence S.   II. Kassin, Saul M.
III. Willis, Cynthia E.   IV. Series.
KF8972.I5 1987   347.73'752   87-23371
ISBN 0-8039-3167-0   347.307752
ISBN 0-8039-3064-X (pbk.)

Contents

Overview

Jury trials have long fascinated and mystified the public, the news media, and legal scholars. Even those of us who have actually served on juries often cannot fully describe what a dramatic experience it is. While the process of forming a verdict is subtle and complex, it is also capable of measurement and understanding. Jurors are people and verdicts are their behavior. Only with an appreciation for state-of-the-art psychology, its concepts, and its research, can we fully understand their role in the courtroom drama.

In the last decade and a half, psychologists and other social scientists have begun to study these processes systematically. One of the merits of the empirical approach is that it can provide data that help resolve controversial issues. Does jury selection "work"? Are jurors able to make unbiased judgments? Should complex civil cases be determined by an experienced judge rather than a set of novice jurors? Does it make any difference in verdicts if the size of the jury is reduced or the decision rule is changed?

Each of these is a challenging question, for which there is plausible speculation to support a variety of answers. This book is a collection of articles from the professional literature—mostly psychological journals and law reviews—relevant to the above questions. The book is divided into four sections, each on a different aspect of jury process. Each section contains three or four reprinted articles, plus an introduction and summary prepared by the editors for this volume. The latter materials place the articles in an appropriate context, bring the issue up to date, and provide conclusions.

Designed for a broad interdisciplinary audience, *In the Jury Box: Controversies in the Courtroom* is of use as a supplement in undergraduate psychology-and-law courses and criminal justice courses. It also has value for advanced general psychology courses and honors courses that aim to provide students a mix of theory, empirical research, and applications to policy issues.

Legal scholars, trial judges, and practicing attorneys will find in this collection of reprinted articles a number of provocative ideas relevant to trial work.

Preface

In the last two decades social psychologists and other social scientists have been increasingly responsive to the demand that they make their studies relevant to the real world. The courtroom has become one of the prime real-world settings for the testing of their theories and the application of their concepts.

When one discipline "invades the turf" of another, controversy is inevitable. Every discipline has its own view, its way of describing the world, its way of gaining new knowledge about the world. There is a temptation to conclude that one discipline's view is "correct" and another's is "faulty," when, in actuality, each may be perceiving the same phenomenon through different conceptual filters.

The purpose of this book is to highlight some of the controversies that emerge when social scientists examine the behavior of jurors and juries. We have identified four aspects of the jury trial process that, we believe, are justifiably entitled "controversial" because there remains for each a difference of opinion within disciplines or between disciplines. The four topics are jury selection, jury bias, jury competence, and the recent Supreme Court decisions that reduce the size of juries and permit less-than-unanimous verdicts. We have selected, for reprinting, three or four articles for each section; some of these articles are reviews of the literature; many are reports of empirical studies; a few reflect opinions of experts in the field. Most of these articles were originally published in psychological journals; a few are from law reviews. Authors of these articles come from a variety of disciplines: social psychology, journalism, experimental psychology, communications, and the legal profession.

Several special features have been employed to increase the value of the book as a learning device. Each section contains an introduction and a summary written for this volume. The purposes of the introductions are to define the concepts under study, to place them in a historical perspective, and to alert the reader to the significant aspects and relationships in the selections that follow. The purposes of the summaries are to highlight the basic findings in the articles, to describe other recent work on the issue, to attempt to resolve conflicting findings, and to point out unanswered questions. Original bibliographies have been retained, so that readers can pursue the topic in more depth if they wish.

This book of readings has a multitude of uses. In conjunction with its companion volume, *On the Witness Stand: Controversies in the Courtroom*, the material in this volume is appropriate for the increasing number of undergraduate courses on the psychology of the law or the psychology of the criminal justice system. A significant proportion of the coverage in such courses relates to the trial process and specifically to jury trials. Textbooks appropriate for such courses cover the issues examined in this volume and often refer to the specific articles reprinted in this book; the supplementary use of this book and its companion book provides further detail on findings, more extensive reviews of the literature, and expositions of methodology. Another use of this book is in social issues courses and advanced social psychology courses that concentrate on recent applied research topics. A further application is in law school courses in trial advocacy and similar courses that seek collections of empirical work relevant to the task of the trial attorney. Scholars may find the compilation of recent articles from a variety of sources to be a useful resource for teaching and research ideas.

We wish to thank a number of people who assisted in the preparation of this book. Charles T. Hendrix, Executive Editor for Sage Publications, Inc., supported our pleas for this rather different approach to psychology and the law; he was quite helpful in adapting to our needs to produce a comprehensive set of materials. Julie A. Allison assisted in the collection of articles and preparation of introductions and summaries. We especially want to thank the authors and the publishers of the selections for permission to reprint this material. We have benefited from our reading of these articles and are pleased to assist in providing the opportunity for others to do so, too.

—*Lawrence S. Wrightsman*
University of Kansas
—*Saul M. Kassin*
Williams College
—*Cynthia E. Willis*
University of Kansas

SECTION I

JURY SELECTION
Introduction

Jury selection is an inevitable aspect of American trials. As long as attorneys are granted peremptory challenges—the opportunity to dismiss a certain number of prospective jurors without giving reasons why—decisions must be made about which persons to strike.

What is the goal of jury selection? Do social scientists have insights that aid attorneys in the jury selection process? What devices may attorneys use as they determine which panel members to dismiss? May they inquire into the personalities and values of prospective jurors and, if so, do these qualities predict how the jurors will behave during deliberations? Do potential jurors reflect their biases through their nonverbal behavior during the *voir dire*—the way they sit, where they look, how their voices sound when they answer questions? And finally, does "jury selection" make any difference; that is, do the juries that attorneys or social scientists select render different verdicts from those that would have been randomly chosen?

Many of these questions can be answered through the empirical research methods used by psychologists and other social scientists. The purpose of this section is to examine these questions by reprinting, first, a case history of social scientists selecting a jury, then a critique of the procedure, and finally, a careful empirical comparison of two methods of jury selection.

As chapter 1 indicates, some social scientists have not been content to play only the role of the researcher. They have brought both their political sympathies and their methodological skills to the aid of defense attorneys in the selection of the trial jury in some of the most highly publicized trials against war protesters. The trial described in chapter 1, the "Harrisburg Seven" trial, in 1972, was the first highly publicized one in which the techniques of "scientific jury selection" were employed. These procedures—including a community survey of demographic relationships to prevailing attitudes as well as the procedures used in assessing individual prospective jurors—are described fully in this chapter.

"Scientific jury selection" has been scrutinized, evaluated, and criticized on a number of grounds. Apparently disregarding the fact that from time immemorial attorneys have relied on their own hunches, stereotypes, and unfounded assumptions in striking "biased" jurors, some critics have charged that the procedures are unethical. A more comprehensive and reasonable evaluation is presented in chapter 2 by Michael J. Saks, formerly of Boston College and now on the faculty of the University of Iowa School of Law.

This chapter recommends caution about overgeneralizing the impact of scientific jury selection. It also notes that "no evidence exists to support the apparent widely held belief that scientific jury selection is a power(ful) tool. . . . Suppose each of the worrisome cases had been tried before two juries—one selected the scientific way and one selected the old way. We could then compare the verdicts delivered by scientific juries with those delivered by the conventional juries." More recently, such a comparison has been carried out, and is reprinted as chapter 3. In this empirical study, Irwin A. Horowitz of the University of Toledo used four different criminal cases to determine if juries selected by social science methods produced verdicts different from those of juries selected by methods that lawyers conventionally used.

In the section summary, we will describe both the effectiveness and the ethical appropriateness of such activities by social scientists.

1

RECIPE FOR A JURY

JAY SCHULMAN
Columbia University
PHILLIP SHAVER
University of Denver
ROBERT COLMAN
BARBARA EMRICH
RICHARD CHRISTIE
Columbia University

A group of social scientists helped Ramsey Clark, Leonard Boudin and other defense attorneys in the conspiracy trial of the Harrisburg Seven. Their problem: Could a few favorable jurors be found, in a fundamentally conservative area, to try unpopular antiwar activists? The defendants, from Philip Berrigan to Eqbal Ahmad, were dramatically accused of plotting to raid draft boards, blow up heating tunnels in Washington, and kidnap Henry Kissinger. Here is the researchers'

REPRINTED WITH PERMISSION FROM *PSYCHOLOGY TODAY* MAGAZINE
Copyright © 1973 American Psychological Association

report of what they did, right and wrong, and what they learned about the American jury system.

In late November 1970, J. Edgar Hoover appealed to Congress for additional funds to control antiwar protesters and militants. The "East Coast Conspiracy to Save Lives," he said, made up of Catholic priests, nuns, and students, was plotting to kidnap a "highly placed Government official" and to blow up underground electrical conduits in Washington, DC. Hoover named Philip and Daniel Berrigan, Catholic priests, as principal leaders of the plot.

The Berrigan brothers had been irritating the FBI for several years. As members of the loose-knit Catholic "Resistance," they had been involved in many antiwar protests. In October of 1967 Philip and three friends poured blood—the Catholic symbol of purity—on draft-board records in Baltimore; this was the first of more than 25 such raids by the Resistance. The following May, Philip, Daniel, and seven others destroyed Selective Service records at Catonsville, Maryland, with homemade napalm. The dramatic trial of the Catonsville Nine led to a three-year prison sentence for Daniel Berrigan, and a three-and-a-half year sentence for Philip (to run concurrently with the six-year term he drew for the Baltimore raid). Philip was sent to Lewisburg Federal Penitentiary in late April 1970; and after eluding the FBI for four months, Daniel was caught in August and sent to the Danbury, Connecticut, Federal Correctional Institution, where Philip was later transferred.

But Hoover did not give up. The brothers continued to pester him by sending out antiwar messages, recruiting convicts to their cause, and staying in contact with other protesters even while they were in prison. Hoover's statement to Congress was followed by a decision in the Justice Department to prepare an indictment that provided names and specific charges. Accused in the final indictment were:

— Father Philip Berrigan, 48 (Daniel was listed in the original indictment but later dropped)
— Sister Elizabeth McAlister, 32, a New York nun who was closely involved with Philip Berrigan
— Father Joseph Wenderoth, 35, a member of the East Coast Conspiracy to Save Lives
— John Theodore Glick, 22, also a member of the East Coast Conspiracy, who was later tried separately
— Father Neil R. McLaughlin, 30
— Anthony Scoblick, 30, an ex-priest
— Mary Cain Scoblick, 32, an ex-nun
— Eqbal Ahmad, 40, a Pakistani who described himself as "odd man out" of this group of resisters

The government had itemized all of the draft-board raids that the defendants, individually or severally, had taken credit for or been suspected of. The indictment then accused the seven of conspiring to raid draft boards and destroy records; of conspiring to kidnap presidential advisor Henry Kissinger (the "high Government official" Hoover had mentioned); and of conspiring to blow up heating tunnels in Washington. Finally, Berrigan and McAlister were charged with several counts of smuggling letters in and out of Lewisburg Prison, where Berrigan was serving time for the Catonsville protest.

The government apparently chose Harrisburg, Pennsylvania, as a site for the trial because it is in a politically conservative area. The indictment had specifically mentioned draft-board raids in Philadelphia, New York, Rochester, and "other parts of the United States," but the Justice Department preferred the middle judicial district of Pennsylvania.

Even within the middle district, the government had a choice among Harrisburg, Lewisburg, and Scranton. Lewisburg is a college town, and Scranton contains a higher proportion of Catholics, Democrats, and sometimes militant mine workers than the government presumably found desirable. Harrisburg, by contrast, has three Republicans for every two Democrats; an unusually low proportion of Catholics and an unusually high proportion of fundamentalist religious sects; several military installations and war-related industries; and an active Ku Klux Klan.

Federal District Judge R. Dixon Herman, 60, a recent Nixon appointee, presided over the trial, which promised to be the most important of his career. The prosecution was led by William S. Lynch, 44, on leave from his regular duties as head of the Organized Crime and Racketeering Section in the Criminal Division of the Justice Department (he characterized the defendants as "more dangerous" than organized criminals and argued against reduced bail). Assisting Lynch were William Connelly, Phillip Krajewski, Paul Killion, and S. John Cottone. The Justice Department insisted that the all-Catholic team was "pure coincidence," but it is more likely that it wanted to head off accusations of anti-Catholicism.

Seven lawyers formed the defense team: former Attorney General Ramsey Clark; Paul O'Dwyer, who had been Democratic candidate for the U.S. Senate from New York; appellate lawyer Leonard Boudin and his associate Diane Schulder; Terry Lenzner, former head of legal services for the Office of Economic Opportunity; J. Thomas Menaker, from a wealthy Harrisburg law firm; and the Reverend William Cunningham, Professor of Criminal Law at Loyola.

The trial began on January 24, 1972, more than a year after the original indictment. The case hinged on the testimony and credibility of Boyd F. Douglas, Jr., an FBI informer who had smuggled letters between Philip Berrigan and Elizabeth McAlister. Douglas had been part of a Lewisburg Prison-Bucknell University study program. At the college, he played the part of an antiwar activist and informed on a number of persons, including two young women to whom he proposed marriage in the process of getting their help. Douglas was on the stand for 14 days of testimony and cross-examination.

The letters between Berrigan and McAlister added an emotional element to the trial. The prosecution read passages to support its charge that the two were conspiring; the defense argued that the two were close friends, in love, who wanted to keep each other encouraged about the resistance movement.

Lynch rested the Government's case on March 23, having presented 64 witnesses. Of these, only Douglas had been crucial to the kidnap-bombing charge. Ramsey Clark argued for a directed verdict of acquittal, on the grounds that the Government had presented "such flimsy evidence"; but Judge Herman denied his motion.

The next day, Clark stunned the court with an opening statement that "the defendants continue to proclaim their innocence—and the defense rests." The defense had decided abruptly not to call any witnesses, not even to let the defendants state their own case.

The jurors began their deliberations on Thursday, March 30, and reached a decision after seven days. They found Father Berrigan and Sister McAlister guilty of smuggling letters. But they were hopelessly deadlocked on the principal charges of conspiracy; 10 voted for acquittal, 2 voted guilty. The government's $2 million effort ended in a mistrial on those counts.

"It was a bitter end for J. Edgar Hoover's great kidnap-bombing conspiracy case," noted reporters Jack Nelson and Ronald J. Ostrow (The FBI and the Berrigans). "Even [William F. Buckley's] National Review called it 'the greatest Federal fizzle of recent years.'"

Unlike the trial of the Catonsville Nine, the Harrisburg conspiracy trial was not a morality play. There was no clear principle or political action at stake that would make going to jail a moral victory for the defendants.

Moreover, the scales of justice were by no means balanced in this case. We felt that the government's use of publicity (e.g., Hoover's original provocative announcement), its reliance on informers and agent provocateurs, its choice of Harrisburg, and its attempts to discredit and silence antiwar activists made it unlikely that the defendants would receive a fair trial. By *fair* we meant simply a trial in which the *jury would assume them innocent unless proven guilty beyond a reasonable doubt.*

All of these reasons, along with our strong antiwar feelings, led us, a coalition of social scientists, activists, and citizens, to offer assistance to the defense. We focused our efforts on the selection of a jury that would be less conservative than the Justice Department had anticipated.

There were few precedents for collaboration between lawyers and social scientists. For example, Jeffrey M. Paige, a sociologist at the University of California at Berkeley, and students had conducted a telephone survey to provide evidence that the Angela Davis trial should be moved. Their effort was successful. Also in the Davis case, black psychologists Harold Dent, Thomas Hilliard, William Pierce, and William Hayes systematically observed jurors, evaluating them for her lawyers. Dennis McElrath and Walter Goldfrank of the University of California, Santa Cruz, made a similar survey in Monterey county after guards were killed in Soledad Prison. They interviewed a number of "opinion leaders" and found that most of them assumed that the black prisoners who had been charged with murder were in fact guilty.

We expected that the characteristics of the jury would be critical to the outcome of the trial for several reasons. The complexity of the formal charges left considerable room for the jurors' ideological and moral predilections to influence their verdict. The jurors would have to consider the government's evidence for several very different alleged overt acts and then interpret the vague concept of conspiracy.

THE PHONE SURVEY

We decided first to survey registered voters in the area around Harrisburg, the population from which the jury ultimately would be selected.

The Harrisburg Defense Committee obtained the demographic characteristics of persons in the existing jury wheel or panel (e.g. sex, age, education, occupation, and race). We wanted to compare the panel with a random sample of registered voters. If the panel represented currently registered voters, the two groups should be statistically similar.

With the help of the defense committee and the Harrisburg Center for Peace and Justice (a group that had formed some time before to deal with political issues), we got the most recent list of voters registered in the 11 counties of the middle judicial district of Pennsylvania. From these we drew a proportional sample of 1,236 people to be interviewed by telephone. The interviewers were students, members of the peace movement, and other citizens, and they completed 840 phone calls. Respondents were generally quite willing to be interviewed. In addition to demographic questions, we asked respondents whom they would favor for president in the 1972 election, to give us a better feel for political attitudes in the area.

We found that members of the random sample were, on the average, younger than people in the available panel. Partly on the basis of this evidence, which defense lawyers presented to Judge R. Dixon Herman, a new panel was selected before a jury was chosen.

THE IN-DEPTH SURVEY

The success of the phone-interview project led us to believe that it would be useful to conduct longer interviews with a subset of our sample. We trained 45 volunteers from Harrisburg and York to do face-to-face interviewing in respondents' homes. Although a few of the volunteers were young and had long hair, most were older and looked "straight." With the help of these people, the interviewing was completed at no cost.

Because time was limited (this was late autumn 1971 and the trial was due to start at the beginning of 1972) we reinterviewed 252 people from our original group of 840, concentrating on the four counties around Harrisburg. This group was representative of potential jury members. We focused on a variety of issues that we thought would be relevant to a juror's attitudes and ability to be impartial.

(1) *Media contact.* The respondent's choice of newspapers, magazines, radio and television stations, and his or her degree of contact with these media.

(2) *Knowledge of the defendants and their case.* We asked respondents whether and what they had heard about some "people in the news lately." Philip Berrigan and Elizabeth McAlister were embedded in a list containing Henry Kissinger, Johnny Carson, Spiro Agnew, Angela Davis, Sophia Loren, Martha Mitchell, Joe Namath, and Hugh Scott.

(3) *The greatest Americans during the past 10 to 15 years,* An open-ended probe designed to reveal the respondent's values.

(4) *Trust in government.* Over the past few years, the University of Michigan's Survey Research Center has found a remarkable decline in trust of the government, which seems to be closely linked to dissatisfaction with the government's handling of the Vietnam War. We used the center's three standard "trust" questions: "How much of the time do you think you can trust the Government in Washington to do what is right?"; "Do you feel that the people running the Government are smart people who usually know what they are doing?"; and "Would you say the Government is pretty much run for a few big interests looking out for themselves, or is it run for the benefit of the people?"

(5) *Ages and activities of respondents' children.*

(6) *Religious attitudes and commitment.*

(7) *Spare-time activities,* such as hunting, community-service work, and so on.

(8) *Organization memberships,* such as the Veterans of Foreign Wars, the American Legion, volunteer police and fire departments, the Kiwanis, the Masons, and the Lions.

(9) *Attitudes that were potentially related to the trial.* We asked for extent of agreement with eight statements, such as "The right to private property is sacred"; "People should support their country even when they feel strongly that Federal authorities are wrong"; "Police should not hesitate to use force to maintain order"; and "If the authorities go to the trouble of bringing someone to trial in a court, the person is almost always guilty."

(10) *Scale of acceptable antiwar activities.* To assess the respondent's support or rejection of the defendants' views and actions, we asked seven questions that indicate a person's degree of tolerance for protest activities. The scale ran from "Accepted what the Government is doing and keep quiet about one's feelings" to "Become part of a revolutionary group which attempts to stop the Government from carrying on the war by bombing buildings or kidnapping officials."

THE "BAD" CHARACTERISTICS

Some of the findings turned out to be most useful. We discovered, for example, that religion was significantly related to all the attitudes that concerned us. We therefore recommended that the lawyers should ask prospective jurors about religion, which they had been reluctant to do; and that certain religious categories—for example, Episcopalians, Presbyterians, Methodists, and fundamentalists—were "bad" enough from our point of view to warrant exclusion from the jury unless there were strong reasons to the contrary. (The "better" religions were Catholic, Brethren, and Lutheran.)

Education and contact with metropolitan news media, which usually are linked with liberal attitudes, were associated in our sample with *conservatism*. College-educated people, especially over 30, were more likely to be Republicans, to be businessmen, to be members of local civic organizations. They were more likely to read metropolitan newspapers, but were also more likely to read conservative magazines. Later we learned that liberal college-educated people and younger college graduates tend to leave Harrisburg for more liberal pastures. This fact was by no means obvious to us or to the defense lawyers before the survey, and it was to play an important part in the jury selection.

The sample was unusually conservative and trusting in government—some 80 percent showed trust compared with a national level of 45 percent to 50 percent. Low trust in government was a good sign for our position, since it related to liberal attitudes. Thus we suggested that the lawyers attempt to assess prospective jurors' trust in government.

The most popular magazine was *Reader's Digest*, which 39 percent of the sample read. The "great Americans of the last 10 to 15 years" included various U.S. presidents, Spiro Agnew, Bob Hope, Billy Graham, and three astronauts. (More liberal members of the sample mentioned Martin Luther King, Jr., Ralph Bunche, and Ralph Nader.) Whereas 93 percent of the sample could identify Johnny Carson, 37 percent had heard of Philip Berrigan. On key attitudes, 87 percent agreed that the right to private property is sacred; 65 percent thought one should support the country even when it is wrong; and 81 percent believed that police should use violence if necessary to maintain order.

THE IDEAL JUROR

Although sex and political party were not important predictors of attitudes, Democrats and women were slightly more liberal on several questions. When we looked at all of the background characteristics and attitudes from the survey, we could picture our ideal juror: a female Democrat with no religious preference and a white-collar job or a *skilled* blue-collar job. Further, a "good" defense juror would sympathize with some elements of the defendants' views regarding the Vietnam War, at least tolerate the rights of citizens to resist government policies nonviolently, and give signs that he or she would presume the defendants to be innocent until proven guilty.

EXAMINING PROSPECTIVE JURORS

In a federal case, unlike most state cases, the trial judge has complete control over the selection process. He decides which questions are to be asked, by whom, and to what depth; he also determines the number of peremptory challenges (dismissals without explanation) available to each side and the rules for their use. If a federal judge wills it, a jury for an important case can be chosen in several hours, as happened in the Dr. Benjamin Spock case.

We were not optimistic about the prospect of our questions being asked, considering that Judge Herman himself had many of the characteristics that identified a person as an undesirable juror. William O'Rourke described him as "a Moose, a Lion, a Mason, an aviator, a hunter, a fisherman, a Legionnaire, a veteran." Even so, he allowed the defense great latitude in influencing the composition of the jury, and he allowed the defense 28 peremptory challenges, to the government's six.

Moreover, Judge Herman also allowed the attorneys to frame their own questions, to address them directly to the prospective jurors, and to follow up and probe as they desired with only occasional interruption. It was our impression that Judge Herman had gone to great lengths to avoid successful defense appeals to higher courts on grounds of a biased jury selection.

On the first day of jury selection we met with the defense lawyers and presented a long memo that explained our survey results and suggested questions that the lawyers should ask. Our survey had led us to expect that at least four out of five persons who would qualify as jurors would be opposed to the defendants. So we stressed the importance of questioning the jury panel for as long as possible, getting unfavorable people rejected for cause, and holding out for the statistically rare but desirable people sketched by our survey findings.

EXCUSING THE WELL-SCHOOLED

During the first day, Judge Herman questioned the panel of jurors as a group—focusing primarily on their biases, exposure to pretrial publicity, and their varied reasons for not wanting to serve on the jury.

Many people excused themselves immediately because they had read about the trial and had already had some thoughts about it. We expected the better-educated, more widely read people to be conservative; so we were pleased when they excused themselves. Nevertheless, the defense lawyers were uneasy. Their intuitions, like ours earlier, were that well-informed prospective jurors would be more "reasonable," open-minded, and liberal than the average.

To compare the survey with our hunches, we called the people who had excused themselves on the first day. We reached 20 of them. Of these, 14 admitted that they were biased against the defendants, 1 leaned in their favor, and 5 refused to answer our questions. The 14 who favored a guilty verdict explained that the defendants weren't "doing what they should be doing as Christians"; or that priests and nuns and teachers should have nothing to do with political issues; or that "If they were accused on 20 to 30 counts, they must be guilty." One interviewee said: "When I saw the demonstrators outside the courthouse, that trash, I felt they [the defendants] must be guilty if that trash was following them around."

On the basis of our calls, the defense lawyers decided not to object to Judge Herman's procedure, since it seemed that it worked in favor of the defendants.

If a person passed the judge's questions, Prosecuting Attorney William Lynch took over. Lynch seldom took more than five minutes to question a prospective juror. In Harrisburg, he seemed to think, one juror was almost as good as another from the government's point of view.

Ramsey Clark led off the defense questions in a folksy and comfortable manner, asking about the juror's family, connections with the military, and so on. Next, Thomas Menaker, the local defense lawyer, asked the person about his or her job, where he or she had gone to school, where he or she lived, what church he or she attended, and so on; that is, most of the important demographic questions from our survey. Since Menaker had lived in the Harrisburg area all his life, it was easy for him to ask such questions in the course of conversation. Finally, Leonard Boudin and Paul O'Dwyer probed the person's attitudes toward the government and the war.

SELECTING THE JURORS

It took three weeks to thin down the panel of 465 prospective jurors to 46. Peremptory challenges on both sides—6 and 28—would then reduce this number to 12. (Six alternates were also selected from the 465, but they did not play a role in the trial.) Of the 46, the defense had rated 14 as "very good" or "good" from its vantage point. The rest were quite conservative. Even some of the 14 would be classed as conservative by national standards, although the defense lawyers had used their latitude in questioning successfully to reduce the government's advantage. The judge excused 22 people for probable bias as a result of the defense lawyers' examinations. Only 2 were excused at the request of the prosecution.

The judge's decision to sequester the jury, which the defense had opposed, was a big help to the defense. For whatever reasons (age, infirmity, potential business losses), "bad" defense jurors seemed more likely than good ones to opt out of jury service by stating the escape formula, "I have formed an opinion." The prospect of sequestration for four to five months upped the ante for prospective jurors who, as one of them said, "wanted to show those defendants." Thus Judge Herman's desire to protect the jurors from harassment by demonstrators, friends of the defendants, and sympathetic reporters, helped to provide a better jury for the defendants.

THE RATING SYSTEM

After each court session, the defense (some 15 to 16 lawyers, defendants, and social scientists) retired to a conference room to unbend, talk about new developments, and discuss and rate prospective jurors on a one- to five-point scale. A rating of one signified a very good defense juror; two, a good defense juror; three, a juror who showed both negatives and positives or could not be placed; four and five, undesirable defense jurors. The lawyers decided to rate all blacks as two unless there was compelling information to the contrary. The purpose of the ratings was to guide our use of peremptory challenges.

Ramsey Clark acted as rating setter, discussion leader, and bookkeeper through all of the hectic rating sessions. Other key participants in these discussions were Tom Menaker, the Harrisburg lawyer; Jay Schulman; and the only non-Catholic defendant, Eqbal Ahmad.

Menaker was the one person among the defense lawyers with direct experience of behavioral cues, styles, and attitudes in different elements of the local population. Through his extensive community and legal contacts, he developed "third-party" information on the backgrounds and attitudes of prospective jurors.

Although the Catholic defendants also wanted the best possible jury, their experiences and sensitivity led them to view jurors in ways different from ours. Sometimes they would express an opinion without fighting for it, in the hope that others would pick it up. Sometimes they left the matter to the "experts." Often they simply expressed faith in the capacities of individual jurors, regardless of their backgrounds and dispositions. It seemed as if some of the defendants wanted jurors whose souls could be won.

Eqbal Ahmad was quite different. A Pakistani, veteran journalist and observer of North Africa, believer in the necessity of violent revolutions in Third-World nations, Princeton Ph.D. in political science, Ahmad was the cultural and political outsider in the group of defendants. His academic background, his marginality, and his politics disposed him to take jury selection very seriously. He thus took a more active role than the other defendants in discussing and rating prospective jurors.

THE DEFENSE VOTES

When the panel of 46 prospective jurors was complete, the defense had rated 8 jurors as one, 6 jurors as two, 15 jurors as three, and 17 jurors as four and five. At the last minute, however, the defense had to change one of its twos to a five. An elderly woman had lured us by announcing that her 90-year-old mother had told her, "Daughter, you go down to that court and do justice to both the defendants and the government." We thought she would be fair and independent. Fortunately, she had mentioned to an acquaintance that she really wanted to get on the jury to "show those Catholic priests and nuns." The acquaintance told this to someone else who passed it on to Menaker, who told us about it.

We anticipated that the government would use its peremptory challenges to eliminate six of our eight first choices, since all of these persons obviously were sympathetic to the defense. In fact, both sides appeared to agree on five characteristics of very good *defense* jurors:

(1) being under 30 years old; the closer to 18, the better
(2) being black
(3) possessing elements of a counterculture style of life
(4) showing strong opposition to the Vietnam War and sympathy for the defendants
(5) having a son or close male relative who was of or near draft age

Two factors underlie these five elements: opposition to authority and a social style in which maternalism exceeds patriarchy, whether in males or females. Youths, blacks who are oriented to "improving the lot of the race," and persons who adopt elements of the counterculture share an opposition to established forms of authority and power.

Indeed, Lynch peremptorily challenged six of our eight best candidates: a black woman, a black state civil-rights-enforcement official, a young blue-collar "hippie", a man who had boldly announced that Ramsey Clark was one of his heroes, and two women who had expressed strong antiwar views.

THE BENIGN SEVEN

Lynch's challenges left us seven jurors whom we considered to be "good" from the standpoint of the defense, two first choices and five second choices. They were, in order:

(1) Pauline Portzline, a housewife in her late 40s or early 50s, whose son-in-law had been killed in Vietnam. Concerning the war, she had said: "I wasn't too much opposed to it at first, but the last few years I've been against it." We considered this statement to be a good sign. She listed no church affiliation.

(2) Robert Foresman, a Lutheran, state-employed instructor of firemen, about 45 years old, married to a Catholic. Foresman mentioned that he "remembered reading that priests and nuns were planning to zip off with Henry Kissinger," and he went on to say that this struck him as ridiculous. Under questioning by defense lawyers he said he was convinced that the Vietnam War was a waste.

(3) June Jackson, a Presbyterian in her early 40s, a nonpracticing pharmacist, and mother of three. She gave no specific answers that implied that her values coincided with those of the defendants, but her answers to the lawyers' questions reflected intelligence, refinement, sensitivity, and tolerance.

(4) Vera Thompson, a black Methodist in her late 40s and mother of two sons, one of whom had served as a medic in Vietnam. Thompson had been a semiskilled factory worker. Boudin and O'Dwyer asked her few questions, presumably because she was black, but she had impressed us as a wise and lively personality. We were not sure what to expect from her.

(5) Jo-An (Tracy) Stanovich, 31, a Methodist housewife. Menaker wanted her on the jury because the two of them had played together as children 20 years earlier. She seemed independent and reasonable, but we probably would not have favored her had it not been for Menaker's comments.

(6) Kathryn Schwartz, 68, mother of six children, including four older sons who were conscientious objectors on religious grounds. She and they were members of the United Brethren in Christ Church, which is formally a pacifist church. Under questioning, Schwartz made it clear that her sons had made their own decisions, without her influence. Unfortunately, the defense lawyers stopped questioning her as soon as they learned that she had four CO sons. This proved to be a serious mistake.

(7) Lawrence Evans, a Lutheran in his 50s, owner of two grocery stores. He said that he "couldn't be against hippies because I have some sons who look like that." On the war, he said, "More could be done and should be done to end the war. . . . I don't know whether we should be there or not."

About priests and nuns who oppose the Vietnam war, Evans declared, "The church people should do more of that." In retrospect, we wonder if Evans deliberately misrepresented his feelings. Unfortunately, we believed him and gave him a positive rating, despite his unfavorable occupational status as owner of a business. Even more than Kathryn Schwartz, Evans proved to be a terrible mistake.

SIZING UP THE MAYBES

At this point, the defense had to evaluate the 15 jurors rated three and identify the five best ones. Then we had to take into account alternative compositions of the jury, with the group dynamics that would result in each case. For example, who were the likely candidates for jury foreman? Who would be most likely to be elected? What would be the effects of an all-woman jury? Did it make sense to have one man with 11 women or should we select two males if we were to have any?

One problem in choosing among the possible jurors was the question of how far we should follow survey data and how far we should rely on impressions from the questioning of the panel. Often we compromised. The main use of surveys is to sort out *types of people,* not to pick out *individuals,* which was the issue at hand. The great danger and temptation was to use the survey results to select jurors mechanically. To paraphrase a defense lawyer, we had to avoid following "Saint Social Science" dogmatically.

First, we considered the young people in their 20s and 30s. We concentrated our attention on five women because they composed a possible jury subgroup. We wanted to choose at least three of these women who, along with Tracy Stanovich (a second choice), would likely seek out each other's company during the long sequestration. Also, we anticipated that one or more of these women would have a negative reaction to Boyd Douglas, the government's key witness.

Our first candidate fit the demographic requirements perfectly: She was young, white-collar, a member of the United Brethren Church, and married to a Catholic schoolteacher. However, we were suspicious on other grounds. She had told the judge that she restricted her newspaper reading almost entirely to the sports pages; and she had said, "I have no objections to [longhairs] if they keep themselves neat. If they look like they come out of a ragbag, I would give more weight to clean people." Also, when the defense asked about the propriety of Ahmad opposing the Vietnam War although an alien, she replied, "There are enough people in the United States questioning United States's institutions. We don't need an alien doing so!" This woman impressed us as a strong individual with a low tolerance for ambiguity and dissent and highly accepting of authority, even though she matched some prodefense survey characteristics. We rejected her.

The three women we chose also posed difficult decisions.

Ann Burnett was an enigma. Single, in her middle 20s, a social service technician, she had had three years at a women's liberal arts college. Lynch, suspicious, had asked his favorite screening question, "Have you ever read the *Harrisburg Independent Press* [a paper favorable to the defense]"? Burnett answered, "I saw the *HIP* on a table at work, glanced at it, but didn't read it since it looked dull."

By our survey criteria, she was a "natural." However, she had confounded the defense by her contradictory answers on the witness stand. She told Boudin, "Sometimes I feel that the war is wrong and at other times I feel that it is justified." She explained, "Whatever one person has, property, pride, freedom, you want to defend it. Suppose we were invaded. I don't know. We haven't been invaded. I don't feel I could kill anyone. It has been said that this war gives people a choice of government. I don't accept or reject this argument." The defense raters had concluded that Burnett had no coherent opinions or she was deliberately creating a smokescreen to disguise her real sentiments. Fortunately, our scouts in the community learned that she had dated—among others—a black man, read a good deal of social and political philosophy, and liked elements of the counterculture.

Patricia Schafer, 31, posed a different problem for us. Her life experience generally ran counter to what we wanted, but her testimony suggested open-mindedness and her demography, including a stated lack of religious affiliation, was favorable. She and her family had lived for at least 10 years near military bases in the United States and Thailand (her husband worked on military installations). Yet Schafer's answers to defense lawyers were promising. She said, "The war [in Vietnam] seemed very remote while I was in Thailand. I'm very glad they're bringing the boys back, that there's an end of war in sight." Schafer was entitled to a statutory exemption from jury service because she had a child living at home. She said she wasn't going to request an excuse because "I take this duty very seriously . . . if all of us ask for excuses, what type of jury would it be?"

Ahmad was convinced from his eye-contact with Schafer that she felt empathy with him rather than prejudice or hostility. Paul Hare, a sociologist specializing in group dynamics, believed that her expression of concern about fair trials was a better indicator of her values than her living near American military bases. While some defendants and lawyers expressed strong doubts about Schafer, others inferred that she genuinely wanted to serve as a citizen in a democracy.

The third woman we chose was Nancy Leidy, a Methodist in her early 20s who worked as a typist. She had been married only four months, yet she was willing to be part of a sequestered jury that would separate her from her husband for four or five months. The puzzled defense lawyers pressed her for reasons. All she would say was that she would not be bothered by sequestration and that her husband would be able to cope. Leidy made only one comment that gave us a clue to her values: "We'll always have war. I'd like to see the young men come home. We could have followed a different policy in Vietnam. I mean total involvement or total withdrawal."

Yet Leidy appeared to be a resolute, task-oriented young woman who would display good judgment. We thought that her desire to be on the jury was consistent with these personality characteristics. We guessed that she and her husband thought of her jury service as a chance to garner a considerable nest egg (jurors are paid $20 per day). We did not think she would hold out for conviction if 10 or 11 of the other jurors were for acquittal.

Now we needed two more jurors, and one of them had to be a Catholic. Paul O'Dwyer had argued strongly, with the Catholic defendants' concurrence, that there had to be at least one Catholic on the jury in order to inhibit expression of anti-Catholic sentiments. We agreed, since our survey showed that Catholics would make "better" defense jurors than Protestants.

There were two possibilities: a self-confident, upwardly mobile man in his mid-30s, whose sister was a Franciscan nun; and an assertive woman of the same age who worked as a bookkeeper. We preferred Frances Yacklich on a variety of grounds. She had expressed ire at people who come to conclusions without knowing the facts; she seemed to have a deep opposition to the war; and she placed human life over property in her hierarchy of values. She dismissed the rights of aliens to protest U.S. policy, but we thought this objection was minor compared with the counts against the other Catholic. He worked for a company that insisted that its managers adhere to political and social conservatism. He also seemed very aggressive and dominating; so we felt that he might have a disproportionate impact on a predominantly female jury.

WEIGHING HAROLD SHEETS

We made our last choice from among three older men, and decided on Harold Sheets, a Methodist tax accountant in his 50s. Sheets read newspapers and a national news magazine but told the judge, "I don't make any conclusions in this case or in any other case from what I read in publications."

Sheets posed a number of difficulties for us, and the raters disagreed strongly on his suitability. He had told the court that sequestration would impose an extreme hardship on him. He explained that he had just joined a tax firm to prepare for retirement in a year, and that he would have to see clients and maintain accounts. There is much experimental evidence that when people are seriously deprived, they become very angry, and that they take out their anger on those whom they hold responsible for their deprivation. (Small group experts Robert Helmreich of the University of Texas and Philip Zimbardo of Stanford University had provided affidavits supporting this point, to aid the defense's contention that the jury should not be sequestered.) Sheets felt that if he went on a sequestered jury, his retirement plans would be put in jeopardy. He would be understandably furious, we thought, and could well take out his anger on the defendants.

Further, Sheets was a high-status, authoritative, fact-minded older man. Doubtless he would be a very strong candidate for foreman of the jury and a major influence on the other jurors. Our survey findings also pointed away from choosing a Methodist, college-graduate professional, unless there were compelling indications to the contrary.

Eventually, however, Menaker received information that Sheets could weather the financial effects of sequestration better than we had thought. Some people who knew Sheets told Menaker that they thought he would not mind serving on the jury; moreover, that he would be a tough but fair-minded juror. Even so, the social scientists favored a more grandfatherly man who had a sense of humor and a strong inner self, but we were outvoted.

At the final meeting of the defense team, all new information was discussed. Schulman summarized the pros and cons on each juror in category three, and everyone argued for their favorites. Then they ranked each of the possibilities and voting began. The second round of voting yielded an overwhelming decision for the five we have described—Burnett, Schafer, Leidy, Yacklich, and Sheets. The jury was complete.

HOW THE JURORS SAW THE TRIAL

In the tale of Rashomon, four travelers describe the same event. The story comes out four different ways. An event is one thing; interpretation of it is quite another.

We have been able to piece together much of what happened during deliberations thanks to Paul Cowan, a journalist who interviewed seven of the jurors after the trial. The following account is based on these interviews.

In the Harrisburg trial, the lawyers for both sides were sure that the jurors were reacting to a witness or a cross-examination as the lawyers did. The jurors, however, often had very different reactions.

The defense lawyers believed, for instance, that they had destroyed Boyd Douglas's testimony with their incisive cross-examinations. The reality was more complex. Most of the women jurors were suspicious of Douglas on sight and dismissed his testimony almost completely. For instance, Stanovich said that "his whole attitude, his general look" bothered her: "What's this person with his $200 suit and silk tie?" Burnett thought that Douglas was like a "smirky little kid." But Sheets and Foresman said that they were not put off by the way Douglas looked. Foresman didn't trust Douglas, but was rather attracted to him anyway.

Several times the defense thought it had accomplished a devastating exposure of Douglas's duplicity, while the jurors had a positive or, at worst, ho-hum response. At one point O'Dwyer had gotten Douglas to admit that having proposed marriage to a Bucknell senior, he had induced her to join a protest demonstration and then had blithely informed on her to FBI agents.

This revelation had little effect on the jurors. Stanovich thought the young woman and her roommate (to whom Douglas had also proposed marriage) were "sorry looking girls" who "knew what they were getting into." Foresman thought that Douglas had done nothing reprehensible: "Boyd cracked me up. . . . It struck a couple of comical points in my life in which I'd done the same thing over the years. . . . I can remember telling a couple of lies [to girls]."

MOLLY MAYFIELD OF THE FBI

Every FBI informer has a "control" or "handler." Douglas's control was an agent named Mayfield, whose code name was Molly. The defense was concerned that a solid-looking, articulate FBI man would impress the jury whereas Douglas (they thought) had failed.

But the jurors were neither as naive nor as trusting as the defense had imagined. Mayfield didn't even impress Sheets, who had been looking forward to his testimony. Foresman, himself a government employee, thought Mayfield was sincere and trustworthy, but added, "I also think he was the kind of guy that is doing his job." He couldn't really say that Douglas was anything but what he said he was, because to do so would have been a reflection on himself. Jackson said that she was confused by Mayfield's testimony: "I don't know how or why, but I got the feeling that he was lying. Just something about him bothered me. Call it female intuition."

If we had had to pick one juror whom we felt would oppose Mayfield, it would have been Burnett, who supported the defendants. Yet she was impressed by Mayfield, "I really thought he was up front," she said. "Never once did he contradict himself. Anyone who has that kind of mental strength had to be a beautiful guy."

NO DEFENSE FOR THE DEFENSE

The most dramatic moment of the trial was Ramsey Clark's abrupt announcement that there would be no defense. Lynch, who had been preparing his cross-examinations of the defendants for months, was speechless. The jurors were shocked and annoyed; they had expected to hear the defendants and they felt let down.

But here the defense made a wise decision. When the jurors got over their initial reaction, they acknowledged that the defense was right. "Maybe if [the defendants] had gone on the stand," said Jackson, "we would have found them guilty." Foresman agreed that the defense lawyers would have harmed their cause if they had put Phil Berrigan on the stand. "Phil comes off a little bit on the arrogant side . . . if he got a chance to get on his feet, he would say a few things that he wanted to get off his chest that wouldn't help any. If he started ranting and raving with his insinuations, that would have irritated me."

THE JURORS AND THE LAWYERS

The jurors, with the exception of Ann Burnett, regarded Judge Herman highly and identified closely with William Lynch. They liked Lynch and thought that he had done an excellent job with little material. They intimated that they sympathized with Lynch because he and his three courtroom assistants were outmanned by the seven-person defense team.

The defendants and we social scientists were sure that Ramsey Clark was the right man for this jury. We could not have been more wrong, The jurors disliked his style and speech, "I thought he was much too oratorical, too theatrical," said Jackson. "I thought he was ineffective." Foresman was angry that "Clark likened Douglas to Judas in his closing. Did he expect us to see Phil Berrigan as Christ?"

In contrast, the jurors liked Boudin. "Boudin had showmanship, ability to think on his feet," explained Foresman. "He just fascinated me. He has a fabulous mind." Boudin had been the last defense lawyer to cross-examine Boyd Douglas; the defendants, his fellow lawyers, and the press criticized his performance harshly. The jurors saw it differently: it was Boudin, their darling, who had tripped up Douglas.

INSIDE THE JURY ROOM

The jury deliberated for more than 60 hours over seven days (apparently a record for jury deliberation in a federal criminal case) before Harold Sheets, the foreman, reluctantly notified Judge Herman that the jury was hopelessly deadlocked over the all-important conspiracy counts. Earlier, the jury had decided that Father Berrigan and Sister McAlister were guilty of one count of smuggling letters in and out of a Federal prison. They were unhappy about doing so, but felt they had no choice.

Ten jurors voted for acquittal on the three conspiracy counts; Harold Sheets, the accountant; Robert Foresman, the fireman teacher; the four young women, Tracy Stanovich, Ann Burnett, Patricia Schafer, and Nancy Leidy; Frances Yacklich, the Catholic bookkeeper; June Jackson, the Presbyterian pharmacist; Pauline Portzline, the first-choice housewife who had been sympathetic to the defendants; and Vera Thompson, the lone black on the jury. The two jurors who held out for conviction were Lawrence Evans, the retired grocery-store owner, and Kathryn Schwartz, the mother of four conscientious-objector sons. We were faced with a tragic irony. While we had argued and debated for hours about *third*-choice jurors, it was two of our *second* choices who hung the jury.

On the first day, Harold Sheets outlined procedures by which he wanted the jury to operate. At this point Lawrence Evans pronounced the defendants guilty by the will of God. He had earlier confided to Mrs. Thompson that he expected the deliberations to be over by 5:00 p.m. that afternoon; so he could attend a hockey game the next day.

Evans began to shout that it was necessary to find the defendants guilty to satisfy God's will and to save the children and grandchildren of America. Evans asserted that the defendants had to be guilty if the government had brought them to trial; he banged on the table for emphasis. He implored his fellow jurors to throw the defendants in jail and be done with the thing. He appealed to their religious convictions, threatening them with the wrath of God. Not once, said the other jurors, did he offer reasons to support his assertion of the defendants' guilt.

Foresman thought later that some of his flip remarks might have triggered Evans's outburst: "I started making cracks. I thought, and said, 'This outfit's going to kidnap Henry Kissinger? Whoever thought such a screwy thing?' I think that irritated him. I think that really set him off. He said to me, 'The government doesn't make any mistakes.' I blew right back at him, 'My God, you're a businessman. You ought to know better than that.' He started to explode at me. I lost my temper and let him have it right back. Neither he nor any man on the face of this earth could tell me how to think."

Foresman had not made up his mind about guilt or innocence before deliberations began. "[Evans] attempted to make me feel guilty if I voted any way but the way he voted. He made so much noise that one of the marshals outside of the door came in and told him to hold himself more in check. What aggravated me was that I was just beginning to put together what had to be done. I wanted to assemble this in my own mind and proceed in my own way as to how I was going to determine what the verdict was going to be. I felt we should have a calm atmosphere so that we could come out with a good, concrete, solid, rational, verdict that everyone would participate in. Starting off with such a deep, emotional outburst was, to me, the worst thing that could have happened."

Most of the jurors were more frightened and dismayed by the nature of Evans's outburst than they were by what he said. Ann Burnett, one of the jurors who felt most adamant about the innocence of the defendants, recalled, "I got really scared. He nearly had a stroke. Veins were standing out at you." She remembered, "The door wasn't even shut yet. He hollered out, 'They're all guilty!' But then he should have been able to sit down and tell us why. He was never able to do that the full time, over 60 hours. When he started shouting, it hit me that we had wasted the whole thing."

THROWING PAPERS

Tracy Stanovich reported that she was sick throughout the deliberations, and couldn't eat or sleep. She recalled: "[Evans] said he was going to jump out of the window if we didn't find them guilty. I turned around and said 'By gum Larry, I can't get the window open.' We heard that for about an hour-and-a-half, him yelling and screaming. The big thing that I didn't like was that he threw papers into Pat's [Patricia Schafer] face." She explained, "[Pat] had asked him for his proof. Larry said, 'This is the proof' and picked up the papers from the table and threw them in her face."

Stanovich described Evans's attack on other jurors. "He started saying to Frances [Yacklich], 'You're voting for acquittal because you're Catholic and they're Catholic.' Frances was very upset. He told every one of us except Kathryn [Schwartz] that we were animals. Then he'd say to Kathryn, 'We'll stick together. We have to do God's work.'"

Harold Sheets, whose social values are very conservative and who did not arrive at a conclusion of innocence until the fifth day of deliberations, agreed that Evans's outburst was "very very harmful." He explained, "Here the jury goes in there and, boom, someone says, 'Slap them in jail and let's get out of here.' I was mad right then. I assumed the responsibility [as foreman] of trying to bring order out of chaos in this thing and to get a decision. Not by knocking anybody over the head and making him do it but by reason, and that drains an awful lot out of you. You don't sleep well at night."

ROCK OF AGES

The jury was sequestered at a motor hotel in Harrisburg. The night of the first day of deliberations, June Jackson heard noises coming from Evans's room, which was next to hers, and went to the wall to listen. She heard Evans marching to and fro, singing verses of "Rock of Ages" and speaking to God. Evans's colloquy with God explained that he had allowed himself to be persuaded by his fellow jurors on a previous case to vote for acquittal, and that a week later God had shown his wrath by striking the acquitted defendant dead of a heart attack. This time, promised Evans, he would heed God's word no matter what.

Up most of the night, Jackson sought out Harold Sheets next morning to tell him what had happened and to ask for his help. Sheets listened, tried to dispel her fears, and asked the chief marshal to have her room changed. His request was denied. Sheets and Foresman briefly considered the possibility of asking the judge for a replacement for Evans, but they decided that they shouldn't do so.

THE DEBATE ON CONSPIRACY

In spite of the explosive start, Sheets was able to guide the jury through four days of hard work. Element by element, they analyzed

Judge Herman's complicated charge on the meaning of conspiracy law. Most jurors concluded that the defendants should be found guilty of conspiracy only if they were guilty of all three counts: conspiring to raid draft boards, *and* conspiring to kidnap Henry Kissinger, *and* conspiring to blow up heating tunnels. Evans maintained, with Prosecutor Lynch, that the defendants should be found guilty of conspiracy if they were guilty of any *one* of the three counts of conspiracy.

The first vote showed nine for acquittal and three for conviction. Vera Thompson changed her vote from guilty to innocent on the basis of many back-and-forth discussions. Thompson said that she changed her mind because of Pat Schafer's blackboard diagram, which distinguished between ideas and actions and tied the legal concept of conspiracy to *acts* of conspiracy.

We believe that the jurors' decision to convict two of the defendants on counts of smuggling contraband is a clue to how they would have voted on the key conspiracy count *if* (1)Judge Herman had been able to formulate and state his charge on conspiracy law sharply and clearly *and* (2) the government lawyers had provided evidence that the defendants had taken one overt action to carry out the kidnapping or the bombing.

In a postverdict press conference, Lawrence Evans accused Ann Burnett of being unwilling to convict even if the defendants were guilty. She disagreed: "If I felt the evidence showed they were guilty, I sure as hell would have voted guilty. You couldn't have voted guilty under that indictment. I was going by the definition the judge gave us."

THE ELUSIVE CONSENSUS

The jury began deliberations on a Thursday afternoon. By Monday, everyone's mind was fixed. Sheets, the foreman, would not give up. He took full responsibility for prolonging the deliberations another two days. He explained, "I was foreman of that jury and I just couldn't close it. I fought for almost two days to get a decision. I thought what a horrible thing this is, for us to come out of here locked."

Sheets maintained the hope that he could engage Larry Evans in a rational exchange of views. "He would not enter into discussion with me and I [tried] sincerely and with great patience. I said I would reiterate all of my thinking that brought me to my decision. Which I did. It took me 20 minutes to do it. I got no response. He sat there and listened to me but he did not come up with his own mental process, or cause, which he used in arriving at his own decision. He was profoundly set in his own religion course." (Each of the seven jurors Cowan talked to was convinced that had Evans changed his vote, Kathryn Schwartz would have followed suit.)

Instead, while Sheets struggled to keep the deliberations going on a rational course, Evans alternately isolated himself in the back of the jury room, and came forth to badger, tease, and confront certain jurors.

The deliberations had begun with a confrontation between Evans and Foresman, and they ended in the same way. The two men, both being Lutherans, had attended church services together the previous Sunday. Evans had sought to impress Foresman with the depth of his religious commitment and his religious knowledge; he also lost no opportunity to make Foresman feel guilty about his vote.

As Foresman tells it: "I just got tired of his bullshit. I just jumped up, ran over to him and told him, 'you're never going to convince me with that method. Mister, you're way out in left field. Who the hell do you think you are telling me how to think.'" June Jackson thought Foresman's outburst provided an important lesson: that violence and emotionality beget more violence and emotionality, which are dehumanizing. "I loved Fuzzy [Foresman]," she said, "and here Larry had reduced him to an animal." Foresman himself said later that he felt his outburst had cost him his dignity, and had given Evans the gift of consolation.

THE SOCIAL PSYCHOLOGY OF SEQUESTRATION

A relationship emerged between a person's role in the jury social organization and the strength of his or her vote for acquittal or conviction. In the jury, as in other social situations, there was a correlation between *social marginality* and the ability to persist or adhere to personal convictions in the face of strong group pressure.

For instance, Burnett and Yacklich were the two jurors most strongly committed to a not-guilty verdict; they might well have held out for acquittal and the majority followed Evans and Schwartz for conviction. Burnett's aggressive personal style, plus her skepticism about some conventional social values, made her somewhat of an outsider in the small society that was the jury. Frances Yacklich likewise was not part of the jury's informal leadership group. In fact, three of the four jurors who were committed to a verdict were isolates, that is, they were only marginally affiliated with the jury social system.

The key members of the jury, those with the greatest potential for influence, were Sheets, Schafer, Foresman, and Stanovich. These were the best-liked and most respected jurors. Indeed, the evidence we have suggests that Pat Schafer could have been elected jury foreman if the jurors were not so accustomed to male authority. Another four jurors were integrated within the social network—Jackson, Portzline, Leidy, and Thompson—and thus they were susceptible to influence during the deliberations. If anything, Evan's unceasing attempts to influence these jurors increased their willingness to stick it out for the defendants.

On the other hand, it appeared that Evans was successful in influencing Schwartz's vote because he was able to appeal to her religious fervor and conservative sentiments.

Because all four jury leaders argued and voted for acquittal, the jurors who followed and liked them were not thrown into conflict. Jackson, Leidy, and Portzline could vote their conscience and still be in agreement with the jurors they liked and respected. It is probable that Thompson changed her vote from guilty to innocent because people with whom she was socially affiliated pressured her to do so, as well as because of the logic of their arguments.

Conversely, we think that had there been full social support behind a vote for conviction, Thompson would not have changed her vote, and Jackson, Leidy, and Portzline would have gone along with the group. Had there been a split in the ranks of the four leaders, the jury surely would have been deadlocked earlier than it was.

VERDICT SURVEY AMONG NONJURORS

While the jury was deliberating, we reinterviewed a number of persons from the original in-depth survey, in order to get their reactions to the trial. From the original 252 respondents, we chose 96 who were rough matches with the real jurors. We then organized a small group of faithful telephone interviewers, who successfully contacted 83 people during the time that the jury was sequestered.

Of the 83, 7 refused to answer questions, 3 others gave unclear responses, and 12 said they didn't know enough about the case to make decisions. The remaining 61 gave us their opinions on three issues: *Do you think that the defendants really (1) intended to kidnap*

Henry Kissinger? (2) planned to blow up tunnels? (3) conspired to raid draft boards?

We classified 28 respondents as having "low-to-moderate presumption of guilt." Although only one person thought that the defendants were guilty of *none* of the three charges, most thought they were guilty of the draft-board charges but said maybe to the other two. (Since several of the defendants had admitted raiding draft boards, most people took this as proof of guilt even though the charge at hand was *conspiracy*.) The remaining 33 respondents had "high presumption of guilt." All believed the defendants were guilty of conspiracy to raid draft boards; and guilty of one or both of the other charges.

It is difficult to compare these respondents with the actual jury since the questions we asked did not correspond perfectly to the task set for the real jurors. The jurors had to decide whether all of the evidence taken together indicated a conspiracy and whether the government had actually *proven* its case against the defendants. Also, we cannot separate the effects of the trial itself from effects due to the jurors' person characteristics. Nevertheless, the overwhelming majority of our respondents presumed some guilt on the part of the defendants, whereas the real jury voted 10 to 2 for acquittal.

THE PRESUMPTION OF GUILT

We wanted to identify the strongest factors that related to a person's perception of the defendants' guilt or innocence. Age and political preference made little difference, but sex did: Women were more lenient. Only 37 percent of the women respondents thought the defendants were guilty on all or most counts, compared with 57 percent of the men. Still, our most accurate prediction came from knowing only the education and religion of a respondent. Of the 22 respondents with high school educations and the "right" religion from the defense standpoint, only four showed a strong presumption of guilt. In contrast, of the 51 respondents who did not meet these criteria, 29 showed strong presumption of guilt.

If the criteria we discovered on this follow-up study had been rigidly applied to the real jury selection, we would automatically have eliminated the two jurors who voted for conviction: Evans because he had too much education and Schwartz because she had too little. However, we would have made other mistakes if we had adhered rigidly to the survey data. For example, we would have rejected several of the other jurors who voted for acquittal.

VERDICTS AND THE MEDIA

It is perhaps more significant for the future to ask how our respondents' opinions related to their exposure to the media. This is relevant to the matter of sequestration and to the possible effect of delay, as in the Daniel Ellsberg case, between jury selection and the onset of a trial.

So we asked respondents whether they had read about the trial in newspapers, heard about it on radio or TV, or talked about it with people they knew. The results showed clearly that presumption of guilt was significantly associated with talking about the case, reading about it in newspapers, and less strongly, with hearing about it on radio or television.

Four months before the jury was selected we had asked these same respondents to identity 12 people who had been in the news. One of these was Philip Berrigan. Of the people who eventually expressed a strong presumption of guilt, 40 percent had correctly identified Berrigan before the trial; the corresponding proportions for the low-presumption and undecided categories were 15 percent and 8 percent, respectively. Further, high-guilt and low-guilt respondents did not differ significantly prior to the trial in the number of daily newspapers they read or in their TV and radio listening habits. The high-guilt group, however, was more attuned to information about the trial, both before it began and while it lasted.

In Harrisburg, then, a person's exposure to the media was likely to be associated with antidefense attitudes. On the basis of these data, Schulman prepared a brief that was later used in the Ellsberg case. The first jury selected for that trial was released for four months pending the outcome of various defense appeals. Schulman's brief, on the relationship between exposure to media and presumption of guilt, was one of the factors in the decision to dismiss that jury.

ISSUES AND IMPLICATIONS

This study raises a number of major issues: practical, political, ethical, and scientific. Most of our questions remain unanswered, although we know much more than we did before the Harrisburg project began.

For example, the jury's decision was more favorable to the defendants than almost anyone would have predicted. Several factors, however, prevent us from taking full credit or blame.

(1) The government's case. There was no control group in our experiment. Thus we don't know what effect the trial itself had on the jurors. In their eyes, the government failed to prove most of its charges ("the government's case," summarized Vera Thompson, "was like a pregnant woman who is constantly trying to give birth but can't for some reason"). Perhaps that feeling alone accounted for the 10-2 vote for acquittal. Indeed, Pat Schafer was furious with reporters for their reiterated doubts that the defendants would be able to find a fair and impartial jury. Of course, such doubts were precisely what motivated us to work for the defense. Schafer felt that the 10-2 vote demonstrated the essential decency of middle Americans. In a sense, she is right: Both the Nixon administration and its radical critics misrepresented and misunderstood the values and psychodynamics of these Americans.

Cowan's interviews with the jurors support Schafer's opinion. Most of them came to believe that the government had spent two million dollars of the taxpayer's money for nothing. June Jackson was "disillusioned" by government: "How could they have let this idiotic thing come to trial when little laymen like us could see how darn little [they] had? I realize now they expected to get a biased jury. How stupid do they think people are in the United States? We all have minds." Sheets proposed two theories: Either the government had been unable to submit all of its evidence, or it knew it had no case and was banking on the prejudices of people in the Harrisburg area to win a conviction. Most jurors believed both hypotheses.

On the other hand, 2 of the 12 jurors did vote for conviction on the conspiracy charges. The jury could easily have contained many more persons like Evans and Schwartz, in which case the verdict would have been different even though the evidence would have been unchanged. Some jurors disagreed with Schafer, readily conceding that the Harrisburg jury was atypical, that Evans was much more representative of the values of the middle district than they were.

Without careful screening of prospective jurors, we have every reason to believe that the jury would have consisted of many more individuals who were strongly opposed to the defendants.

(2) The judge's rulings. It was Judge Herman who permitted extended questioning of the jury, which he could have chosen himself. It was also Herman who gave the defense 28 peremptory

challenges and the prosecution 6, and who allowed an unusually wide latitude for questions. All of these factors contributed to the composition and verdict of the jury.

However, we feel justified in concluding that our work did have an effect. We helped induce the judge to update the jury wheel, and this worked in the defense's favor. The evidence of conservatism and progovernment feelings that we found in the Harrisburg area led defense lawyers to file motions objecting to various aspects of the trial.

Further, our work contributed to defense strategy, encouraging the lawyers to examine as many persons as possible and providing them with leads for fruitful questions. We helped to shape the ways in which the lawyers looked at and evaluated prospective jurors.

(3) Sequestration. Leonard Boudin had prepared a brief detailing the high likelihood of conviction in cases with sequestered juries. To our surprise, sequestration helped the defense, possibly for several reasons.

First, we had found that reading or talking about the case was associated with presumption of guilt. Sequestration guarded the jury against prejudicial input from local citizens and news media. Sheets, for example, mentioned after the trial that most of his friends and clients had told his wife that the defendants had to be guilty. "They were very forceful in what they thought," he said. "I figure that 90 percent of them thought that they were guilty."

Second, the jurors knew in advance that they would be sequestered. Since it was relatively easy for them to be excused, they had, in a sense, *chosen* to be locked up. Having done so, they apparently were under pressure to see their choice as meaningful.

Third, the knowledge that sequestration was likely may have meant that only people who were serious about the responsibilities of a juror would choose to continue.

The seven jurors whom Cowan interviewed agreed that sequestration was essential to their being conscientious jurors. Sheets had strongly opposed the judge's decision to sequester the jury, but changed his mind: "I think that I'm a fairly strong person, that I can kind of ferret things out. But I'm not too sure that if we'd been subjected to everything in the press, what that would have done to the progression of my thinking. I'm sure that there would have been peace people trying to get next to us if we'd have been on the outside. I'm not sure how I would have handled it. It could have very well gotten me to the point of not being rational on analyzing the facts. I feel confident that peace people would have gotten me mad."

(4) The limits of social science. It would be foolish and dangerous to maintain that we fully determined the composition of the jury, or that

we knew exactly what we were doing at the time. Some persons, upon hearing about this project, have raised the specter of a future in which computers select jurors on the basis of massive survey studies. This is an unnecessary nightmare. In selecting the Harrisburg jurors, the defense used a complex combination of subjective impressions, hearsay, objective information, and data from our survey. We drew no "prediction equations" and, if we had, they would have been incomplete and invalid. There are no equations precise enough to predict the behavior of *individuals* from group characteristics, especially in a situation as ambiguous as the unfolding of a trial.

Then, too, the lawyers and defendants would not have suspended their own judgment in favor of ours. For good reasons, neither professionals nor laymen wholeheartedly trust social scientists who are operating in novel situations, and we would not want them to. The primary function of social scientists in juror selection is to clarify questions and to suggest ways in which data might be gathered to answer them.

We had studied attitudes toward the alleged crimes of the defendants on the assumption that these attitudes would color the way in which jurors would interpret testimony. But Cowan's interviews with the actual jurors, and our interviews with prospective jurors who were excused, suggest that the psychological and interpersonal processes involved in reaching a verdict were much more complex than anything we could have predicted.

For example, most of the jurors took their role as fair decision makers more seriously than we anticipated. Most of them tried earnestly to consider the defendants "innocent until proven guilty." It seems wise to consider a person's conception of the role of juror as a distinct characteristic when assessing jurors. A person like Harold Sheets, for example, may be fair because he believes this role requires fair play, even though he disapproves of the defendants on many grounds.

RECOMMENDATIONS TO DEFENDERS

Surveys of the kind we conducted appear to be worthwhile; and with the help of committed volunteers, researchers can obtain results of high quality for very little cost (about $450 in our case). We conclude that defense teams should consider the following issues in selecting jurors:

(1) Attitudes toward the defendants and their alleged crimes will often relate to demographic and personality variables, but patterns found in one area may not resemble patterns found in another. While the relationships that turn up may indicate fruitful lines of questioning and suggest *general* rules for jury selection, one should never apply these rules blindly.

(2) Assessment of ratings. We made some errors in rating prospective jurors: for example, Evans, Schwartz, and Sheets. We analyzed Cowan's interviews with real jurors and interviewed 21 prospective jurors who had been excused during the questioning. We found that our mistakes could have been avoided.

The big problem with our one-through-five rating scheme was that we did not score *systematically* each prospective juror on *both* key background characteristics and key attitudes. Had we done so, our rating mistakes would have shown up as discrepant cases, that is, as persons good on one indicator and bad on the other. When this happens, the defense team should make an all-out effort to get additional information to resolve the inconsistency. For example, Evans expressed prodefense attitudes that seemed incompatible with this demography. We were seduced by the impression he created and did not seek further information about him.

(3) Individual conceptions of the juror's role. Although we did not consider this factor during the questioning of the Harrisburg jury, lawyers could identify jurors who conceived of their tasks as deciding whether the prosecution has presented sufficient evidence, rather than as deciding whether the defendants are guilty or innocent.

(4) Composition of the jury. We considered two aspects of jury composition that proved very useful: the number of women and the issue of dominance. As we had predicted, the cluster of young women we selected proved more lenient toward the defendants and interacted supportively. We also predicted the balance of dominant individuals fairly accurately.

We recommend that defense teams rank each juror systematically on a dominance scale and use these ratings to guide the use of peremptory challenges.

(5) Behavioral cues. Paul Hare and his coworkers have evidence from observations of juror interaction in the Harrisburg courtroom that nonverbal behavior (for example, eye contact, body orientation, facial expressions, dress) could have given us important information. By neglecting the nonverbal behavior of prospective jurors, we missed opportunities to detect attitudes, probably subgroups within the jury, and bias. We should have noted these factors systematically.

(6) Special characteristics of the trial. Defense lawyers usually know what testimony will arise during a trial, and they must try to anticipate jurors' reactions. They may know about other factors (such as sequestration) whose effects can be considered in advance.

(7) The right to extended questioning of prospective jurors. Our experience in Harrisburg has sensitized us to the difficulty of selecting an impartial jury, whether the venue is Camden, Los Angeles, Boston, or Gainesville. To increase the chances for a fair jury, federal trial rules should be revised to give both defense and prosecution the right to extended questioning, now standard procedure in many states.

WHAT ABOUT ETHICS?

Our contribution to the defense effort was within the law; we did no "jury tampering." We spoke with none of the prospective jurors before their appearance in the courtroom. And we agreed before the trial that if anyone from our survey sample was called as a prospective juror, we would not provide defense lawyers with specific information about that person. If our behavior was improper, the impropriety was an ethical, not a legal, matter.

Is it ethical, for instance, for social scientists to take sides in a dispute, in negotiations, or in any social interaction? The question has already been answered positively by market researchers, military and industrial psychologists, private political pollsters, and many other social scientists engaged in applied research. But we cannot settle ethical questions by precedent.

In the Harrisburg trial, we believed strongly that the defendants' right to presumption of innocence was seriously threatened. The government chose a conservative location for the trial. J. Edgar Hoover proclaimed the defendants' guilt long before the trial began. William Lynch made public some of the controversial Berrigan-McAlister letters. As in most criminal and political trials, the investigatory and financial resources of the government far outweighed those of the defendants. And the trial raised a host of constitutional questions, from wire-tapping to conspiracy law. For these reasons we believed, and still believe, that our partisanship was proper.

Many people would disagree with the implication that it is difficult to receive a fair trial in the United States when one is opposed by the government. They point to the government's failure to obtain convictions in recent political trials (for example, the Berrigans,

Angela Davis, the Black Panthers) as evidence of the fairness of the current court system. However, these trials were highly visible, they drew unusually fine legal talent (sometimes volunteered without pay), and the assistance of many people, including social scientists, who would not ordinarily be available to defendants in criminal cases. Our experience in Harrisburg has convinced us that social scientists should give more rather than less assistance to defendants.

However, we have been bothered by two ethical questions concerning research and the possible extensions of our work.

In introducing ourselves to respondents, we said that we were researchers interested in the Harrisburg area because it was to be the site of an important trial. We had decided not to tell respondents that the information they gave might be used to help the defendants, since we feared that to do so would seriously bias our results. This omission clearly violated the principle that research subjects should know the uses to which their data will be put. We went ahead with the deception only after we had concluded that it was extremely unlikely that our procedure could harm the respondents. Since most of the people we interviewed were political conservatives, they probably would not have cooperated with us if they had known our intentions. The public should consider that today a person can be interviewed without knowing whether his answers will help elect a candidate whom he favors or opposes, promote a product that will help or harm him, design television programs that will entertain or deceive him, or assist the cause of antiwar activists whose freedom he might like to restrict.

The second ethical question concerns who will benefit from our procedures in the long run. We depended upon energetic volunteers. In less-celebrated cases, most defendants would lack the organization and money required to apply social research to jury selection. The Justice Department might also adopt our methods, thus turning our efforts into a weapon against defendants.

There is no comforting solution to this problem. While the FBI seems unsuited for carrying out social research, it is possible for the organization to change. And while people are likely to give biased answers (especially about "trust in government," and so on) to interviewers who reveal that they are FBI agents, it is conceivable that the agents might not identify themselves as such.

Social science methods are used in all kinds of legal activities, and since our methods were standard in psychology and sociology, someone was bound to use them soon. We believe it is the duty of those who are concerned with the rights of defendants to be sure that sophisticated methods are not reserved to the government.

GETTING HANDS DIRTY

It seems to us that if social scientists wish to take an active and adversary role in trials, they should turn to criminal law. The opportunities for direct, practical research are enormous.

The presence of scientific observers in courts may help to guard defendants' rights and regularize procedures. Social scientists can serve a major role in phrasing questions and gathering information. They can help determine the extent of racial prejudice in the courts, assess misapplication of procedural safeguards, and appraise the effectiveness of public defenders. Experiments can examine anything from witness credibility to the effectiveness of various defense strategies. Certainly research could discover some of the differences among 3-, 6-, and 12-person juries, and this is critically important at a time when new laws are reducing the size of many juries. (*Editors' note*: See section 4, article II, for a study on this issue.)

Such work will be effective only if social scientists are willing to get their hands dirty, to take sides, to enter directly into the processes they study.

Social scientists need to be more concerned about their own values, about the impact of their findings, about the relationship between their work and the goals of the people it serves. Too often, research has served only government and industry. Social scientists must commit themselves to work for those who have limited resources, to look at social processes from their perspective, to become trustworthy in their eyes. It is our impression that if these conditions were fulfilled, both social science and the needs of people would be better served.

2

SOCIAL SCIENTISTS CAN'T RIG JURIES

MICHAEL J. SAKS
School of Law, University of Iowa

Helped by social scientists, defense attorneys picked juries that acquitted John Mitchell, the Harrisburg Seven, and the defendants at Wounded Knee. But a careful look suggests that the quality of the evidence, not the personal characteristics of the jury, makes the most difference in the outcome of a trial.

Scientific jury selection was born in the winter of 1971-1972, the child of antiwar activism, social science's renewed search for social relevance, and the slow pragmatism of lawyers. Philip Berrigan and seven other defendants were indicted by the federal government and charged with raiding a number of draft boards, of conspiring to kidnap Henry Kissinger, and conspiring to blow up heating tunnels in Washington, DC. It was another in the government's continuing series of conspiracy trials against antiwar and other activist groups. The trial was convened in Harrisburg, Pennsylvania, an area with an unusually conservative and progovernment citizenry.

A group of social scientists joined with the team of defense attorneys headed by Ramsey Clark to select from that inordinately conservative population a jury that would be more favorable to the defendants. The social scientists worked without remuneration. They were aided by an army of volunteers who helped gather the demographic and attitudinal data that would make the scientific jury selection possible. In spirit and in style the first scientific selection was another type of antiwar rally. The trial ended in a hung jury, split 10 to 2 in favor of the defense, and the government dropped the charges (see the previous article for details).

The use of social science expertise in jury selection has been growing since the trial of the Harrisburg Seven. Social scientists have helped and are helping lawyers select juries in the trials of the Camden 28, the Gainesville Eight, the Angela Davis trial, the trial of Indian militants from Wounded Knee (see "The Notion of Conspiracy Is Not Tasty to Americans," A Conversation with June L. Tapp, by Gordon Bermant, *Psychology Today*, May 1975) and defendants in the Attica prosecutions. The most publicized use of scientific jury selection was in the trial of former Attorney General John Mitchell and Maurice Stans. After failing to come to terms with the Harrisburg Seven team of social scientists, the defense turned to Marty Herbst, a market-research consultant, who did the job for them.

Many concerned people have noted that no defendants who have used scientific jury selection have been convicted, except on the most trivial of the charges in their indictments. They have interpreted this fact to mean that the techniques are effective and powerful, and have suggested that its power may be a threat to our system of trial by jury and to justice itself.

A NEW BITE FROM THE APPLE

Critics worry that if the outcome of a trial can be manipulated simply by choosing jurors labeled acceptable by social scientists, then trial by jury would cease to function impartially and ultimately have to be abandoned. Amitai Etzioni, a prominent sociologist, has also argued that scientific jury selection threatens the integrity of the jury system, increases the advantages of the rich and celebrated over the poor and obscure, and may prompt the state to hire its own social scientists to increase further the government's already sizable advantages in a criminal proceeding. Writes Etzioni: "Man has taken a new bite from the apple of knowledge, and it is doubtful whether we all will be better for it."

The advent of scientific jury selection has come quite late. The necessary techniques for measuring attitudes have been in existence since the late 1920s and the necessary mathematical techniques for a good bit longer than that. By 1950, the development of standardized attitude and personality scales and studies of the relationships between various demographic characteristics (such as sex, age, race, religion) and attitudes were well under way. By the time computers became a common part of the social science arsenal, around 1960, the potential for selecting juries scientifically went from feasible to easy.

The law provides for a two-stage process for the selection of jurors. From the eligible population, known as the *venire,* a pool of prospective jurors is drawn. The pool usually comes from voter-registration lists and is intended to be a representative cross-section of the population. Persons who would be overburdened by serving or who are not able to perform the juror role competently (such as a person who does not speak English) are excused.

From this pool will be drawn the jurors for each jury trial, be it civil or criminal. Jurors receive a *voir dire* examination, in which they are questioned, sometimes by the judge, sometimes by the prosecuting and defense attorneys to determine their fitness to serve. Prospective jurors are placed on the jury unless a challenge is made against them. The respective attorneys may challenge for cause, a process in which the judge is asked to exclude a prospective juror for reasons put forth by the challenging attorney. If the judge agrees, the juror is excluded from that case. Or the attorneys may use one of a limited number of peremptory challenges to exclude a juror without having to state reasons and without requiring the judge's consent. The defense is usually given a larger number of peremptory challenges than the prosecution. It is through these challenges that attorneys can influence the composition of the jury that is finally impaneled.

The purpose of *voir dire* is to eliminate jurors whose biases may interfere with a fair consideration of the evidence. Of course, both advocates try to find and impanel jurors who are most favorable to their side. For centuries, lawyers have relied upon intuition, superstition, past personal experience, old wives' tales, and various combinations of these to try to figure out which prospective jurors will be most favorable to their side. Scientific jury selection allows these decisions to be made with the benefit of knowledge acquired through the use of systematic empirical (i.e., "scientific") methods.

Taking into consideration the issues on which the case is likely to hinge, the social scientists design questionnaires that include:

* scales previously developed and validated to measure attitudes related to the crucial issues of the case, such as a trust-in-government measure;
* new attitude and information items written for the particular case at hand, such as knowledge of the defendants and their case; and
* measures of background characteristics including personality; demographic characteristics, such as sex, occupation, race, education, socioeconomic status; media contact and preferences; spare-time activities, and organizational memberships.

Interviewers use these questionnaires to collect data from a sample of the population from which the juror pool will be drawn. They do not approach any of the prospective jurors themselves. By correlating the background characteristics with the attitude measures, it is possible to uncover the important variables that predict the population's attitudes. It might be found, for example, that females are more favorable to the defense than males; young people more than older people; egalitarians more than authoritarians; readers of *The New York Times* more than readers of the New York *Daily News*; Elks more than Masons; and that level of education, introversion, age, political affiliation, and two dozen other things are not at all related to the critical attitudes.

JURORS SOMETIMES LIE

The reason for surveying the local jurisdiction rather than examining national trends is that each community may have its own unusual circumstances which make, say, women more amenable to the defense's case in Harrisburg, but men more defense-prone in Gainesville. It is best to know what is happening in the particular community where the case is being tried instead of relying on general trends, which may not hold in that locality. Moreover, key attitudes change not only with geography but also with the passage of time or the rise of a new case to activate new issues.

One benefit of obtaining demographic correlates of attitudes related to the trial is that during *voir dire*, jurors sometimes lie. They may say they are not biased against protesting priests when they actually are and want to be on the jury to punish the defendant. But background characteristics cannot be falsified. If the juror is a 54-year-old male registered Republican who is the proprietor of a sporting-goods store, computer printouts will tell what he is likely to believe, even if he won't. On the other hand, the data tell only about the probabilities for the population, not how any particular 54-year-old male Republican entrepreneur will vote. Like a baseball manager deciding on which pinch hitter to use, the social scientist cannot know if on a particular occasion player A will outhit player B. But he can know that against pitcher X left-handed hitters have, on the average, done better than right-handed hitters, and play the percentages accordingly. In the long run, he will come out ahead.

The social scientists in the Harrisburg case have warned against placing too much faith in such technology as attitude scales and prediction equations. In the courtroom, they also observed the prospective jurors and tried to discern which way each one leaned. They relied on nonverbal behavior, what jurors said and how they said it, and on appearance and "vibrations." The attorneys, of course, did the same thing in their own way, as they would have even without the social scientists. So did the defendants. The results of these intuitive judgments were compared to the statistical findings and when both agreed, the defense team could be confident that a favorable juror had been identified. When the human and computerized indicators did not concur, the juror in question could be skipped over or investigated further.

While such caution agrees with the common sense of most of us, the caution is probably in the wrong direction. Intuitive, instinctive judgments, when put to the test, have proved notoriously unreliable. Even professional people watchers, such as psychiatrists and clinical psychologists, have produced a surprisingly poor track record. Studies show that professional training, when it has any effect at all on the accuracy of predictions about people, tends to *reduce* judgmental accuracy. Moreover, when the same information is available to a human decision maker and a mathematical model, almost without exception the mathematical model makes more reliable and accurate predictions. After 60 studies comparing clinical versus statistical prediction, the humans beat the computer only once. These findings were as much of a shock (and offense to the human ego) to the people who discovered them as to you who read about them. The original intention was to aid human decision makers by providing a floor of statistical accuracy below which they could not fall. But the floor turned out to be a ceiling. We are indeed fallible creatures. In the Harrisburg trial, one of the two jurors who held out for conviction had been vetoed by the computer. That advice, however, was overruled by Ramsey Clark, who felt certain the juror was a good choice.

STIFLING PREJUDICE

Fortunately, we need not choose between trusting the humans and trusting the technology. Both are available for use. If only jurors who are approved by both methods are selected, then many questionable jurors, who would have been picked by one or the other and turned out to be wrong, would be safely excluded. The wisdom of using both and looking for agreement is obvious.

During and between *voir dire* sessions, the social scientists and attorneys compare notes, classify jurors according to how favorable they seem, and make their selections. The selections are based largely, but not entirely, upon predictions of jurors' predispositions. The defense in the Harrisburg Seven trial also considered the probable dynamics of the group that would become the jury. Since the defendants were mostly Catholic, it would be desirable to place at least one Catholic on the jury, so that an expression of anti-Catholic prejudice by other jurors would be inhibited. Also taken into account was social science knowledge about dominance and marginality in members of small groups: who was most likely to be selected foreman, who would be least influential but also most resistant to pressure from other jurors, and the effects of possible sequestration on certain jurors.

The line between the "scientific" and "unscientific" is often a fuzzy one, but the distinction throws some light on the technology we are discussing. Science is one of the many human enterprises. Its distinguishing characteristic is that it is obsessed with systematic empirical verification of its hypotheses. That contrasts with the relatively haphazard way most of us most of the time settle on our beliefs, relying upon evidence that does not lend unambiguous support or upon no empirical evidence at all. The process of using the findings of social science to select jurors is not itself science, but rather is the application of findings previously obtained through use of the scientific method. Like engineering and medicine, it is not science, but borrows from science. Almost of necessity, applications themselves cannot be science. That is why the applications are regarded as scientific and are given the label *technology*. When the borrowings from science combine with other sources of knowledge, the resulting enterprise is called an *art*.

To the extent that social scientists rely on their professional and clinical experience to intuit jurors' leanings, they are probably going to be less accurate than trial lawyers who have had more experience in that setting. Prison officials have been found to make more accurate predictions of dangerousness than psychiatrists, and mental patients were found better able than the institution's staff to detect the true status of researchers who infiltrated mental hospitals.

HEAD NODS, BODY LEAN

Research on nonverbal behavior shows it to be most subtle and often quite unrevealing. In a lengthy series of experiments, social-psychologist Robert Love of American University tried unsuccessfully to establish a consistent relationship between nonverbal behavior and attitudes. He finally found that people display reliable nonverbal patterns that correlate with attitudes only when they actively try to do so. And even then it required repeated studies of videotapes of the subjects, counting the number of eye blinks, timing the use of head nods, protractor measuring of body lean. Jurors who wish to conceal their real attitudes are therefore able to do so nonverbally as well as verbally.

Still, there are verified, reliable techniques and they are being used. These techniques are worrying many lawyers, social scientists, and others concerned with the health of the jury system. A defense of scientific jury selection might begin by pointing out that it is thoroughly legal. Prospective jurors are not themselves approached or tampered with. They are merely compared to statistical profiles of the population from which they were drawn. They are questioned only during *voir dire*, and only to the extent permitted by the trial judge, as has been the way for generations. All that has changed is that lawyers can now know the hidden meaning of the answers and of jurors' background characteristics.

The practice of *voir dire* has been part of the jury system for centuries. And for those centuries lawyers have sought to impanel the most favorable possible jury for their clients. This has always been widely regarded as a proper goal for the lawyer. Why should the fact that he has finally been given the means to achieve that goal be so objectionable? If the goal is good, why has the ability to achieve it become bad? Of course, we may actually have mistaken goals, which becomes obvious to us only after we learn to achieve them. The problem lies not in the technology but in the goals we have chosen, and the goal of scientific jury selection is not, I think, an unwise one.

The intent is to impanel an impartial jury, that is, a jury whose members do not have biases that would make them unable to weigh the evidence fairly. Jurors are supposed to reach a verdict shaped by the weight of the evidence. The strategy for achieving that goal—allowing both advocates some opportunity to exclude from the jury persons thought to be biased against their side—also seems to me a wise and workable one. Instead of guessing at who will be biased and who will not, lawyers can make informed judgments. If both sides have social science help, each will exclude jurors favorable to the other side more effectively, and the final panel will consist of the neutral jurors, the very ones who will be most able to do what the jury is intended to do. Thus juror attitudes and personality would play a minimal role in determining the outcome of the trial. Evidence would be permitted to play the greatest possible role. Thus scientific jury selection would make the goal of impartial jury decisions more attainable than has ever before been possible.

But, the critics would interject, the presence of such expertise on both sides is a fantasy that ignores the realities of justice in America. Today only the wealthy and celebrated have such help, and tomorrow the only additional people to have it will be prosecutors, and they will use it routinely. And it is probable that this criticism is entirely true. But it does not demonstrate some evil inherent in scientific jury selection. It points instead to a fundamental inequity in our courts. All resources will be unevenly distributed in a system in which those with wealth or the right friends can obtain services unavailable to the average citizen. This is not the fault of the resources or their inventors. The rich can hire lawyers who are likely to be better than the prosecutors, and the poor must settle for legal aid attorneys who in many instances will be less able than the prosecutors.

TRADITIONAL INEQUITIES

It was only as recently as 1963, in *Gideon v. Wainwright,* that the defendant's right to have any counsel at all was firmly established. As I will discuss shortly, trial evidence is and has always been a far more important determinant of the verdict than who sits on the jury. The ability to prepare a strong case is of primary importance. In addition to a good lawyer, that depends upon investigators. The prosecution has its investigators. They are called police detectives. And the rich have their private investigators. The evidence they provide is often of vital importance. So the greatest and most serious inequities—greater or lesser access to attorneys and to investigators—already exist and have for centuries.

I have saved for last what is perhaps the most interesting reason for not worrying excessively about scientific jury selection: the empirical reason. No evidence exists to support the apparent widely held belief that scientific jury selection is a power tool. What has most people upset is the fact that no one who has used it has lost a case. By the standards for evaluating empirical evidence used by the same social scientists who developed the basic principles for the techniques, this seemingly impressive evidence is really no evidence at all. Suppose each of the worrisome cases had been tried before *two* juries—one selected the scientific way and one selected the old way. We could then compare the verdicts delivered by the scientific juries with those delivered by the conventional juries. We know that all of the scientifically selected juries refused to convict. Would the conventional juries in these trials all have convicted? Or would they all have acquitted? Or would some have convicted and some have acquitted and if so, how many would have done which? To know how effective scientific jury selection is, we need to know the answers to these questions. Without such comparisons we simply cannot know.

The focus of controversy on the jury selection process has obscured other critical determinants of trial outcome, such as the nature of the case. If all of our fraternal-twin juries refuse to convict, it might have been because in none of the trials was a strong case made against the defendants. Every one of these trials could be characterized as political, and nearly every count in every case was a charge of conspiracy. Virtually every recent political trial conducted by the government, whether the defense used scientific jury selection or not (such as the Chicago Seven trial and the Panther 21 conspiracy trial), has failed to result in conviction. (Perhaps prosecutorial judgment falters when ideological fervor wells up.) And conspiracy charges are also very difficult to prove.

None of this is to say that scientific jury selection did not have an important effect on verdicts in the cases in which it was used. It says only that we cannot know what the impact was because the necessary comparisons could not be made. The social scientists at Harrisburg understood all of this and, true to their training, they endeavored to measure the effectiveness of their selections. While the actual jury was deliberating, they reinterviewed a subsample of people from their original survey of the community. Fifty-four percent revealed a high presumption of the defendants' guilt. In contrast, only 17 percent (2 of 12) of the actual jurors voted to convict. But the surveyed citizens differed from the selected jurors in a very important way. The surveyed citizens had not heard the evidence—or lack of it.

A LOSING BET

In nontechnical reports of the findings and doings of social scientists working on jury selection, you will read that females are more favorable to the defense than males are. Does that mean that zero percent of females would vote to convict while 100 percent of males would? Or does it mean that 65 percent of females will be conviction prone while 67 percent of males will be similarly disposed? The difference is important for a realistic understanding of scientific jury selection. In the first illustration, the selections are a certainty. The second shows more correctly how the social scientist is really playing the odds. Male-juror A may be one of the 33 percent of males who would acquit, and female-juror B may be one of the 65 percent of females who would convict. The defense would pick juror B because she was the best bet, but they would lose that bet. Scientific jury selection helps one make educated bets. It is not magic. In fact, it appears to be a relatively weak device.

In one of the most extensive studies of jurors and their decision-making behavior, Rita James Simon studied jurors in Chicago, St. Louis, and Minneapolis. She examined the relationship between a juror's vote and his or her education, occupation, sex, income, religion, ethnicity, and age. Only education and ethnicity were able to predict jurors' votes, and they did not do so nearly as well as the characteristics of the evidence in the cases being heard. After also looking at the attitudes of the jurors, Simon concluded: "The sharp lack of findings in this chapter rival in interest any data we have. Three efforts were made to relate attitudes to verdict, and each ended in failure."

I studied 480 jurors in Columbus, Ohio. Each was shown the same videotaped trial, deliberated as a part of a jury, and rendered a verdict. The predictor variables I examined included the jurors' attitudes toward criminals, jurors' personal value systems, their socioeconomic status and level of education, and whether they were left- or right-handed. These predictors were correlated with their degree of certainty of guilt prior to deliberation and their vote to convict or acquit.

HEREDITY OR ENVIRONMENT?

Out of the 27 predictors, the best was whether the jurors believed crime was mainly the product of "bad people" or "bad social conditions." But surprisingly, those who believed that bad social conditions cause crime were *more* likely to regard the defendant as guilty. The best predictor could account for only 9 percent of the variance in the jurors' judgments. Using a multiple-predictor format, the four best predictors in linear combination (belief that crime is caused by bad people versus social conditions, how much they value leadership, and political-party preference) accounted for less than 13 percent of the variance. None of the remaining variables could add as much as 1 percent to the predictive accuracy.

Robert Buckhout, director of the Center for Responsive Psychology in New York, studied a sample of municipal court jurors in California. He compared the demographic and personality characteristics of jurors voting guilty to those voting not guilty. They showed no significant differences in age, income, education, or on such personality measures as need for social approval, dogmatism, or Machiavellianism. The only significant discriminator between jurors voting guilty and those voting not guilty was how the jurors felt about the prosecutor. Those voting guilty liked him more than those voting not guilty. Such an index does not seem likely to be useful in selecting jurors. In court, face-to-face with the prosecutor and defense attorneys, jurors are not likely to state their preferences candidly even if the judge would allow the question to be asked.

Research by Herman Mitchell and Donn Byrne, fairly often cited by social scientists interested in jury behavior, found that measures of authoritarianism did not distinguish conviction-prone jurors from those likely to acquit. They found instead that high authoritarians were more likely to acquit defendants that they saw as similar to themselves and to convict those they saw as different, while low authoritarians did not respond with such seesaw preferences. The problem for the defendant, then, may not be to select nonauthoritarians from the jury pool (because there was no overall difference in the way authoritarians and egalitarians voted). The problem is: Do you take authoritarians and hope that they'll like you rather than dislike you, or do you go with egalitarians and know that their personal reaction to you will not affect their decision?

All these findings are statistically significant, which means that the effects found are highly unlikely to be the product of chance. They are real, but not strong. What this means is that scientific jury selection can help, but it is not going to come close to determining absolutely the outcome of a trial. If the evidence against the defendant is very strong or very weak, it isn't going to matter who is on the jury. If the evidence is close, then scientific jury selection could make the difference.

Carol Werner of the University of Utah, Tom Ostrom of Ohio State, and I asked a sample of former jurors to indicate their certainty of the defendant's guilt or innocence in a series of hypothetical cases. They were given cases in which the alleged crime differed, in which the amount of evidence against the defendant differed, and in which the strength of the evidence varied—it was either moderately or highly incriminating.

We also tested the jurors with a scale of attitudes toward the defendant in order to classify them as either favorable or unfavorable to the defense. Our scale did predict significantly how the jurors would respond. Jurors designated as antidefendant gave an average rating of guilty of 58, while prodefendant jurors gave ratings that averaged –20. That is a spread of 78 points. But the point spread between average certainty of guilt in response to moderately incriminating evidence compared with highly incriminating evidence was 172 points. And hearing one item of evidence compared with six items of evidence produced a difference of 143 points. Looking at the proportion of variance accounted for by each of the independent variables, we find that the amount of evidence was more than three times as powerful as attitudes toward the defendant in determining a juror's verdict. The jurors' characteristics made a difference, but far less than the characteristics of the trial evidence.

THE LINE WITH THE EVIDENCE

Virginia Boehm, a research psychologist for the State of New York, studied jury bias and the ability of an instrument called LAQ (Legal Attitudes Questionnaire) to predict which way jurors were leaning.

The study found that persons classified by the LAQ as authoritarian were significantly more likely to convict than persons classified as antiauthoritarian. But how much more likely? Boehm wisely used two forms of trial evidence, one that favored the defense and one that favored the prosecution. Examining the verdicts of jurors who "erred," that is, who voted guilty when the evidence favored the defense or voted leniently when the evidence favored the prosecution, Boehm found that four-fifths of those designated by the LAQ as antiauthoritarians erred leniently, while only one-third of the authoritarians did so. But what is often overlooked is that only 38 percent of *all* the jurors erred. Only 28 percent erred in the direction predicted by the LAQ. Most important, and most overlooked, is that fully 62 percent of the jurors voted exactly in line with the trial evidence.

Probably the best-known research on juries is Harry Kalven and Hans Ziesel's report on work from the Chicago Jury Project in their book, *The American Jury.* They found that in 78 percent of a national sample of several thousand cases, the judge and jury agreed on the verdict. In 64 percent, when the jury believed the defendant was guilty, so did the judge; and in 14 percent, both agreed the defendant was not guilty. This substantial agreement is not an accident. By and large, both judge and jury respond to the trial evidence, and thus arrive at the same verdict.

A CORE PERSONALITY?

In our culture it has been popularly believed for a long time that personal characteristics make a major difference in people's behavior. That belief apparently is wrong. However important genetics, personality, and attitudes may be, they are generally not as important as situational factors.

The old Freudian theory that we have a core personality that manifests itself throughout our behavior in different situations and circumstances is either inadequate, relatively trivial, or simply wrong. After decades of looking for the core-personality types, and finding none, it began to occur to the searchers that perhaps little was there to be found. Behavior changes dramatically from situation to situation. One would therefore be more effective by controlling the key-stimulus characteristics of the jury situation—the evidence—rather than the characteristics of the people in the situation. These notions are upsetting to many people because they take them to mean that we are not unique individuals with our own autonomous direction in life, that instead we are impotent rats responding to environmental stimuli. The nicer way of stating the case is that we are all unique individuals, but our differences are vastly overshadowed by our similarities. Moreover, the range of situations we are likely to encounter is far more varied than the range of human beings who will encounter them. From the viewpoint of one concerned about the fate of our system of justice and the jury's place in that system, this view is optimistic. It means that jurors have been and will continue to be much more responsive to the evidence placed before them than to their own personalities and attitudes.

No lawyer would be harming his client by taking advantage of scientific jury selection. But if he wanted to have an even greater influence over the outcome of the trial, he ought to hire social scientists to help build and structure the evidence to be presented. Curiously enough, if there is anything social psychologists know about, it is the process of persuasion, which they have studied intensively for many years. One has to wonder why no lawyers or social psychologists have thought to consult with each other on that instead of playing around with the less important chapter of jury selection.

3

JUROR SELECTION
A Comparison of Two Methods in Several Criminal Cases[1]

IRWIN A. HOROWITZ[2]
University of Toledo

The Sixth Amendment of the United States Constitution guarantees the criminal defendant the right to a trial by an "impartial jury." In order to secure this right, the Federal courts have granted both prosecution and defense the opportunity to exclude certain prospective jurors by challenge, either for cause or peremptorily. The Federal Rules of Criminal Procedure provide an interrogation of prospective jurors known as the voir dire, in order that these challenges may be utilized intelligently (Cooper, 1976).

The voir dire, "truth talk," is the stage of the jury selection process aimed at obtaining the least biased jury possible (Moskitis, 1976).

From *Journal of Applied Social Psychology* (1980) *10*(1), 86-99. Reprinted with permission of the publisher.

Potential jurors are questioned by the judge or the prosecution and defense counsel or by both counsel and judge, depending upon the court. Challenges may be put for *cause*, when a juror demonstrates clearly, during the voir dire examination that he or she cannot render an impartial verdict; *peremptorily*, when counsel suspects, for whatever reason although not sufficient cause, the juror will not be impartial; and *to the array*, a rare occurrence, when counsel feels that the entire panel may be biased.

Clearly, lawyers attempt to exercise their challenges in order to secure a jury which will be favorable to their client. Furthermore, lawyers utilize the voir dire to implant the defense (or prosecution) theory of the case and to stifle any incipient prejudice toward their client that is not strong enough to warrant the exercise of a challenge. Weeding out biased jurors and indoctrination of jurors are seen, currently, as the two major tactical purposes of the voir dire. This study is concerned with the use of the voir dire in the service of securing a favorable jury.

The voir dire has been utilized to secure a favorable jury since the medieval period in England. To aid lawyers in this endeavor, an extensive legal literature and related folklore is available (Wildman, 1966). Recently, scientific techniques have increasingly been used in the selection of jurors with apparently great success (Saks, 1976; Schulman, Shaver, Colman, Emrich, & Christie, 1973). The use of social science methodology to obtain acquittals in a number of publicized cases, including the Harrisburg seven, the Joan Little case, and the conspiracy trial of John Mitchell and Maurice Stans, has raised a number of ethical (Etzioni, 1974) and constitutional (Cooper, 1976; Moskitis, 1976) concerns.

Moskitis (1976) has argued that the use of social science methodology to secure biased jurors by the prosecution violates a defendant's Fourteenth Amendment right to due process and, further, violates the Sixth Amendment right to a trial by an impartial jury drawn from a cross-section of the community. The use of social science techniques by the defense, would, in Moskitis's (1976) view, be a threat to the state's right to a fair trial before an impartial panel. Etzioni (1974) has voiced particular concern that the state, with all the resources at its disposal, would employ its data gathering powers in conjunction with scientific jury selection methodology to violate the integrity of the jury system. In any event, as Etzioni points out, the use of scientific jury selection has given an inordinate advantage to those individuals who, by virtue of notoriety or wealth, can command a large legal defense fund.

It should be noted that the techniques employed by social scientists in juror selection do not differ radically from those traditionally employed by lawyers, regardless of the heat generated by the current controversy (Christie, 1976). The social scientists do appear to offer a comprehensive methodology in the service of selecting competent and "friendly jurors." Indeed, it has been noted that many trial lawyers are simply not interested in jury selection (Kairys, Schulman, & Harring, 1975). Briefly, the social science technique involves both pretrial and voir dire courtroom procedures (Christie, 1976; Schulman et al., 1973). Research has indicated that biases and dispositions are likely to be present in a potential juror with certain definable demographic and personal characteristics (Stephan, 1975). These data provide counsel with probabilities concerning biases and hence its utility is in primarily the exercise of peremptory challenges.

The first step, typically, involves a survey to be taken of a sample of the population from which the jury will be chosen (Moskitis, 1976). The survey attempts to delineate the community attitudes relevant to the trial. The data obtained from this survey, and from telephone interviews if time allows, are analyzed in terms of the relationships between community attitudes and sentiments and various demographic characteristics in order to obtain a profile of the "friendly juror." A second survey, after the list of veniremen has been issued, may be carried out, unobtrusively, by interviewing friends and neighbors of the panel members in order to increase the probability of selecting "friendly jurors." In the Harrisburg seven trial, for example, the ideal juror was a female Democrat, who held sympathetic views with the anti-war movement, who did not have a religious preference, and held a skilled-blue-collar job or a white-collar-position (Schulman et al., 1973).

The voir dire procedure is based, in great part, on the friendly juror profile analysis. The voir dire examination is designed to elicit potential jurors' favorable or unfavorable attitudes toward the defendant. Questions are designed to discover the extent of the jurors' authoritarian tendencies, as research has indicated that authoritarians are conviction prone (Stephen, 1975). Kinesic and paralinguistic analysis of the individual's responses during examination by counsel are also considered useful. If a potential juror is a good match with the initial friendly juror profile, exhibits appropriate body language and paralinguistic cues, he or she will be chosen to serve by the defense team. Clearly, after challenges for cause have been exhausted, the primary purpose of the friendly juror ratings of the veniremen would be in the judicious use of the defense's allotted peremptory challenges.

While constitutional and ethical concerns relative to the use of social science methodology in selecting jurors abound, there is little empirical evidence that these techniques are effective or indeed are any more effective than the methods and hunches traditionally employed by trial lawyers (Berk, 1976). The findings that various defendants have been acquitted when the defense availed itself of social science techniques do not, obviously, validate the efficacy of the procedures. A large defense fund buys not only social scientists but also expensive and skilled lawyers. Furthermore, a large proportion of these trials involved a conspiracy charge which is exceedingly difficult to sustain.

The effectiveness of the social science technique of juror selection has simply not been empirically demonstrated. The efficacy of this selection procedure depends, in part, on how good these techniques are, and on how effective the lawyers are in the absence of these techniques. We know something of the lawyer's performance in selecting jurors using conventional methods. Zeisel and Diamond (1976) report an experiment carried out in the U.S. District Court for the Northern District of Illinois in which a series of cases were tried in the presence of three juries: the actual jury and two experimental juries. One of these experimental juries was comprised of those potential jurors who were challenged peremptorily by either defense or prosecution. These jurors did not know which side excused them from serving. The second of these experimental juries was the "English jury," chosen at random, without being questioned by counsel or the court.

The two experimental juries sat through the trial and deliberated a final verdict. While the sources of recognition of a potentially unfavorable juror were not clearly articulated by the lawyers in the trial, both defense and prosecution were able to identify jurors unfavorable to their side. Significantly more jurors challenged by the defense convicted than those removed by the prosecution (Zeisel & Diamond, 1976).

The legal literature does not clearly delineate procedures for discovering juror prejudice during voir dire examination. Keeton (1973) suggests that the lawyer must be cognizant of the following areas: the jurors' organizational membership, including racial, social, political, and occupational affiliations; the juror's personality with particular reference to whether the juror is a "compromiser"; and is the juror strong-willed, or is he likely to make snap judgments and be influenced by bias or prejudice? Obviously, Keeton's (1973) advice is not much different than that offered by the social science model.

Keeton does not, however, offer a coherent method for securing answers to these important questions.

Daugherty (1976) conducted a number of interviews with trial lawyers in Toledo, Ohio, on the question of their theories of juror selection. She reports that while these lawyers rely on hunches, cues, past experience, and hearsay, eventually the focus is on the demographic and personality variables.

Therefore, when a comparison of lawyers' conventional methods of juror selection with the social science method (SSM) is made, we find a certain similarity of assumptions and observations. The personality, behavior, and demographic characteristics of prospective jurors are thought to be important by both approaches. The difference seems to be that the social scientists offer a methodology to secure answers to the same question. Indeed, it has been suggested that a combination of the two methodologies might be the best screening device available.

The SSM would be effective and training thereby facilitated, insofar as the issues of the trial are relevant to the demographic and personality variables which have clearly been demonstrated to affect a juror's decision. Fried, Kaplan, and Klein (1975) argue, for example, that the prosecution should select jurors disposed to side with authority. These authors note that authoritarians, by definition, identify with powerful, high-status sources of information. Authoritarian jurors would therefore tend to heed the state's arguments because they perceive that the prosecution represents legitimized power (Fried et al., 1975).

Although recent work has given greater credence to the utilization of the authoritarian dimension as an important peg of the social science methodology (Bray & Noble, in press), it is not the only one, nor has it proven to be the most powerful. Indeed, an empirical stance is usually assumed by social science proponents because it is clear that the predictive power of various factors differs with different populations, cases, and geographical variables. There does not in fact appear to be a packaged program for the SSM proponent to employ. It is in fact a pastiche of possible predictive relationships among demographic, personality, and attitudinal variables within the venire. Berk, Hennessey, and Swan (1977) have suggested that there is less actuarial and more clinical judgment inherent in the SSM than its proponents indicate.

The present experiment is an attempt to test experimentally the differences between conventional methods of juror selection and systematic SSMs. The comparison of the two methods was made over four separate criminal cases. The cases varied in type of crime and in the strength of predictive relationships from which the systematic social science derives its potential power.

<hr>

METHOD

Subjects

Ninety-six potential jurors, (55 males, 41 females) were recruited from evening classes at the University of Toledo. Evening students were used so that the simulated jurors more closely approximated the demographic profile of actual jurors. These prospective jurors responded to a request for subjects for a study of courtroom procedures. Forty-eight "defense lawyers" (42 males, 6 females) were recruited from students in the University of Toledo Law School. These students were part of a study in "juror selection procedures."

Design

Two factors were combined to yield a 2×4 design. The design compared two methods of juror selection within the context of four separate criminal cases.

Procedure

Defense lawyers were trained in one of two methods of juror selection. They were randomly assigned to the SSM or the conventional method (CM). After completion of their training, lawyers were assigned, randomly, to one of four criminal cases. They were given a written summary of the case which detailed the evidence and the witnesses to be heard. All lawyers were instructed to screen the jurors during a voir dire examination held in a moot courtroom so as to select those most likely to acquit their client. There were six lawyers for each of the eight experimental conditions.

The 96 prospective jurors (veniremen) were asked, prior to the experimental sessions, to complete a "juror information sheet" which requested the following: name, age, occupation, marital status, sex, and residence. Jurors were randomly assigned to one of the eight experimental conditions (12 jurors for each cell). After completion of the voir dire examination, jurors heard an audiotape of the case to which they were assigned and reached individual decisions as to degree of guilt or innocence.

Juror selection training: overview. The assumption underlying the training procedures was that it is imperative to bring subject-lawyers trained in both methods to the same ceiling of proficiency. Previous research (Horowitz, 1977) and the suggestions of Meehl (1954) and Hold (1968) indicated that it is necessary to expend more effort in training lawyers in the conventional method than in the apparently more easily applied actuarial or SSM.

SSM. Defense lawyers randomly assigned to SSM were given training in the application of social science technique to juror selection. These subjects were told that they would be assigned to one of four criminal cases, and that their task would be to predict jurors' probable verdicts.

The instruction was comprised, in part, of a 90-minute lecture in the SSM technique. The major portion of the lecture was given by a social psychologist. The lecture contained a section on the theoretical assumptions underlying the selection of jurors with appropriate references to empirical verification of their assumptions. In particular, the relationship between authoritarianism and conviction-proneness was covered in detail with a special reference to the Witherspoon (1968) decision. Illustrations from major criminal cases in which the SSM was used were employed. In essence, then, these lawyer-subjects were instructed in the use of various personality and demographic data as they related to juror selection. Subjects further were given reprints of relevant articles concerning SSM to read. A section on the application of kinesic and paralinguistic cues completed the lecture.

All lawyers trained in the SSM were given profiles of possible jurors ranging from a profile of the "most friendly juror" to the "most unfriendly juror." These profiles were constructed from an attitude questionnaire given to 205 students in evening classes at the University of Toledo, the venire from which actual jurors were sampled. This questionnaire was devised, based on the Schulman et al. (1973) model, to measure potential jurors' attitudes with regard to the issues of whichever criminal case the lawyers were assigned. Data pertaining to potential jurors' demographics, media preferences, organizational memberships were collected. Further, the demographics gleaned from the 96 jurors' information forms was also utilized here.

In addition, the SSM trainees were given a preexperimental practice session. Trainees were also provided with a calculus, based upon the variables which were most likely to predict a juror's probable response. A separate calculus was devised for each of the four criminal cases used in the experiment. The calculus was an attempt to have the trainees represent quantitatively the following factors: the demographic and attitudinal variables, empirically derived from the separate pretrial questionnaires for each case, predicting jurors' probable verdict; a weighting of the jurors' nonverbal responses during the voir dire; and the lawyers' evaluation of the jurors's response to the voir dire interrogation.[3]

The training of lawyer-subjects in the SSM mode required that they fully comprehended the rationale and thus be able to temper and alter the application of the calculus by their own judgments and evaluations, as suggested by their training experience.

All subjects trained in the SSM mode were instructed to employ this method alone in their selection of jurors. They were informed that the purpose of the research was to test the effectiveness of various selection procedures and that use of non-SSM information would hinder the outcome of the research.

CM training procedure. Previous research (Horowitz, 1977) has suggested that a training session comparable in length and detail to the SSM or the CM was not sufficient to produce equal proficiency for both selection techniques due to previous discussed differences between actuarial and clinical approaches (Meehl, 1956). Therefore, a somewhat more involved technique was employed to train CM practitioners. The essence of the program was modeled upon techniques used to train students in clinical psychology, to wit: lectures, readings, observations, practicum, and critique.

Initially, lawyers were given a lecture on juror selection models conventionally utilized by trial lawyers. Readings, particularly Keeton (1973) and Wildman (1966), were assigned. In addition, a videotape of a lecture given by a local trial lawyer based upon his reflections and experiences within the context of local conditions was shown (Horowitz, 1977).

Lawyers were then exposed to actual courtroom voir dire sessions to observe well-known local attorneys interrogate potential jurors. These practicing attorneys utilized what has been termed the conventional method (Daugherty, 1976). Trainees were able to compare their choices with that of the attorney and discuss discrepancies.

Finally, these trainees were shown a videotape of a voir dire examination of potential jurors and were asked to select a jury. Feedback was given as to the accuracy of their choices and a critique offered.

All CM trainees were instructed to employ only the selection method in which they had been instructed in their juror screening task. They were informed that their task was to predict jurors' probable verdict.

Criminal Cases

Sixty students in various psychology classes were asked to read accounts of 22 different crimes, 2 for each 11 crime clusters identified by Richards, Smith, and Gutman (1975). Following a procedure suggested by Fried et al. (1975), subjects' standard beyond which there was no longer a reasonable doubt of guilt was calculated. Subjects' standard of reasonable doubt was correlated with their authoritarianism score as indicated by their responses to Byrne's (1974) acquiescence-free version of the F-scale. Subjects also responded to a survey questionnaire, following Christie (1976), which gathered information pertaining to demographics, attitudes concerning relevant criminal issues, organizational memberships, and media preferences.

Four criminal cases were chosen based on observed differences between high and low authoritarians and differences in demographic and attitudinal variables between those subjects indicating a high threshold of reasonable doubt and those with a low threshold of reasonable doubt.

The cases were chosen on dimensions which either increased or decreased differences between SSM and CM. On the assumption that SSM would be most effective when the predictive relationships between demographics and probable guilty verdicts were strong, as indicated by previous research and by the preexperimental investigation relating demographics, attitudinal, and personality factors to reasonable doubt levels, two criminal cases were chosen. Strong relationships between probable guilty verdicts and both attitudinal and personality variables also dictated the choice of those two criminal cases. The two cases were (1) *the sale of illegal drugs*[4] and (2) a military *court martial* adapted from Hamilton (1976).

Case (3) involved a *murder* and the preexperimental data indicated, given the nature of the case, moderate to weak predictive relationships. Case (4), *drunk driving,* did not have significant relationships between the various predictive variables and probable guilty verdicts attached to it. Each case was prerated by law students for evidentiary closeness prior to the study. All four cases were rated as close to the threshold of reasonable doubt.

The Voir Dire Examination

The voir dire examination was carried out in eight separate sessions corresponding to the eight experimental conditions. Four 3rd-year law students (all males), one for each crime, conducted the voir dire. Each "interrogating lawyer" was trained in either the SSM or the CM.

The voir dire was carried out in a moot courtroom setting. The 6 defense lawyers randomly assigned to the experimental condition listened to the interrogation, and all 12 jurors randomly assigned to the condition were present but were interrogated individually.

Examination of each juror was conducted according to guidelines offered by Garry (1976) and Keeton (1973) and the advice of Law School professors.[5] Lawyer-subjects were allowed to ask questions by writing a note to the interrogating attorney. The lawyer-subjects could not directly ask questions, but could do so only through the person of the interrogation attorney. The four male interrogating attorneys were chosen on the basis of their performances in a Trial Practice course. They were thoroughly trained in both selection cases and thoroughly familiar with cases to which they were assigned. Their training was aimed at minimizing, as far as is possible, any significant differences among these four interrogators.

Since the defense lawyers were trained in only one of the two selection methods, and since they did have the opportunity to ask questions, indirectly, of the potential jurors, it was decided not to have CM and SSM rate the same jurors. It was probable that the two selection methods would indicate different kinds of questions and thus elicit different information from the jurors. While error variance would have been reduced had all defense lawyer subjects rated the same jurors, the elicitation of information not in accordance with one or the other training procedures would have been a confounding factor. CM subjects could have availed themselves of SSM-related information and the reverse would also be possible. Furthermore, total standardization of the voir dire would, to some extent, vitiate the ability of subjects trained in each of the methods to utilize the unique characteristics of that method to elicit differential information.

The Measures

The lawyer-subjects were instructed that their task was to predict the juror's probable verdict. Both juror and lawyer were given a 6-point, bracketed scale. Points 1 through 3 indicated a not guilty verdict, with confidence being the highest at one and lowest at three. Points four through six indicated a guilty verdict, with higher numbers denoting increasing confidence in that verdict.

Lawyers were asked to use the 6-point scale to predict as each juror finished the voir dire interrogation.

Jurors listened to an audiotape of the case they were assigned to after completion of the voir dire and then were asked for their verdict on the 6-point scale. There was not any deliberation among jurors.

The 6-point verdict-confidence scale was chosen as the major measure rather than a simple guilty-not guilty dichotomy because it was felt that a degree of sensitivity was gained by the use of this scale. The scale allows one to deal with near misses, far misses, and predictions that fall in between the extremes. Further, it allows for whatever differences the two approaches to juror selection generate to be more clearly observed.

Dependent measure. Each lawyer-subject made a prediction concerning each juror's probable verdict on the same 6-point scale the juror used to indicate his or her verdict after listening to the audiotape of the case. For each juror, the six lawyer-subjects' predictions were averaged and compared to that individual juror's verdict, thus yielding a difference score. Analyses were performed on these difference scores.

RESULTS

Analysis of difference scores. A 2 × 4 analysis of variance was performed on the difference scores. The analysis yielded a significant main effect for criminal cases, $F(3, 88) = 2.63, p < .05$, and a significant cases × jurors selection methods interaction, $F(3, 88) = 4.27, p < .001$. The methods main effect did not reach significance, $F < 1.00$. An *F-max* test for heterogeneity of variance was not significant ($F = 1.96, p > .05$).

Table 1 presents the mean difference scores for all experimental conditions and presents the results of a Duncan Multiple Comparison Test performed on all eight means. Lawyers using SSM were more effective in predicting jurors' verdicts in both the drug and court martial cases. Lawyers using CM were more effective in predicting jurors' verdicts in the murder case. Both methods were most ineffective in the drunk-driving case and neither method had an advantage in this case. The best predictions occurred in the murder case using CM and in the court martial case utilizing SSM. Overall, it proved easier to accurately predict jurors' responses in the murder and court martial cases.

DISCUSSION

In the present study, the SSM proved to be more effective than the CM in juror selection in two of four criminal cases, the sales of illegal drugs, and a military court martial. The predictive relationships derived from surveys and demographic studies, and moot in-court ratings of jurors, held most strongly in these two cases, and therefore it

TABLE 3.1
Mean Difference Scores for Both Selection Methods
for Four Criminal Cases

Juror selection method	Criminal Case			
	Drugs	Court martial	Murder	Drunk driving
CM	1.27^c	0.84^b	0.54^a	1.15^c
SSM	0.75^b	0.61^a	0.84^b	1.19^c

Note: Means which do not share a common subscript differ significantly ($p < .05$) by Duncan multiple-range test. The lower the difference score, the more accurate the prediction. Six lawyers and 12 jurors comprised each experimental condition.

was expected that the SSM would be most effective in these two instances. Lawyer-subjects using the CM of juror selection were more effective in predicting jurors' verdicts in the murder trial. The predictive relationships relied upon in the SSM were only mildly relevant in this instance. Both methods were relatively ineffective in predicting jurors' responses in the drunk-driving case. Overall, lawyer-subjects were best able to predict jurors' verdicts in the court martial and murder cases.

Clearly, then, the effectiveness of the SSM depends upon its use in cases in which the actuarial data on which its profiles are based appear to be fairly strong. When these predictive relationships are less powerful, the SSM proved to be inferior to, or no better than, the conventional methods of juror selection. Therefore, in this laboratory-conducted experimental study, the effectiveness of juror selection methods was dependent upon an appropriate interaction with the specific variables of the criminal case.

The most serious problem one has in conducting a laboratory study of issues such as were raised in this instance is, of course, the problem of ecological validity. Have we appropriately and faithfully simulated the two juror selection methods? Clearly, the lawyer-subjects were not trained social scientists nor were they trained and experienced lawyers. Clearly, the present methodology, despite very careful attention given to the training of the lawyer-subjects, was not able to bring them up to the level of either experienced lawyers or Ph.D.-level sociologists. Indeed, the entire strategy was to keep subjects as neutral as possible in order that the differences between the methodologies were reflected most clearly.

It must be noted that in the present study lawyers made predictions about the verdict rendered by each juror. This system does not deal with the possible impact of group pressures which might alter these verdicts if jurors were permitted to deliberate before reaching a verdict. Selection methods would have to account for the impact of social interaction influences on the juror's ultimate decisions.

The power of the SSM resides in its potential ability to generate predictions from very little data, such as the jurors' race, sex, residences, etc. Indeed, one suspects as the data base increases the differences between SSM and CM narrow and disappear. That is, if the voir dire was not limited, as is very common, and was true in the present study, and if enough questions are asked of potential jurors, both methods would converge on the same jurors.

The present study favored the SSM insofar as the voir dire was relatively limited in its scope and on the assumption that actuarial techniques are more easily applied than clinical techniques. On the other hand, SSM proponents could argue that the methodology was slighted to the degree that the power of the method is dependent upon the analysis of the juror profiles done in the courtroom and in conjunction with psychological analysis of the jurors' responses at the time of the voir dire investigation. While the present study endeavored to simulate this aspect of SSM, the lawyer-subjects were not experienced sociologists.

CM proponents may feel that the fact that the CM did not prove to be superior to SSM was due simply to bad clinical performances or inadequately trained lawyer-subjects.

The constitutional issues raised earlier could be dealt with by removing the pretrial differential in information between SSM and other methods. To do this, one simply makes the pre-voir dire information available to both sides. Moskitis (1976) points out that present laws fail to allow for discovery of pre-voir dire investigative information, thus neglecting to curb both adversarial imbalances and possible invasions of privacy. Indeed, as some commentators have noted (Cooper, 1976), the unbridled use of such investigations may, in fact, constitute an undue invasion of privacy. Another option would be to allow for in-depth probing voir dire. While there is the possibility of abuse in this procedure, cases with particularly sensitive issues of bias would benefit from an expanded voir dire. This would likely reduce any differences between selection methods.

In summary, this study represents an experimental and empirical demonstration of the differential effectiveness of the SSM of juror selection and CMs of selection. The data indicated that when the voir dire examination is limited, as was the case in this experiment, and parenthetically is true of most voir dire examinations, and the predictive relationships used by SSM are relatively strong, the SSM was an effective utilizer of scant biographical and demographic data in predicting jurors' responses. The more intuitive, conventional approach was better than SSM when the critical predictive relationships were weak or absent. Overall, the SSM was not superior to CM.

NOTES

1. The research was supported by a grant from the University of Toledo Graduate School.

2. Requests for reprints should be sent to Dr. Irwin A. Horowitz, Department of Psychology, University of Toledo, Toledo, Ohio 43606.

3. A more detailed description of the training is available upon request from the author.

4. A detailed description of each case and the procedures for selecting these cases is available upon request from the author.

5. Professor Thomas E. Willging of the Toledo University Law faculty was very helpful at this stage of the research and throughout the project.

REFERENCES

Berk, R. A. Social science and jury selection: A case study of a civil suit. In G. Bermant, C. Nemeth, & N. Vidmar (Eds.), *Psychology and the law.* New York: Lexington Books, 1976.

Berk, R. A., Hennessy, M., & Swan, J. The vagaries and vulgarities of "scientific" jury selection. *Evaluation Quarterly,* 1977 1(1).

Bray, R. M., & Noble, A. M. Authoritarianism and decisions of mock juries: Evidence of jury bias and group polarization. *Journal of Personality and Social Psychology,* in press.

Byrne, D. *An introduction to personality: Research, theory, and applications* (2nd ed.). Englewood Cliffs, NJ: Prentice-Hall, 1974.

Christie, R. Probability vs. precedence: The social psychology of jury selection. In G. Bermant, C. Nemeth, & N. Vidmar (Eds), *Psychology and the law.* New York: Lexington Books, 1976.

Cooper, L. Voir dire in federal criminal trials: Protecting the defendant's right to an impartial jury. *Indiana Law Journal,* 1976, 269-280.

Daugherty, M. *Juror selection methods of trial lawyers: Interview with ten Toldeo attorneys.* Unpublished manuscript, University of Toledo, 1976.

Etzioni, A. Creating an imbalance, *Trial,* 1974, **10**, 28-30.

Fried, M., Kaplan, J. J., & Klein, K. W. Juror selection: An analysis of voir dire. In R. J. Simon (Ed.), *The jury system in America*. Newbury Park, CA: Sage Publications, 1975.

Garry, C. Voir dire. *Trial Offering*, 1976, **37G**, 34.

Hamilton, V. L. Individual differences in ascriptions of responsibility, guilt, and appropriate punishment. In G. Bermant, C. Nemeth, & N. Vidmar (Eds.), *Psychology and the law*. New York: Lexington Books, 1976.

Holt, R. R. Assessing personality, In. I. C. Janis, G. F. Mahl, J. Kagan, & R. R. Holt (Eds.), *Personality*. New York: Harcourt, Brace & World, 1968.

Horowitz, I. A. *Juror selection: The impact of voir dire, social science methods of selection and the evidence on juror's verdict*. Unpublished manuscript, University of Toledo, 1977.

Kairys, D., Schulman, J., & Harring, S. (Eds.) *The jury system: New methods for reducing prejudice*. Prepared by the National Jury Project and the National Lawyer's Guild. Philadelphia: Philadelphia Resistance Print Shop, 1975.

Keeton, R. E. *Trial tactics and methods* (2nd ed.). Boston: Little, Brown, 1973.

Meehl, P. E. *Clinical versus statistical prediction*. Minneapolis: University of Minnesota Press, 1954.

Meehl, P. E. Wanted—A good cookbook. *American Psychologist*, 1956, **11**, 263-272.

Moskitis, R. L. The constitutional need for discovery of pre-voir dire juror studies. *Southern California Law Review*, 1976, **49**, 597-633.

Richards, L. G., Smith, D., & Gutman, I. *On the conception of crimes*. Paper presented at the Psychonomic Society Meetings, November, 1975.

Saks, M. Social scientists can't rig juries. *Psychology Today*, 1976, January, 48-57.

Schulman, J., Shaver, P., Colman, R., Emrich, B., & Christie, R. Recipe for a jury. *Psychology Today*, 1973, May, 37-44.

Stephan, C. Selective characteristics of jurors and litigants: Their influences on juries' verdicts. In R. J. Simon (Ed.), *The jury system in America*. Newbury Park, CA: Sage Publications, 1975.

Taylor v. Louisiana (419 U.S. 522) 1975.

Wildman, M. Selecting the jury—Defense view. *American Jurisprudence Trials*, 1966, U.S., 249-285.

Witherspoon v. Illinois. *Supreme Court Reporter*, 1968, **88**, 177-178.

Ziesel, H., & Diamond, S. S. The jury selection in the Mitchell-Stans conspiracy trial. *American Bar Foundation Research Journal*, 1976, **1**, 151-174.

SECTION I

SUMMARY

Two distinguishable issues regarding the psychologist's role in jury selection are worth further discussion here. One is the matter of propriety or ethics; the second deals with the effectiveness of "scientific" jury selection, in comparison with traditional methods or, for that matter, no selection at all.

Is it ethical for social scientists to aid one side—usually it has been the defense—in a criminal trial? Richard Christie (1976), one of the social scientists on the Harrisburg Seven defense team, offers two kinds of justification. One is that the social scientists' techniques are not that different from the traditional approach of attorneys; he writes, "The techniques used by those of us working with lawyers on jury selection are in no way a radical departure from more traditional legal practice; they are more a matter of degree or style than of kind" (pp. 265-266). But as chapter 3 notes, there *are* significant differences; in assessing the characteristics of the venire, lawyers traditionally use their experience with previous jury pools, whereas social scientists carry out surveys and demographic studies. In making observations of prospective jurors, lawyers typically rely upon intuition, seasoned by their own past experience; social scientists try to make systematic ratings. Finally, in trying to compose the actual jury, lawyers often focus on the selection of key jurors, whereas social scientists more systematically apply the findings from research on small group dynamics.

A second kind of justification, offered by Christie (1976) and also exemplified by chapter 1, rests on the social scientists' beliefs that the defendant's rights to a fair trial have already been jeopardized. With regard to the trial of the Harrisburg Seven, Schulman and his coauthors noted in chapter 1 some of the ways that the government slanted matters toward an eventual guilty verdict. Implicit in the justification is a view that in an adversary system, each side must use whatever devices that are within legal limits to compensate for the bias resulting from partisanship by the other side.

The original reason for having a jury pool larger than the actual number of jurors needed was to encourage the development of a fair and impartial jury. Given the adversarial nature of the process, attorneys for each side attempt to dismiss those potential jurors who would have been biased against their case. Christie (1976) concludes that most potential jurors in political trials are biased in favor of the prosecution. Taking this view, we may conclude the following: Acting as consultants to the attorneys, social scientists face no ethical dilemmas in facilitating the selection of favorable jurors, as long as they do the best job they can with the methods they have available. This narrow view assumes, of course, that each side is equally effective in identifying and eliminating those potential jurors who are unsympathetic to its case. But rarely do both sides devote equal effort and equal ability to jury selection, and the outcome often is a jury slanted in either one direction or the other.

Kairys, Schulman, and Harring (1975) make the bald statement that "Most criminal lawyers are not interested in jury selection." While our experiences advising attorneys would contradict that claim, certainly lawyers differ in their ability to select the kind of jurors they want. Furthermore, to our knowledge, there has never been a criminal trial in which *both* sides employed social scientists to assist in jury selection. So the hoped-for goal that the adversary system would permit a "balancing out" rarely occurs.

On the matter of the effectiveness of jury selection, the limited evidence that is available suggests that both the traditional methods used by attorneys and "scientific jury selection" are more effective than a random-selection procedure. In one study that used a simulated personal injury case, a social scientist (Strodtbeck, reported by Zeisel & Diamond, 1976) asked experienced trial attorneys to rank jurors according to the size of the damage award that each might advocate in jury deliberations. He then compared their rankings with the actual awards proposed by these jurors. Strodtbeck found that lawyers of both types—representing plaintiffs and defendants—were good at predicting the variations in awards. Another study by a team of psychologists and lawyers (Padawer-Singer, Singer, & Singer, 1974)·

also concluded that the *voir dire* served its purpose for the attorneys; compared with unexamined jurors, those they selected were more sympathetic about mitigating circumstances, were less influenced by negative pretrial information, and were more concerned about following the law set forth by the judge.

In a different type of study, Zeisel and Diamond (1978) assessed lawyers' skills in jury selection by looking at how prospective jurors who were challenged *would have* voted. For 12 criminal trials conducted at the U.S. District Court of Northern Illinois, the researchers asked those venire members who had been excused to remain "shadow jurors"; that is, they watched the trial from the spectator section of the courtroom and then rendered their own verdicts. With this device, a comparison could be made between the decisions of actual juries composed solely of those who had survived the *voir dire* and hypothetical juries composed simply of the first 12 venire members. (These latter "juries on paper" thus were made up of both real jurors and those who had been excused.) After analyzing the results, the researchers concluded that in 3 of the 12 cases, the ultimate verdicts were affected by the defense attorney's efficient use of peremptory challenges, and concluded that trial attorneys apparently win at least some of their cases with the help of their own actions during *voir dire*.

Chapter 3 indicates that when the two methods are compared head to head, neither approach is consistently superior to the other. But the method of "scientific jury selection" appeared to be more effective in those cases in which there were clear-cut relationships between personality or demographic variables and jurors' votes. In the real world there is no reason why both approaches cannot be employed in collaboration. Attorneys bring to trials a wealth of experience with the nuances of courtroom interaction; social scientists bring a systematic way to analyze impressions.

REFERENCES

Christie, R. (1976). Probability v. precedence: The social psychology of jury selection. In G. Bermant, C. Nemeth, & N. Vidmar (Eds.), *Psychology and the law: Research frontiers.* (pp. 265-281). Lexington, MA: Lexington Books.

Kairys, D., Shulman, J., & Harring, S. (1975). *The jury system: New methods for reducing prejudice.* Philadelphia, PA: Philadelphia Resistance Print Shop.

Padawer-Singer, A. M., Singer, A., & Singer, S. (1974). Voir dire by two lawyers: An essential safeguard. *Judicature, 57*, 386-391.

Zeisel, H., & Diamond, S. S. (1976). The jury selection in the Mitchell-Stans conspiracy trial. *American Bar Foundation Research Journal, 1*, 151-174.

Zeisel, H., & Diamond, S. S. (1978). The effect of peremptory challenges on jury and verdict: An experiment in a federal district court. *Stanford Law Review, 30*, 491-529.

SECTION II

THE BIASED JUROR
Introduction

Jury selection practices have always aroused controversy. Should lawyers be allowed, during the voir dire, to pry into personal matters such as a juror's religious preference, political affiliation, likes and dislikes, or family history? Should judges or attorneys conduct the questioning? Should prospective jurors be questioned individually or together as a group, in public or in private? The entire practice of rounding up a *representative* collection of citizens, and then removing from that panel those who are not *impartial*, is founded on the assumption that jurors may be so biased that they could not reach decisions based on an objective evaluation of the evidence. Few scholars or practitioners would deny that when jurors enter the courtroom they are tainted in some way by their personal backgrounds, beliefs, and experiences. That raises two important questions—what are the characteristics of a biased juror, and are jury verdicts hopelessly contaminated by these nonevidentiary factors? This section consists of three chapters that address these issues.

What kinds of people become biased jurors? Trial lawyers have their own intuitive theories. Clarence Darrow, for example, thought that Irish and Italian jurors were good for the defense, while Scottish, Scandinavian, and German jurors were not (quoted in Sutherland & Cressey, 1966, p. 442). In the meantime, psychologists interested in the relationship between personality and decision making have conducted a good deal of research on juries. Lawyers and psychologists are rarely on the same track. But there is one topic they agree on—authoritarianism and juror bias. This section thus opens with a study by Bray and Noble (1978). It demonstrates rather convincingly that mock juries composed of relatively authoritarian individuals were more likely to convict than those composed of nonauthoritarian individuals. Does that feeling signal the danger that jury verdicts are based on nonrational factors? The chapter by Myers (1979) addresses this very question. In that piece, Myers reports on an archival study of 201 jury trials. Looking at the available records on these cases, Myers finds that, as a general rule, verdicts were based more on the integrity of the evidence than on extraneous or irrelevant factors. In the final chapter in this section, Kaplan and Miller (1978) offer one possible explanation for the apparent discrepancy between the bias of individual jurors on the one hand, and the fairness of jury verdicts on the other. It will be seen that these investigators offer a theoretical framework and research that delineate the conditions under which verdicts are driven by bias versus trial evidence.

REFERENCE

Sutherland, E. H., & Cressey, D. R. (1966). *Principles of criminology* (7th ed.). Philadelphia: Lippincott.

4

AUTHORITARIANISM AND DECISIONS OF MOCK JURIES
Evidence of Jury Bias and Group Polarization

ROBERT M. BRAY
AUDREY M. NOBLE
University of Kentucky

Several investigations of judicial decision making have focused recently on the relationship of authoritarianism and juror performance (e.g., Berg & Vidmar, 1975; Boehm, 1968; Crosson, 1967; Jurow, 1971;

Authors' Note: Portions of this research were supported by a summer research fellowship from the Graduate School of the University of Kentucky to the first author. Appreciation is extended to Steve Kaiser for help in collecting the data. Some of these data were presented at the Midwestern Psychological Association Meeting, Chicago, May 1978. Requests for reprints should be sent to Robert M. Bray, Department of Psychology, University of Kentucky, Lexington, Kentucky 40506.

Mitchell & Byrne, 1973; Kagehiro & Werner, Note 1; Kirby & Lamberth, Note 2; Lineberry, Becker & Lammers, Note 3; Vidmar, Note 4). The characterization of high authoritarians as conservative, rigid, and punitive toward those who violate conventional values (Adorno, Frenkel-Brunswik, Levinson, & Sanford, 1950) suggests that as jurors they may convict more frequently and render more severe punishment than low authoritarians. Whether high authoritarians exhibit a bias toward such harshness is of particular concern for trials involving capital punishment. Because capital-trial jurors generally forswear scruples against the death penalty, it has been argued that such "death-qualified" juries are inclined to be composed of politically conservative or authoritarian jurors. In *Witherspoon v. Illinois* (1968), for example, the petitioner requested the Supreme Court to set aside his conviction and death penalty arguing that (a) the jury that found him guilty favored the death penalty, (b) jurors favoring the death penalty have highly authoritarian, dogmatic, and conservative personalities, and (c) highly authoritarian, dogmatic, and conservative jurors are more likely to favor a guilty than a not guilty verdict. The Court agreed with the first argument and reversed the death sentence. However, it let stand the guilty verdict on the basis of fragmentary evidence linking high authoritarianism and the tendency to convict.

Since the Court's ruling, despite several additional studies on the issue (e.g., Berg & Vidmar, 1975; Jurow, 1971; Mitchell & Byrne, 1973; Kagehiro & Werner, Note 1; Kirby & Lamberth, Note 2; Lineberry, Becker, & Lammers, Note 3), the claim that high authoritarians are more likely to render guilty verdicts remains unsettled. Davis, Bray, and Holt (1977), in their review of jury research, concluded that "for judgments of punitiveness high authoritarians tend to be more harsh than low authoritarians, but for judgments of guilt the influence of authoritarianism remains to be clarified" (p. 336). Elwork and Sales (in press) reached a similar conclusion in their literature review.

Not only is the evidence on authoritarianism and the tendency to convict tentative, it has generally been confined to judgments of individual jurors prior to group deliberations. Although group decisions have frequently been omitted in mock-trial research, their importance has received recent emphasis (Davis et al., 1977; Foss, 1976; Jurow, 1971; Vidmar, Note 4). The necessity of considering group decisions is further underscored in view of conflicting hypotheses about how high and low authoritarians will behave in group settings. Some researchers (e.g., Boehm, 1968; Kirby & Lamberth, Note 2) have argued that high authoritarians reach verdicts early in a trial (e.g., after hearing the prosecution arguments) and are more resistant to change in the face of new information than are low authoritarians. Thus in a group, high authoritarians should hold firmly to their initial position and not readily alter their verdicts. In contrast, other research on conformity and social influence suggests that high authoritarians are more susceptible to influence attempts than are low authoritarians (see Kirscht & Dillehay, 1967, for a review). Consequently, group interactions should produce more verdict changes for high than for low authoritarians.

One purpose of the present investigation was to examine again the relationship between juror authoritarianism and judicial decisions of guilt and punishment and to extend prior research by assessing this relationship among both individual jurors and deliberating juries.

Another concern of our study was to extend research efforts on the group polarization hypothesis in simulated juries. Briefly, the polarization hypothesis argues that group interaction tends to enhance choice tendencies initially favored in the subject population. Thus if predominant sentiment among individual jurors is toward a guilty (not guilty) verdict, that sentiment should be more predominant following discussion. Myers and Lamm (1976) have recently argued that the group polarization phenomenon appears to be general across a variety of tasks including jury decisions. Nonetheless, they acknowledge that while some studies (e.g., Myers & Kaplan, 1976; Vidmar, Note 4) are consistent with the polarization phenomenon, as a whole, the findings "from experimental simulations of the jury process, do not lend themselves to clear-cut generalizations" (p. 606).

Thus in our investigation, we sought to provide additional evidence of group polarization in simulated juries composed of low or high authoritarians. We hypothesized that high-authoritarian jurors would vote guilty more often and recommend more severe punishment than low authoritarians and predicted that group deliberations would polarize postdiscussion juror judgments in the direction initially favored by the subject population. We also expected that high-authoritarian juries would convict more often and give longer sentences than low-authoritarian juries and that these jury decisions would be polarized relative to the individual predeliberation judgments. Finally, we explored the question of verdict changes but offered no specific predictions, in view of the conflicting literature.

METHOD

Subjects

Participants were 280 students (160 females and 118 males) enrolled in an introductory psychology course or a beginning social psychology class. Each student participated for 2 hours to earn extra credit. From the total sample, 264 persons were divided into 44 six-person juries, while the remaining 16 subjects performed an alternate task during the deliberations. Only data from the six-person juries were analyzed.

To classify participants as high or low authoritarians, a 22-item acquiescence-free version of the F scale (Byrne, 1974) was administered to a large number of students early in the semester. Using a 4-point response format ("strongly agree" to "strongly disagree") the pretested sample obtained a mean F score of 49.19 and a standard deviation of 8.49. Persons scoring at least one-half a standard deviation above and below the mean were designated as high and low authoritarians, respectively.

Procedure

Approximately 36 to 48 persons, either all high or all low authoritarians, appeared at each experimental session. The experimenter met the subjects in a classroom, explained that they were to act as jurors for the case, and instructed them not to take notes or discuss the proceeding prior to deliberations. Participants then listened to a 30-minute audio recording of a murder trial, based on a case tried in Illinois. Two male defendants, while in a drunken state, purportedly murdered a female in her Chicago apartment; she had presumably rebuffed their advances in a nightclub earlier the same evening. The trial concluded with the judge instructing the jurors regarding the law that should guide them in reaching a verdict of guilt or innocence.

Following the trial, jurors individually completed a questionnaire. They first made judgments about the guilt of the defendants on a dichotomous guilty-not guilty scale. Jurors were then asked to assume that the defendants were guilty, regardless of their prior verdict, and to recommend a prison sentence from 14 years (the minimum sentence for the crime in Illinois) to 99 years. No additional instructions were given about specific factors to weigh (e.g., type of person, past history) in determining sentences. Jurors also indicated on a 7-point scale how similar they found themselves to the defendants.

For deliberations, six-person juries were randomly composed except that an effort was made to balance sex composition of the groups.[1] An arbitrarily appointed foreperson read instructions explaining that five of the six jurors must agree in order to declare a verdict, after which the jury began deliberations. Juries failing to reach a verdict after 45 minutes were considered hung. Juries were also asked to reach a decision about the appropriate sentence for the defendants, assuming them guilty.

Following deliberations, jurors again gave individual judgments of guilt and punishment. In addition, they rated on a 6-point scale the importance of the foreperson in the jury verdict. Finally, they indicated on a 7-point scale the likelihood of their voting guilty for a murder charge (given that the evidence pointed toward guilt) if death were a potential penalty.

RESULTS

Manipulation of Authoritarianism

A Sex × Authoritarianism unweighted-means analysis of variance was computed on participants' F scores to verify the effectiveness of the pretest selection procedure. The results showed a strong effect only for authoritarianism, $F(1, 253) = 1266.60$, $p < .001$. The means for the male low and high authoritarians were 39.66 and 59.33, respectively; comparable means for females were 39.74 and 58.55

Juror Decisions

Before and after deliberations, jurors made judgments about whether the defendant was guilty or not guilty. These responses were examined in a Sex × Authoritarianism (high or low) × Deliberation (pre-or post-) multidimensional chi-square analysis with repeated measures on the last factor. This analysis followed the general linear model approach to nonmetric data (Grizzle, Starmet, & Koch, 1969; Kritzer, 1973) and used the procedure for repeated measurement designs reported by Lehnen and Koch (1974). The results showed significant effects for authoritarianism, $\chi^2 (1) = 15.53$, $p < .001$, and for deliberations, $\chi^2 (1) = 15.00$, $p < .001$. As shown in Table 1, high authoritarians voted guilty significantly more often than low authoritarians, both before and after deliberations. Further, after deliberations there was a shift toward fewer guilty verdicts for high and low authoritarians.

To assess whether high- or low-authoritarian jurors were more likely to alter their verdicts because of deliberation, prediscussion-postdiscussion verdict changes were examined. Verdict shifts appearing in Table 2 show that jurors changed in both directions, although most changers shifted toward a not guilty verdict. Further, the large majority of jurors did not change from their initial verdict, a result that may reflect the strength of the evidence favoring acquittal. A chi-square test showed that high authoritarians changed significantly more than low authoritarians, $\chi^2(2) = 8.81$, $p < .02$.

TABLE 4.1

Percentage of Individual Jurors Voting Guilty
Before and After Deliberations

	Predeliberation						Postdeliberation					
	Male		Female		Total		Male		Female		Total	
Authoritarian	%	n	%	n	%	n	%	n	%	n	%	n
Low	33		17		25		21		8		14	
		61		64		125		61		64		125
High	42		48		45		33		33		33	
		48		84		132		48		84		132

Note: Either pre- or postdeliberation responses were missing for seven participants. Percentages are rounded to the nearest whole number.

Jurors were also asked both before and after deliberations to indicate an appropriate sentence under the assumption that the defendant had been found guilty. To examine these data, a 2(sex) $\times$ 2 (authoritarianism) $\times$ 2(deliberation) unweighted-means analysis of variance was computed with repeated measures on the last factor. The results showed significant effects for authoritarianism, $F(1, 257) = 60.30$, $p < .001$, and for the Authoritarianism $\times$ Deliberation interaction $F(1, 157) = 25.68, p < .001$.[2] The mean sentences are presented in Table 3. As can be seen from the marginals, high authoritarians gave significantly longer sentences than low authoritarians. More interestingly, the interaction shows a polarization effect; low authoritarians gave more *lenient* sentences after deliberations than before, whereas high authoritarians gave more *severe* sentences after deliberations than before.

Jury Decisions

Jury verdicts, displayed in Table 4, were examined with an Authoritarianism $\times$ Verdict chi-square test. The results showed that high authoritarians reached verdicts of guilty significantly more often than low authoritarians, $\chi^2(2) = 9.02, p < .02$.[3] As shown in Table 4, although most juries reached a not guilty verdict, all that reached a guilty verdict were high authoritarians.

Juries were also asked to sentence the defendants assuming they had been found guilty. A one-way analysis of variance showed high authoritarians recommending significantly more years in prison than low authoritarians, $F(1, 38) = 13.90, p < .001$ (see Table 3).[4]

Juror Perceptions

Prior to deliberations, jurors reported on a 7-point scale how similar they were to the defendants. A Sex $\times$ Authoritarianism unweighted-

TABLE 4.2
Prediscussion-Postdiscussion Verdict Changes for
Low- and High-Authoritarian Jurors

	Direction of change					
	Not guilty → Guilty[a]		Guilty → Not guilty[a]		No change	
Authoritarian	%	n	%	n	%	n
Low	1.6	2	12.0	15	86.4	108
High	7.6	10	19.7	26	72.7	96
M	4.7		16.0		79.4	
Total		12		41		204

Note: Total N = 257; either prediscussion or postdiscussion verdict data were missing for seven jurors.
a. Label to left of arrow indicates predeliberation verdict; label to right of arrow indicates postdeliberation verdict.

means analysis of variance showed significant differences for sex, $F(1, 259) = 6.31$, $p < .02$, and for authoritarianism, $F(1, 259) = 9.06$, $p < .003$. Generally, all jurors considered themselves quite dissimilar to the defendants ($M = 2.14$). Females rated themselves as significantly less similar ($M = 1.96$) than did males ($M = 2.33$), a finding that may reflect, in part, the fact that the defendants were males. High authoritarians ($M = 1.92$) judged themselves significantly less similar to the defendants than did low authoritarians ($M = 2.37$).[5]

After deliberations, jurors indicated on a 6-point scale the importance of the foreperson in influencing their jury's verdict. A Sex × Authoritarianism analysis of variance showed a significant effect for authoritarianism, $F(1, 256) = 5.47$, $p < .02$. High authoritarians ($M = 3.16$) rated the foreperson as significantly more influential than low authoritarians ($M = 2.70$).

Finally, jurors indicated on a 7-point scale the likelihood of their voting guilty for a murder charge (given strong evidence pointing to guilt) if death were a potential penalty. A Sex × Authoritarianism analysis of variance showed a strong effect for authoritarianism, $F(1, 260) = 35.39$, $p < .001$, with highs ($M = 4.60$) being significantly more likely to vote guilty than lows ($M = 3.11$).

DISCUSSION

In the present experiment, high authoritarians imposed longer sentences and reached more guilty verdicts than low authoritarians.

TABLE 4.3
Juror and Jury Mean Sentences in Years

| | Authoritarian | |
Response	Low	High
Predeliberation[a]	38.07	56.36
Postdeliberation[a]	28.58	67.70
M	33.33	62.03
Jury	34.75	72.90

Note: Range of sentences was 14-99 years.
a. Mean responses of individual jurors.

These results occurred both for individual jurors and, perhaps more important, among interacting jury members; for the latter, all guilty verdicts were returned by high authoritarians. More severe punishment by high authoritarians is consistent with results of previous investigations (e.g., Berg & Vidmar, 1975; Jurow, 1971; Mitchell & Byrne, 1973; Kirby & Lamberth, Note 2; Lineberry, Beckers & Lammers, Note 3). More interestingly, our results for guilty verdicts offer support for the widely held but generally untested notion that high-authoritarian juries are more inclined than low-authoritarian juries to find a defendant guilty (see Davis et al., 1977; Elwork & Sales, in press).

That these results should obtain in the present study but not in prior research aimed at testing the same basic question (at least for nondeliberating jurors) is worthy of comment. An analysis of this earlier research suggests two possible explanations. The first is that in some studies (e.g., Berg & Vidmar, 1975; Mitchell & Byrne, 1973), the distribution of sentiment about the case was highly skewed. Thus the evidence may have been sufficiently convincing that no differences emerged. The second explanation concerns the use of a median split to define "high" and "low" authoritarians, a procedure followed in many of the studies (e.g., Berg & Vidmar, 1975; Jurow, 1971; Mitchell & Byrne, 1973; Kagehiro & Werner, Note 1; Lineberry, Becker, & Lammers, Note 3; Vidmar, Note 4). With this technique, subjects from the middle portion of the F-scale distribution get classified as either high or low authoritarians. This practice increases within-group variability (see Jurow, 1971, as an extreme example) and may have "washed out" differences that would be apparent if midrange responders were eliminated.

Although we recommend caution in generalizing to actual trials, we note that these findings linking authoritarianism and guilt have

TABLE 4.4
Verdicts for Low- and High-Authoritarian Juries

Authori- tarian	Jury verdict					
	Guilty		Not guilty		Hung	
	%	n	%	n	%	n
Low	0	0	90	19	10	2
High	35	8	61	14	4	1
M	18		75		7	
Total		8		33		3

Note: Percentages are rounded to the nearest whole number.

potential implications for trials involving capital punishment, the type of trial where juries containing all high authoritarians would most likely be empaneled. This follows from selection criteria in which capital-trial jurors must indicate their willingness to consider all potential penalties and must not be irrevocably committed before the trial has begun to vote against the death penalty (cf. Witherspoon v. Illinois, 1968). In this regard, Jurow (1971) reported that low authoritarians were most opposed to the death penalty, whereas high authoritarians were most favorable toward it. Our data also provide some support for this view. High authoritarians reported that they would be more likely than low authoritarians to convict when death was a potential penalty. Considered together, these findings suggest that to the extent that greater endorsement of the death penalty by high authoritarians results in their being selected as capital-trial jurors, such juries are inclined to convict a defendant. One implication is that consideration be directed to the procedures for selecting capital-trial jurors to ensure that an impartial jury is empaneled (cf. Jurow, 1971).

Another aspect of our data concerns prediscussion-postdiscussion shifts in juror judgments that are interesting in two regards. First, for verdicts of guilt, high authoritarians changed more than low authoritarians. This finding runs counter to the hypothesis that high authoritarians exhibit greater resistance to change (e.g., Boehm, 1968; Kirby & Lamberth, Note 2) and at a minimum suggests that they are not closed minded. Second, the shifts in judgments for guilt and sentencing offer support for the polarization hypothesis in a jury paradigm (Myers & Lamm, 1976) in that the jurors moved in the direction of choice tendencies initially favored. However, for guilt verdicts the use of a single case restricted movement to one direction.

Our data extend prior research based on short written summaries (see Myers & Lamm, 1976) in that we used complex case material more similar to that occurring in the courtroom. We did not focus explicitly on a mechanism to account for the shifts in judgments. However, the polarization pattern of our results suggests that jury deliberations were likely characterized by general processes of informational influence and/or interpersonal comparison, currently favored explanations for polarization (Burnstein & Vinokur, 1977; Myers & Lamm, 1976; Sanders & Baron, 1977).

In concluding, we note along with Kerr et al. (1976) that our present laboratory simulation differed in a number of ways from the usual courtroom situation and that results reported here are more properly viewed as suggestive rather than definitive. Nonetheless, in our favor we note that (a) other research using nonstudents is consistent with our data in showing greater punitiveness by high authoritarians (e.g. Jurow, 1971) and (b) since our jurors were drawn from a homogeneous student population, we might expect the pattern of decisions observed to be even more predominant in the general population, in view of its greater range of high- and low-authoritarian tendencies (Elwork & Sales, in press.)

NOTES

1. The distribution of juries by sex composition (M, F) for low authoritarians was as follows: 3 juries had 1M, 5F; 5 juries had 2M, 4F; 4 juries had 3M, 3F; 8 juries had 4M, 2F; 1 jury had 5M, 1F. For high authoritarians, 1 jury had 0M, 6F; 3 juries had 1M, 5F; 12 juries had 2M, 4F; 5 juries had 3M, 3F; 2 juries had 4M, 2F.

2. In this analysis, subjects were asked to assume guilt regardless of their actual verdict and then to impose a sentence. To examine whether verdicts of guilt affected sentences, Sex $\times$ Authoritarianism $\times$ Verdict (guilty or not guilty) least squares analyses of variance were conducted for pre- and postdeliberation judgments of sentencing. The results showed significant effects only for authoritarianism for predeliberation sentences, $F(1, 251) = 16.24, p < .001$, and again for postdeliberation sentences, $F(1, 251) = 87.73, p < .001$. There was no effect for the verdict variable in either analysis ($Fs < 1$), indicating that subjects' sentences were not systematically affected by their verdicts of guilt. Further, an analysis of sentences using only jurors who voted guilty produced the same effects and pattern of results as those obtained from all subjects.

3. There were several small expected frequencies in this analysis because of the low number of juries voting guilty or ending hung. After the elimination of hung juries to produce acceptable expected frequencies, a subsequent Authoritarianism $\times$ Verdict chi-square analysis was carried out. It verified that high authoritarians reached significantly more guilty verdicts than low authoritarians, $\chi^2(1) = 8.58, p < .004$. The distribution of guilty-voting juries by sex composition was 1 jury composed of 1M, 5F; 4 juries with 2M, 4F; and 3 juries with 3M, 3F.

4. To test that jury verdicts did not contaminate sentence recommendations, an Authoritarianism × Verdict analysis of variance was computed (omitting the three hung juries to avoid excessive empty cells). The results showed a main effect for authoritarianism, $F(1, 38) = 8.67$, $p < .006$, but no effect for verdict ($F < 1$).

5. Mitchell and Byrne (1973) observed an interaction between attitude similarity and authoritarianism. To test the extent that similarity affected predeliberation judgments, we computed correlations of authoritarianism with guilt and with sentencing, partialing out effects of similarity. These correlations were .21 and .25, respectively ($ps < .01$). Zero-order correlations for these respective variables were .22 and .26. Thus our results confirm a main effect for authoritarianism and not the interaction obtained by Mitchell and Byrne.

REFERENCE NOTES

1. Kagehiro, D. K., & Werner, C. *Effects of authoritarianism and inadmissibility of evidence on jurors' verdicts.* Paper presented at the annual meeting of the Midwestern Psychological Association, Chicago, May 1977.
2. Kirby, D., & Lamberth, J. *The lawyers' dilemma: The behavior of authoritarian jurors.* Paper presented at the annual meeting of the Midwestern Psychological Association, Chicago, May 1974.
3. Lineberry, M. D., Becker, L. A., & Lammers, H. B. *The influence of defendant-juror attitude similarity, authoritarianism, and strength of evidence on punitiveness and attraction.* Paper presented at the annual meeting of the Midwestern Psychological Association, Chicago, May 1977.
4. Vidmar, N. *Group-induced shifts in simulated jury decisions.* Paper presented at the annual meeting of the Midwestern Psychological Association, Cleveland, Ohio, May 1972.

REFERENCES

Adorno, T. W., Frenkel-Brunswik, E., Levinson, D., & Sanford, R. N. *The authoritarian personality.* New York: Harper, 1950.
Berg, K. S., & Vidmar, N. Authoritarianism and recall of evidence about criminal behavior. *Journal of Research in Personality,* 1975, 9, 147-157.
Boehm, V. Mr. Prejudice, Miss Sympathy, and the authoritarian personality: An application of psychological measuring techniques to the problem of jury bias. *Wisconsin Law Review,* 1968, 734-750.
Burnstein, E., & Vinokur, A. Persuasive argumentation and social comparisons as determinants of attitude polarization. *Journal of Experimental Social Psychology,* 1977, 13, 315-322.
Byrne, D. *An introduction to personality: Research theory and applications* (2nd ed.). Englewood Cliffs, NJ: Prentice-Hall.

Crosson, R. F. An investigation into certain personality variables among capital trial jurors (Doctoral dissertation, Western Reserve University, 1966). *Dissertation Abstracts,* 1967, *27,* 3668B-3669B. (University Microfilms No. 67-4587)

Davis, J. H., Bray, R. M., & Holt, R. W. The empirical study of decision processes in juries: A critical review. In J. L. Tapp & F. J. Levine (Eds.), *Law, justice, and the individual in society: Psychological and legal issues.* New York: Holt, Reinhart & Winston, 1977.

Elwork, A., & Sales, B. D. Psycholegal research on the jury and trial process. In C. Petty, W. Curran, & L. McGarry (Eds.), *Modern legal medicine and forensic science.* Philadelphia: F. A. Davis, in press.

Foss, R. D. Group decision processes in the simulated trial jury. *Sociometry,* 1976, *84,* 323-345.

Grizzle, J., Starmer, F., & Koch, G. G. Analysis of categorical data by linear models. *Biometrics,* 1969, *25,* 489-504.

Jurow, G. L. New data on the effect of a "death-qualified" jury on the guilt determination process. *Harvard Law Review,* 1971, *84,* 567-611.

Kerr, N. L., et al. Guilt beyond a reasonable doubt: Effects of concept definition and assigned decision rule on the judgments of mock jurors. *Journal of Personality and Social Psychology,* 1976, *34,* 282-294.

Kirscht, J. P., & Dillehay, R. C. *Dimensions of authoritarianism: A review of research and theory.* Lexington: University of Kentucky Press, 1967.

Kritzer, H. NONMET: A program for the analysis of nonmetric data by linear models. *Behavioral Science,* 1973, *18,* 74-75.

Lehnen, R. G., & Koch, G. G. The analysis of categorical data from repeated measurement research designs. *Political Methodology,* 1974, *1*(4), 103-123.

Mitchell, H. E., & Byrne, D. The defendant's dilemma: Effects of jurors' attitudes and authoritarianism on judicial decisions. *Journal of Personality and Social Psychology,* 1973, *24,* 123-129.

Myers, D. G., & Kaplan, M. F. Group-induced polarization in simulated juries. *Personality and Social Psychology Bulletin,* 1976, *2,* 63-66.

Myers, D. G., & Lamm, H. The group polarization phenomenon, *Psychological Bulletin,* 1976, *83,* 602-627.

Sanders, G. S., & Baron, R. S. Is social comparison irrelevant for producing choice shifts? *Journal of Experimental Social Psychology,* 1977, *13,* 303-314.

Witherspoon v. Illinois. *United States Reports,* 1968, *391,* 510-542.

5

RULE DEPARTURES AND MAKING LAW
Juries and Their Verdicts

MARTHA A. MYERS
Indianapolis, Indiana

In American law the jury is symbolically significant as a protection against the arbitrary exercise of state power. In the past 150 years, however, jury power has declined considerably (Howe, 1939; Yale Law Journal, 1964; Sheflin, 1972), while criticism of the competence and representativeness of its members has increased.[1] Currently, court officials are reluctant to use juries to adjudicate guilt in many criminal cases (Newman, 1966; Blumberg, 1967). Although this reluctance may stem in part from constraints on office resources, it has an additional source in the pervasive distrust with which officials view jury deliberations and verdicts.

Author's Note, This research was partially funded by Law Enforcement Assistance Administration Grant 76-NI-99-0071. I wish to thank Marion County law enforcement officials for their permission and assistance in collecting these data. Anonymous reviewers provided helpful comments on an earlier draft. Duane F. Alwin, E. M. Beck, and Peter J. Burke provided valuable advice during data analysis. I, of course, assume responsibility for any errors.

From *Law and Society Review* (1979), *13*, 781-797. Copyright © 1979 Law and Society Association.

It is this distrust, and the more general criticism of jury competence, that is of concern in this article. In the first section, I examine the presumption that underlies many criticisms—namely, that juries depart from formal instructions and, in so doing, make or nullify existing law. To determine whether this presumption and the criticisms it generates are warranted, the second section reports the analysis of data obtained from a sample of jury trials.

JURY RULE DEPARTURES

One of the most serious criticisms of the jury bears on the competence of its members to decide issues of fact. Although some socialization is provided by the voir dire (Balch et al., 1976) jurors, it is said, lack the legal training and experience deemed necessary to decide matters of fact. But few critics take the extreme position that lack of legal training and experience renders juries incapable of understanding and following instructions. Indeed, the work of Reed (1965) and others (e.g., Kalven and Zeisel, 1966; Simon, 1967; Elwork et al., 1977) indicates that jurors comprehend instructions, are willing to follow them, and are responsive to changes in them.

Rather, the specific charge is that because they are not professionally trained, jurors permit "irrational," "extralegal," and "extraneous" considerations to affect their verdicts (Newman, 1966; Miller, 1970; Neubauer, 1974). In particular, values or sentiments intrude upon and affect the fact-finding process, with the frequent result that jurors take a "merciful view of the facts" (Devlin, 1965: 21).[2] The intrusion of personal values and sentiments leads juries to add to or override distinctions that law makes. When juries fail to follow judicial instructions they are, in effect, legislating "interstitially," articulating their own legal policies and, in so doing, making new law and nullifying existing law (Jacobsohn, 1977).

The charge that jurors depart from instructions and make law is a serious one, because it implies that they are improperly performing their role as fact-finders.[3] To the extent that juries cannot be trusted to discharge their duty properly, a reliance on such other methods of guilt determination as bench trials and, more frequently, guilty pleas, is seen by law enforcement officials as legitimate and necessary.

Whether rule departures are proper or not depends on one's interpretation of the jury's role (Kadish and Kadish, 1973, Christie, 1974). At its most extreme, a critical stance toward rule departures implies that the jury's role involves a straightforward and strict expectation to follow instructions. This interpretation equates jurors with clerks and gives them no "discretion to disobey" (Kadish and Kadish, 1973; Brooks and Doob, 1975).

Judicial opinions (e.g., *Williams v. Florida,* 1970; Bazelon, J., dissenting in *United States v. Dougherty,* 1972) and theoretical discussions (Kadish and Kadish, 1973) offer a different interpretation of the jury's role. It is not clerklike. Nor does it contain the wide discretionary powers that characterize the roles of the prosecutor and police. Rather, the jury's role is more appropriately conceptualized as a *recourse* role that permits jurors to "evaluate the consequences of adhering to the role's prescribed means in terms of the role's prescribed ends" (Kadish and Kadish, 1973: 61). When these consequences conflict with or preclude attainment of prescribed ends, jurors have the liberty, but not the right, to depart from instructions. For proponents of this interpretation, then, the mere existence of rule departures is neither improper nor subject to criticism. Rather, it is the grounds for these departures, and the nature of the law-making activity that results, which merit scrutiny and can be criticized as improper.

This article does not propose to resolve interpretational issues about the jury's role. Rather, it is concerned with two prior empirical questions that are central to a consideration of those issues. First, do rule departures occur? Second, if such departures occur, of what do they consist and what kinds of rule-making activity do they reflect? Preliminary answers to these questions may serve to ground theoretical debate about the jury's role more firmly in empirical knowledge of how that role is actually performed.

PRIOR RESEARCH

Despite the frequency of allegations about jury rule departures, there is little direct evidence supporting the assertion. The extensive literature on jury decision making has been reviewed elsewhere (Erlanger, 1970; Brooks and Doob, 1975; Kessler, 1975; Stephan, 1975; Colasanto and Sanders, 1978) and will not be discussed here. It is sufficient to note that prior research has shed little light on the issue of rule departures, for two reaons. First, many studies (e.g., Nemeth and Sosis, 1973; Sue et al., 1973) used simulated juries. As a result, their findings may not be generalizable to complex situations in which adjudications of legal responsibility actually affect a defendant's life chances (Hamilton, 1978). Second, studies of actual jury outcomes do not include the range of variables necessary to determine the extent and nature of rule departures. Measures of evidence and witness credibility are often lacking. Thus while there is some indication that "irrelevant" factors such as defendant's socioeconomic status affect verdicts (Broeder, 1965; Judson et al., 1969; Nagel, 1969), the findings could be spurious and must therefore be treated with caution.

The recent work of Eisenstein and Jacob (1977) is an exception to the general trend. It reports that, while jurisdictional variation is considerable, characteristics of the defendant and the offense affect jury verdicts. At times, they find that this effect is stronger than the effects of the evidence in a case. But while this research is more useful than earlier work, it uses only a few measures of evidence and suffers from the absence of data on credibility-related victim characteristics (e.g., race, age, sex, relationship with the defendant). In addition, along with most other researchers, Eisenstein and Jacob fail to explore the possibility that the effects of legally irrelevant factors on verdicts depend on the strength of the evidence in the case. As a result, they could not test the hypothesis proposed by Kalven and Zeisel (1966) that juries consider legally irrelevant factors only under certain circumstances, in particular, when the evidence in a case is "close".

Research using quantitative data does not provide unequivocal support for the contention that juries depart from instructions. Most support for that proposition appears to be anecdotal; at best it is indirect. For example, the influential work of Kalven and Zeisel (1966), which more than any other study purported to document the intrusion of values into the fact-finding process, relied exclusively on self-reported judicial perceptions and interpretations of jury behavior. These perceptions may be accurate, but they require independent validation and are no substitute for direct analyses of jury verdicts themselves.

The analysis reported below is a partial attempt to fill the need for a direct study of jury decision making. It focuses on the product of jury deliberations, the verdict, and seeks to answer the following questions:

(1) To what extent do juries consider the evidence presented to them?
(2) What kinds of evidence, if any, have the strongest effects on verdicts?
(3) To what extent do verdicts reflect the intrusion of values into the fact-finding process? Is this intrusion contingent on the evidence? Does a "close" case "liberate" the jury to consider "extraneous" factors?
(4) To what extent do jury findings reflect sentiments about the defendant

and the law? Of what does the law-making activity of jurors appear to consist?

THE DATA

The original data set was a random sample of 980 defendants charged with felonies in Marion County (Indianapolis), Indiana. The sample excluded crimes without victims (e.g., drug law violations and gambling) and consisted of cases disposed between January, 1974, and June, 1976. Of 980 defendants, 317 (or 32 percent) went to trial; of those who went to trial, 63.4 percent (or 201) were tried by jury. The remainder were dismissed by the court or tried by a judge.[4] Analysis focuses on the 201 cases tried by jury.

The file folder of the assistant prosecutor who tried the case provided most of the information about the criminal event. Where there were missing data, criminal court records, police arrest records, and telephone interviews with victims were used. During the eight-month period of data collection, I was a member of the prosecutor's staff and conducted informal discussions with prosecutor and court personnel. The qualitative data I collected guided categorization of the independent variables and are used to shed light on the findings reported below.

Dependent Variable

Table 1 presents the variables and their frequencies.[5] The dependent variable, verdict, is dichotomized as an acquittal (0) or guilty verdict (1).

Legally Relevant Independent Variables

The first set of independent variables are measures of evidence. Since access to court transcripts was not possible, I obtained information from the assistant prosecutor's notes for case presentation and from a summary sheet of the evidence submitted for the probable cause hearing. It merits emphasis, then, that data on the evidence for each case are not complete. This is particularly true with respect to circumstantial evidence and the testimony of character and corroborative witnesses. Thus the data provide only a first approximation of the case's evidence, and our test for its relevance to jury verdicts is therefore conservative. On the positive side, however, our approximation is a closer one than has previously been possible (see Eisenstein and Jacob, 1977). A wide range of evidence is considered, such as the

TABLE 5.1

Notation, Coding, and Frequencies of Variables

Variable		Coding	Frequencies
Y	Verdict	0 Not guilty	31.3 (63)
		1 Guilty	68.7 (138)
Evidence			
X_1	Victim Identification of Defendant	0 None	33.3 (67)
		1 One or more	66.7 (134)
X_2	Eyewitness(es) Identification of Defendant	0 None	63.7 (128)
		1 One or more	36.3 (73)
X_3	Testimony of Defendant and/or Accomplices	0 None	82.1 (165)
		1 One or more statements	17.9 (36)
X_4	Amount of Expert Testimony	0 None	68.2 (137)
		1 One expert	26.9 (54)
		2 Two or more experts	5.0 (10)
X_5	Recovered Property	0 No property loss	38.8 (78)
		1 Unrecovered loss	35.8 (72)
		2 Recovered loss	25.4 (51)
X_6	Recovered Weapon	0 No weapon used	37.8 (76)
		1 Unrecovered weapon	42.8 (86)
		2 Recovered weapon	19.4 (39)
X_7	Number of Witnesses	Interval	$\overline{X} = 6$
Witness Credibility			
X_8	Defendant Prior Convictions	Interval	$\overline{X} = 2.7$
X_9	Victim Prior Convictions	0 None	85.6 (172)
		1 One or more	14.4 (29)
X_{10}	Prior Victim-defendant Relationship	1 Family or friend	8.0 (16)
		2 Acquaintance	24.9 (50)
		3 Stranger	67.2 (135)
Sympathy-Related Factors			
X_{11}	Defendant Sex	0 Female	4.0 (8)
		1 Male	96.0 (193)
X_{12}	Defendant Age	Interval	$\overline{X} = 27$
X_{13}	Youth/Old Age of Defendant	0 Under 20 or over 45	26.4 (53)
		1 21 to 45	73.6 (148)
X_{14}	Defendant Employment Status	1 Unemployed	45.1 (71)
		2 Employed	52.0 (89)
		3 Self-employed	6.4 (11)
X_{15}	Victim Sex	0 Female	40.8 (81)
		1 Male	59.7 (120)

(continued)

TABLE 5.1 Continued

X_{16}	Victim Age	Interval	$\overline{X}=34$
X_{17}	Youth/Old Age of Victim	0 Under 17 or over 59 1 17 to 59	19.3 (38) 80.7 (159)
X_{18}	Victim Employment Status	1 Unemployed 2 Employed 3 Self-employed	19.5 (32) 57.3 (94) 23.2 (38)

Other Legally Irrelevant Factors

X_{19}	Alleged Victim Conduct[a]	0 No allegation 1 One allegation 2 Two or more allegations	71.1 (143) 19.4 (39) 9.5 (19)
X_{20}	Racial Composition I	0 Other events 1 Black v. white events	65.3 (126) 34.7 (67)
X_{21}	Racial Composition II	0 Other events 1 White v. white events	75.1 (146) 24.9 (48)
X_{22}	Victim Injury	1 None 2 Minor 3 Required hospitalization 4 Fatal	64.7 (130) 15.0 (30) 7.0 (14) 13.4 (27)
X_{23}	Prosecution Charge[b]	Interval	$\overline{X}=17$
X_{24}	Defendant Pretrial Release Status	0 In jail 1 Out on bond	72.1 (145) 27.9 (56)
X_{25}	Bond Amount	Interval	$\overline{X}=\$12,821$
X_{26}	Counsel	0 Court-appointed 1 Privately-retained	47.8 (96) 52.2 (105)

a. The measure for alleged victim conduct is the sum of responses (no = 0; yes = 1) to items regarding: (1) victim provocation; (2) prior victim-defendant conflict; (3) questionable moral character of the victim; and (4) victim's sexual misconduct or potentially criminal behavior.
b. This variable refers to the rank of the most serious prosecution charge. The rank is based on (1) the prison sentence stipulated by law, if given in years (e.g., 20 years); or (2) the mean prison sentence, if the stipulated penalty is given as a range of years (e.g., 10 to 30 years).

presence of eyewitness identification of the defendant and other factors usually thought crucial or indispensable to the determination of guilt.

Following Cleary's (1972) classification, the measures of evidence, as presented in Table 1, are:

(1) testimony of eyewitnesses (victims and others) who identified the defendant (X_1 and X_2)
(2) testimony of the defendant and/or accomplices about their involvement in the crime or lack thereof (X_3)
(3) testimony of experts (such as polygraph examiners) about the victim and defendant, fingerprint and ballistics experts, and psychiatrists giving evidence of the defendant's capacity to stand trial (X_4)

(4) real or demonstrative evidence, that is, material objects in the form of stolen property (X_5) or a recovered weapon (X_6)
(5) the number of witnesses specified in the information or indictment (X_7); this variable provides a rough and indirect indication of the amount of testimonial evidence

The second set of independent variables consists of indicators of *witness* credibility.[6] In actual practice it is difficult to distinguish credibility-related factors from those eliciting sympathy, but the conceptual distinction made by Kalven and Zeisel (1966) is retained. Because a prior record of convictions is a legally permissible consideration when assessing witness credibility, analysis includes the prior conviction record of the defendant (X_8) and victim (X_9). Since few victims (n = 16) had more than one conviction, the measure was dichotomized as no convictions (0) and one or more convictions (1). An interval measure was retained for defendant's conviction record, because the distribution was not seriously skewed.

Instructions also permit a consideration of potential bias against the defendant when assessing the victim's credibility. As an indicator of bias, I use the prior relationship between the victim and defendant (X_{10}). The underlying presumption is that, like official agents (Emerson, 1969; Reiss, 1971; Stanko, 1977), jurors may use prior relationship as a guide to the victim's credibility. They may be more likely to question the motives and doubt the allegations of a victim who knew the defendant prior to the offense.

Legally Irrelevant Independent Variables

The remaining variables attempt to capture in an indirect way two potential jury "sentiments" discussed by Kalven and Zeisel (1966)—namely, those toward the defendant and those about the law. I enlarge the former category to include sentiments toward the victim on the grounds that, just as a sympathetic or attractive defendant may elicit leniency, so too may an unsympathetic or unattractive victim.[7] Similarly, juries may be more likely to convict not only when the defendant is unattractive but also when the victim is seen as attractive or helpless (Landy and Aronson, 1969; Yale Law Journal, 1974; Williams, 1976).

Because they could relate to witness attractiveness and/or helplessness (Kalven and Zeisel, 1966; Williams, 1976), the sex (X_{11}, X_{15}), age (X_{12}, X_{16}), and employment status (X_{13}, X_{18}) of defendants and victims, respectively, are included. Since extremely young or old witnesses may appear particularly sympathetic (Williams, 1976), the effects of age on verdict could be curvilinear. To examine this possibility, both measures of age are dichotomized and dummy-coded (X_{13}, X_{17}).[8] To test for curvilinearity, each dummy variable will be entered into a regression equation that contains all independent variables (including the interval measures for age). The significance of the increment in R^2 produced by the addition of the dummy variable will then be determined.[9]

The second set of "legally irrelevant" variables taps sentiments about the law. It consists of circumstances or characteristics that, while not formally recognized as reducing the defendant's culpability, may predispose jurors to acquit despite the evidence. The first variable (X_{19}) taps the use of victim conduct to assess defendant culpability and subsumes sentiments regarding both self-defense and "contributory fault." A single variable was constructed by summing allegations regarding (1) victim provocation—that is, whether the victim allegedly struck the first blow or began an argument that culminated in his or her own victimization; (2) prior victim-defendant conflict—that is, whether the victim allegedly argued with or harassed the defendant in the past; (3) the questionable moral character of the victim; and (4) the victim's sexual misconduct or potentially criminal behavior.[10] This measure provides some indication of whether juries are more likely to acquit if the victim is seen as partly responsible for, or deserving of, the injury sustained.

The second possible mitigating circumstance, subcultural orientation of the victim and defendant, permits a test of the hypothesis that events involving black defendants and victims are treated more leniently than others, in part because the parties are "disreputable" (Garfinkel, 1949; Wolfgang and Riedel, 1973; Black, 1976). Racial composition is dummy-coded to compare black intraracial events with both black defendant-white victim (X_{20}) and white intraracial events (X_{21}). There were no white defendant-black victim events.

The third possible mitigating circumstance, jury notions of de minimis, tests the hypothesis that acquittal is more likely if the offense is minor and if the harm the victim sustained was not serious. Two indicators are used: (1) the extent of physical injury suffered by the victim (X_{22}) and (2) the legal seriousness of the offense (X_{23}).[11] The latter refers to the rank of the most serious prosecution charge, where rank is based on the prison sentence stipulated in the criminal code. Where the penalty is stipulated as a range of years (e.g., 10-30 years), rank is based on the mean prison sentence (e.g., 20 years).

The final set of legally irrelevant variables is procedural. These variables are included because the literature (e.g., Ares et al., 1963; Roballo et al., 1974; Swigert and Farrell, 1977) suggests their importance to criminal justice outcomes. The defendant's pretrial release status (X_{24}), if known, could be used by jurors in either of two contrasting ways. It could indicate the defendant's presumed dangerousness. If so, having been detained in jail could increase the probability of conviction. Or, alternatively, pretrial release status could indicate the extent to which the defendant has already suffered (by being incarcerated) or has been discriminated against. In this case, having been detained in jail could increase the probability of acquittal (see Bernstein et al., 1977).

To estimate the effect of pretrial release accurately, analysis includes as a control variable the amount of final bond (X_{25}). Type of counsel (X_{26}), whether court-appointed or private, is included to determine whether juries are affected by the character of counsel.

Frequencies

As Table 1 indicates, there was little variation in several independent variables. Cases that proceeded to jury trial involved victims who appeared credible. Few victims had provoked the defendant, engaged in misconduct prior to the crime, or established a conviction record. On the other hand, most defendants had prior convictions and may thus have appeared discreditable. With respect to evidence, expert testimony and statements from defendants and accomplices were relatively rare. This homogeneity suggests considerable screening of cases prior to trial. It also presents problems for analysis, since limited variation could reduce the ability of these variables to account for differences in jury verdicts.

RESULTS

To determine whether the effects of legally irrelevant variables depend on the case's evidence, I constructed an interactive model of jury decision making (see Hanushek and Jackson, 1977: 97-101).[12] First, the values of all variables were incremented by 1 to eliminate zero values. Then, the natural logarithm of the dependent variable was regressed on the natural logarithms of the independent variables. The resulting equation,

$$\log Y = a + b_1 \log X_1 + b_2 \log X_2 + \ldots + b_{26} \log X_{26} + U,$$

estimates a fully multiplicative model, whose functional form is

$$Y = e^a X_1{}^{b1} X_2{}^{b2} \ldots X_{26}{}^{b26} e^u.$$

This model assumes that the change in the dependent variable (Y) associated with the change in a specific independent variable (e.g., X_1) varies with the magnitude *both* of the specific independent variable and of the other independent variables in the equation (X_1 through X_{26}).

The data were then analyzed using dummy variable regression procedures.[13] In contrast to the interactive model, ordinary least squares assume that the effects of the independent variables are additive rather than multiplicative. To determine which model (the interactive or additive) fits the data better, the R^2 of the interactive model was transformed,[14] so that it could be compared with the R^2 of the linear model.

A comparison of the findings of the interactive and additive models revealed no essential differences. The former explained 23.3 percent of the variance in verdict, while the latter explained 27.1 percent. Reasons of parsimony dictate subsequent focus solely on the additive model. Substantively, the lack of difference in explained variance means that the data provide no statistical support for the argument that the effects of legally irrelevant characteristics on verdict depend on the extent or nature of the evidence. The liberation hypothesis proposed by Kalven and Zeisel (1966) receives no support, then, from these data.

The addition of the dummy variables for defendant and victim age (X_{13} and X_{17}) did not significantly increase the proportion of explained variance. The analysis reported below is based, then, on an additive model that excludes these variables. Table 2 presents the coefficients of variables in this model whose effects on verdict were significant at $p < .10$. Before discussing the individual coefficients, it should be noted that while the proportion of explained variance is significant and larger than that typically encountered (see, e.g., Eisenstein and Jacob, 1977), it is nonetheless modest. A majority of the variance remains unexplained, in part because of limits on the information contained in the data to which access was possible.

As Table 2 indicates, juries were more likely to convict if the defendant or accomplice made a statement about involvement in the crime or lack thereof (X_3); a weapon was recovered (X_6); and a large number of witnesses were specified in the indictment or information (X_7). Jury verdicts did *not* depend on eyewitness identification of the defendant (X_1, X_2), on expert testimony (X_4), or the recovery of stolen property (X_5). Taken together, these findings indicate that juries

TABLE 5.2
Regression Coefficients and Related Statistics for
Variables Significant at p < .10 on Verdict (Y)

Variable		r	b (Standard error)	β
X_3	Testimony of Defendant and/or Accomplice	.212	.327 (.120)	.278
X_6	Recovered Weapon	.108	.113 (.063)	.191*
X_7	Number of Witnesses	.223	.041 (.017)	.223
X_8	Defendant Prior Convictions	.182	.049 (.017)	.306
X_{14}	Defendant Employment Status	−.097	−.128 (.076)	−.178*
X_{16}	Victim Age	−.027	−.005 (.003)	−.173*
X_{23}	Prosecution Charge	−.024	−.028 (.011)	−.272
	R^2	.271		
	Number of Cases[a]	134		

*Significant at $.06 < p < .10$.
a. Attrition in the number of cases is due to missing data on one or more independent variables.

accord evidence differential weight. Their selectivity in this regard is surprising, since eyewitness identification and expert testimony are often assumed to be more convincing than other kinds of evidence.

Juries were more likely to convict if the defendant had numerous prior convictions (X_8) and thus may have been potentially discreditable as a witness. In contrast, characteristics related to the *victim's* credibility— namely, prior conviction record (X_9) and relationship with the defendant (X_{10})—had no measurable effect on the verdict.

In general, variables expected to elicit sympathy toward the defendant or victim had more modest effects. Consistent with the findings of Reed (1965) and others (Broeder, 1965; Judson et al., 1969; Nagel, 1969), conviction was slightly more likely if the defendant was unemployed (X_{14}). Juries were also more likely to convict if the victim was young (X_{16}). Though both results could have occurred by chance, they may reflect an underlying sympathy toward young victims and employed defendants.

Juries did not appear to be influenced by the past conduct of the victim (X_{19}) or by the subcultural orientation of victims and defendants ($X_{20,21}$). There was no evidence, then, of greater leniency toward defendants who victimized persons who might have been considered partly deserving of, or responsible for, the injury inflicted on them.

Although juries were not predisposed to acquit if physical injury was minor (X_{22}), they were more likely to acquit if the offense was serious (X_{23}). This reluctance to convict in serious crimes has a number of possible interpretations. It could reflect hesitancy to make an adverse ruling when the ramifications of the ruling would be seriously damaging to the defendant—that is, involve a long period of incarceration—or when the jury believed the punishment was nonetheless disproportionately severe. Instances of such leniency have been reported by Kalven and Zeisel (1966) and, in experimental settings, by Vidmar (1972) and Hester and Smith (1973). A tendency to acquit when the crime is serious might also reflect the use of a higher standard of proof for these crimes. When the crime is not as serious, juries may accept a lower standard of proof. Finally, it is possible that jurors could not decide on, or lacked a sufficient understanding of, alternative lesser-included offenses. Thus the prosecutorial tendency to charge the maximum, in the hope of conviction of a lesser-included offense, may have consequences that are both unanticipated and, from the prosecutor's point of view, adverse.

Apart from its direction, the finding that juries were less likely to convict in more serious crimes is noteworthy in light of the zero-order correlation between prosecution charge and verdict ($r = -.024$). As shown in Table 2, this correlation is small and statistically insignificant. A strong relationship emerged only when the remaining independent variables were controlled. Additional analysis, using stepwise regression, revealed that the partial correlation became significant when the testimony of defendant and/or accomplice (X_3), prior victim-defendant relationship (X_{10}), bond amount (X_{25}), and counsel (X_{26}) were controlled. Thus an unbiased estimate of the effect of prosecution charge on verdict requires the inclusion of both legally relevant and legally irrelevant variables.

Jury verdicts did not depend on the defendant's pretrial release status (X_{24}) or on type of counsel (X_{26}). These findings diverge from those of other studies (e.g., Ares et al., 1963; Roballo et al., 1974; Bernstein et al., 1977; Swigert and Farrell, 1977) that have shown both factors to be important in other jurisdictions and for other decisions made during the prosecution of the defendant.

CONCLUSION

The data provided a preliminary indication of the factors jurors consider. In this jurisdiction, verdicts depended on the evidence, but not all evidence was accorded the same weight (Miller and Boster, 1975). The amount of testimony and whether its source was the defendant or an accomplice, rather than the victim, appeared to be especially persuasive. In contrast, and perhaps because they considered such evidence fallible (see e.g., Buckhout, 1974; Goldstein, 1977), juries did not rely significantly on eyewitness identification or expert testimony.

Juries also assessed the credibility of the defendant. Their rulings tended to be adverse when the defendant was discredited or discreditable. In contrast, juries appeared to be relatively unconcerned both with the evidence offered by victims (namely, eyewitness identification) and with their credibility as witnesses.

Juries exercised their liberty to depart from instructions only in certain circumstances, particularly in cases involving a serious offense, a young victim, and an employed defendant. In adding distinctions— victim's age and defendant's employment status—that the law rarely, if ever, makes, juries were, in a sense, making law. And, to the extent that their reluctance to convict when the crime was serious reflected an opinion that prescribed punishments may be excessive, juries were nullifying existing law. The interesting feature of these results is that, in addition to being motivated by subjective considerations about the defendant (as Kalven and Zeisel, 1966, emphasize), jury departures and law-making activity were motivated by characteristics of the victim and, more strongly, by the prosecutor's allegations about the defendant's criminal behavior (namely, the prosecution charge).

Our findings of substantial rule departures thus challenge the orthodox "clerk" theories of jury decision making. But these departures are more limited in nature and in scope than many revisionists or jury critics would have us believe. Jury discretion, at least in Marion County, Indiana, does not appear to be excessive. Rather, the performance of juries in our sample of cases came closest to what Kadish and Kadish (1973) called a "recourse role," in which rule departures occurred only under fairly specialized circumstances. More definitive conclusions about the extent, and abuse, of jury discretion await the reporting and analysis of information that only jurors themselves can supply.

NOTES

1. For more thorough discussion of recent criticisms of the jury see Kalven and Zeisel (1966), Simon (1967), and Yale Law Journal (1974). The specific issue of jury nullification is discussed in greater detail by Sheflin (1972), Kadish and Kadish (1973), and Christie (1974).

2. While our attention is confined to irrelevant characteristics of the case that juries might consider, a related argument posits that juries are inappropriately swayed by the mode and order in which testimony is presented. For research and discussions of these issues, see Walker et al. (1972), Miller et al. (1974, 1975), and Lawson (1969).

3. The observational literature documents no pervasive distrust or criticisms of judges in their role as fact-finders during bench trials. While this lack of criticism could reflect a desire to maintain smooth working relationships, it could also suggest a more liberal interpretation of the judge's role. Rather than defining it as a recourse or clerk role, prosecutors and other court officials could define the judge's role during trial as discretionary and, consequently, as one that requires no justification for rule departure. Or court officials could simply assume (quite incorrectly, see Newman, 1966) that judges do not depart from the law.

4. Unfortunately, there were too few bench trials in this jurisdiction to reliably compare judicial and jury decision making.

5. Although the independent variables are categorized according to their legal relevance, they will be considered separately during analysis rather than scaled in order to maintain comparability with the work of Kalven and Zeisel (1966).

6. Data on the full range of characteristics that establish credibility were not available. For example, there is no information about the presentational skills of witnesses (Miller et al., 1975). Thus the data provide only an initial and approximate indication of victim and defendant credibility.

7. Given limitations on the data to which access was possible, this set of victim and defendant characteristics is not exhaustive. Rather, it gives a first and indirect approximation of the importance of sympathy factors to jury verdicts.

8. The categories used for defendant's age differed because fewer than two percent were under 17 or over 59 years old. The measures for age were also trichotomized (under 17, 17-59, over 59 for victims and under 20, 20-45, over 45 for defendants). This coding produced essentially the same results as the dichotomization.

9. The test for curvilinearity in the effect of defendant's age, for example, will be

$$F = \frac{(R^2 \text{ with } X_1 \text{ to } X_{26} - R^2 \text{ with all variables but } X_{13})/k}{(1 - R^2 \text{ with } X_1 \text{ to } X_{26})/(N - k - 1)} ,$$

with (k) and (N – k – 1) degrees of freedom, where k is equal to 1, the number of dummy variables. The interval measure of age is included in the equation with the dummy-coded variable to compensate for information lost in recoding (Nie et al., 1975: 376-377).

10. While it would have been preferable to examine the effects of each type of allegation separately, the extreme skew in the distribution of each variable introduced multicollinearity problems and required the construction of a single measure.

11. Although Kalven and Zeisel (1966) emphasized the seriousness of the offense, there is some evidence that the type of crime may affect outcomes and the criteria used

to prosecute the case (Williams, 1976). However, the size of our sample precluded any comparisons by offense type.

12. An alternative procedure would have been an analysis of covariance design in which, for each measure of evidence, interaction terms between the measure and each of the remaining independent variables were constructed. A test for the significance of the increment in R^2 produced by adding these terms to the regression equation would then have been performed. Given our sample size, the number of regressors this procedure involves would have been unwieldy and conducive to the production of misleading inflated coefficients. The procedure described in the text avoids this problem. It has the added virtue of testing a hypothesis about jury decision making that is more general than the liberation hypothesis proposed by Kalven and Zeisel (1966). Specifically, it enables us to test whether the effect each independent variable has on outcome depends on its magnitude and on the magnitude of the remaining variables, evidentiary as well as nonevidentiary. Such a test would not have been possible using analysis of covariance.

13. Since the dependent variable is binary, the assumption of homoskedasticity is difficult if not impossible to meet. Concretely, this means that, while estimates are consistent and unbiased, both they and their standard errors are inefficient (Hanushek and Jackson, 1977: 148, 154). The usual response to this problem is to use a weighted least squares (WLS) solution. Goldberger's (1964: 231-248) "two-round" procedure produces estimated coefficients that are unbiased, consistent, and efficient. The standard errors of the estimates are also efficient. For our sample, WLS produced results that were strikingly similar to those reported in the text. However, conviction was slightly more likely if the victim was a stranger to the defendant, bond was high, and counsel was court-appointed. Since these coefficients were modest, with significance levels between .05 and .10, they do not alter our basic conclusions. The results of the WLS were not reported in the text because the small sample size exacerbated the problems of multicollinearity produced by the weights. Coefficients tended to be artificially inflated and therefore misleading. The results are available to interested readers on request.

14. To obtain an R^2 that could be compared with the R^2 from the linear regression model, we squared the correlation coefficient of the dependent variable with the antilog of the unstandardized predicted scores for the natural logarithm of the dependent variable (Hanuschek and Jackson, 1977: 101).

REFERENCES

Ares, Charles, Ann Rankin, and Herbert Sturz (1963) "The Manhattan Bail Project: An Interim Report on the Use of Pretrial Parole." 38 New York University Law Review 67.

Balch, Robert W., Curt T. Griffiths, Edwin L. Hall, and L. Thomas Winfree (1976) "Socialization of Jurors: Voir Dire as a Rite of Passage," 4 Journal of Criminal Justice 271.

Bernstein, Ilene N., Edward Kick, Jan T. Leung, and Barbara Schulz (1977) "Charge Reduction: An Intermediary Stage in the Process of Labelling Criminal Defendants." 56 Social Forces 362.

Black, Donald (1976) The Behavior of Law. New York: Academic Press.

Blumberg, Abraham S. (1967) *Criminal Justice*. Chicago: Quadrangle Books.

Broeder, Dale W. (1954). "The Functions of the Jury: Facts or Fictions?" 21 *University of Chicago Law Review* 386.

———(1965) "The Negro in Court" 1965 *Duke Law Review* 19.

Brooks, W. Neil and Anthony N. Doob (1975) "Justice and the Jury," 32(3) *Journal of Social Issues* 171.

Buckhout, Robert (1974) "Eyewitness Testimony," 231 *Scientific American* 23 (December).

Christie, George C. (1974) "Lawful Departures from Legal Rules: 'Jury Nullification' and Legitimated Disobedience," 62 *California Law Review* 1289.

Cleary, Edward W. (1972) *McCormick's Handbook of the Law of Evidence* (Second Edition) St. Paul: West

Colasanto, Diane and Joseph Sanders (1978) "Methodological Issues in Simulated Jury Research." Presented at the annual meeting of the Law and Society Association, Minneapolis (May).

Devlin, Patrick (1965) *The Enforcement of Morals*. New York: Oxford University Press.

Eisenstein, James and Herbert Jacob (1977) *Felony Justice: An Organizational Analysis of Criminal Courts*. Boston: Little, Brown.

Elwork, Amiram, Bruce D. Sales, and James J. Alfini (1977) "Juridic Decisions: In Ignorance of the Law or in Light of It?" 1(2) *Law and Human Behavior* 163.

Emerson, Robert M. (1969) *Judging Delinquents: Context and Process in Juvenile Courts*. Chicago: Aldine.

Erlanger, Howard S. (1970) "Jury Research in America: Its Past and Future," 4 *Law and Society Review* 345.

Garfinkel, Harold (1949). "Research Note on Inter- and Intra-racial Homicides," 27 *Social Forces* 370.

Goldberger, Arthur S. (1964). *Econometric Theory*. New York: John Wiley.

Goldstein, Alvin G. (1977) "The Fallibility of the Eyewitness: Psychological Evidence," in Bruce D. Sales (ed.), *Psychology in the Legal Process*. New York: Spectrum.

Hamilton, V. Lee (1978) "Obedience and Responsibility: A Jury Simulation," 36(2) *Journal of Personality and Social Psychology* 126.

Hanushek, Eric A. and John E. Jackson (1977) *Statistical Methods for Social Scientists*. New York: Academic Press.

Hester, Reid K. and Ronald E. Smith (1973) "Effects of a Mandatory Death Penalty on the Decisions of Simulated Jurors as a Function of the Heinousness of the Crime," 1 *Journal of Criminal Justice* 319.

Howe, Mark D. (1939) "Juries as Judges of Criminal Law," 52 *Harvard Law Review* 582.

Jacobsohn, Gary J. (1977) "Citizen Participation in Policy-Making: The Role of the Jury," 39 *Journal of Politics* 73.

Judson, Charles J., James J. Pandell, Jack B. Owens, James McIntosh, and Dale L. Matschullat (1969) "A Study of the California Penalty Jury in First-Degree Murder Cases." 21 *Stanford Law Review* 1297.

Kadish, Mortimer R. and Sanford H. Kadish, (1973) *Discretion to Disobey: A Study of Lawful Departures from Legal Rules.* Stanford: Stanford University Press.

Kalven, Harry and Hans Zeisel (1966) *The American Jury.* Boston: Little, Brown.

Kessler, Joan B. (1975) "The Social Psychology of Jury Deliberations," in Rita J. Simon (ed.), *The Jury System in America.* Newbury Park, CA: Sage.

Landy, David and Elliot Aronson (1969) "The Influence of the Character of the Criminal and His Victim on the Decisions of Simulated Jurors," 5 *Journal of Experimental Social Psychology* 141.

Lawson, Robert (1969). "The Law of Primacy in the Criminal Courtroom," 77 *Journal of Social Psychology* 121.

Miller, Frank (1970) *Prosecution: The Decision to Charge a Suspect With a Crime.* Boston: Little, Brown.

Miller, Gerald, David C. Bender, B. Thomas Florence, and Henry E. Nicholson (1974) "Real vs. Reel: What's the Verdict?" 24 *Journal of Communication* 99.

Miller, Gerald R., David C. Bender, F. Joseph Boster, B. Thomas Florence, Norman E. Fontes, John E. Hocking, and Henry E. Nicholson (1975) "The Effects of Videotape Testimony in Jury Trials: Studies on Juror Decision Marking, Information Retention and Emotional Arousal," 1 *Brigham Young University Law Review* 331.

Miller, Gerald R. and F. Joseph Boster (1975) "Effects of Type of Evidence on Judgments of Likelihood of Conviction and Certainty of Guilt." Unpublished manuscript. Department of Communication, Michigan State University.

Nagel, Stuart S. (1969) *The Legal Process from a Behavioral Perspective.* Homewood, IL: Dorsey.

Nemeth, Charlan and Ruth H. Sosis (1973) "A Simulated Jury Study: Characteristics of the Defendant and the Jurors." 90 *Journal of Social Psychology* 221.

Neubauer, David (1974) *Criminal Justice in Middle America.* Morristown: General Learning Press.

Newman, Donald J. (1966) *Conviction: The Determination of Guilt or Innocence Without Trial.* Boston: Little, Brown.

Nie, Norman H., C. Hadlai Hull, Jean G. Jenkins, Karin Steinbrenner, and Dale H. Bent (1975) *SPSS: Statistical Package for the Social Sciences.* New York: McGraw-Hill

Reed, John P. (1965) "Jury Deliberations, Voting and Verdict Trends," 45 *Southwestern Social Science Quarterly* 361.

Reiss, Albert J., Jr. (1979). *The Police and the Public.* New Haven: Yale University.

Roballo, John, James Hall, and Ronald Peek (1974) *Plaintiff's Memorandum on the Merits.* New York: U.S. District Court 74 Cir. 2113-MEL.

Sheflin, Alan W. (1972) "Jury Nullification: The Right to Say No," 45 *Southern California Law Review* 68.

Simon, Rita J. (1967) *The Jury and the Defense of Insanity.* Boston: Little, Brown.

Stanko, Elizabeth A. (1977) "These are the Cases That Try Themselves," Ph.D. dissertation, Graduate School, the City University of New York.

Stephan, Cookie (1975) "Selective Characteristics of Jurors and Litigants: Their Influence on Juries' Verdicts," in Rita J. Simon (ed.), *The Jury System in America.* Newbury Park, CA: Sage.

Sue, Stanley, Ronald E. Smith, and Cathy Caldwell (1973) "Effects of Inadmissible Evidence on the Decision of Simulated Jurors: A Moral Dilemma," 3 *Journal of Applied Social Psychology* 345.

Swigert, Victoria L. and Ronald A. Farrell (1977) "Normal Homicides and the Law," 42 *American Sociological Review* 16.

Vidmar, Neil (1972) "Effects of Decision Alternatives on the Verdicts and Social Perceptions of Simulated Jurors," 22(2) *Journal of Personality and Social Psychology* 211.

Walker, Laurens, John Thibaut, and Virginia Andreoli (1972) "Order of Presentation at Trial," 82 *Yale Law Journal* 216.

Williams, Kristen M. (1976) "The Effects of Victim Characteristics on the Disposition of Violent Crimes," in William F. McDonald (ed.), *Criminal Justice and the Victim.* Newbury Park, CA: Sage.

Wolfgang, Marvin E. and Marc Riedel (1973) "Race, Judicial Discretion and the Death Penalty." 407 *Annals of the Academy of Political and Social Science* 119.

Yale Law Journal (1964) "Note: The Changing Role of the Jury in the Nineteenth Century," 74 *Yale Law Journal* 170.

———(1974) "Note: Toward Principles of Jury Equity." 83 *Yale Law Journal* 1023.

CASES

United States v. Dougherty, 473 F.2d 1142 (D.C. 1972)
Williams v. Florida, 399 U.S. 78, 100 (1970)

6

REDUCING THE EFFECTS
OF JUROR BIAS

MARTIN F. KAPLAN
LYNN E. MILLER
Northern Illinois University

Bias in jurors is an unwanted component of our jury system. The voir
dire attempts to eliminate from service jurors who profess a specific
interest in the case and who may be unlikely to lay their biases aside. In

Authors' Note, This research was supported by Grant MH 23516 from the Center for
Studies of Crime and Delinquency, National Institute of Mental Health. The assistance
of Gwen Kemmerick in running the first two experiments and of Sharon Krupa in
running the third experiment is greatly appreciated. Appreciation is also due Karl Sorg
and the Lewis University College of Law for their cooperation in conducting the third
experiment. Requests for reprints should be sent to Martin F. Kaplan, Department of
Psychology, Northern Illinois University, DeKalb, Illinois 60115.

From *Journal of Personality and Social Psychology* (1978), 36(12), 1443-1455. Copyright ©
1978 by the American Psychological Association. Reprinted by permission of the
publisher and authors.

addition, attorneys may peremptorily challenge a restricted number of suspect jurors. However, since few persons have led such sheltered lives that they have not formed opinions about the law, or other people, or the issues involved in a case, the assumption of a "tabula rasa" in selected jurors would be naive.

In both actual and simulated juries, a variety of biases have been shown to affect juror verdicts. These effects have been well documented elsewhere (cf. Boehm, 1968; Jurow, 1971; Kalven & Zeisel, 1966; Kaplan & Schersching, 1978; Mitchell & Byrne, 1973; Nagel, 1969), and it would be pointless to detail here the many instances of biasing. The more fundamental questions addressed are (a) How do biases interact with evidential information in producing judgments? and (b) How may the impact of biases on the judgment be reduced?

THEORETICAL ANALYSIS

Some theoretical presumptions will be adopted in attacking these questions and should be made explicit. First, the underlying judgmental processes in juror decision making are seen as theoretically continuous with those found in other person perception tasks. Second, people are viewed primarily as information processors. People try to make sense of their world and continually form, modify, and integrate beliefs about events around them. Third, in the sense-making process, people abstract information from evidence about the object to be judged, from situational conditions surrounding the judgment, and from their residual predispositions. In a jury trial, examples of these three broad categories could be testimonial evidence, witness reliability and judicial instructions, and juror biases, respectively. Finally, this information is represented in the judgmental process by two qualities: scale value and weight. *Scale value* refers to the position of a piece of information on the quantitative judgment dimension, for example, how much of an appearance of guilt does a particular fact possess? *Weight* refers to the importance of a piece of information to the overall judgment, for example, is information relating to motive more important than information relating to opportunity?

Information integration theory (Anderson, 1974; Kaplan, 1975) deals with the integration of separate pieces of information into the overall response. It is simultaneously concerned with the rule by which weighted scale values of pieces of information are combined into a judgmental whole (usually assumed to be an algebraic function) and with the underlying psychological processes implied by that rule. Let us consider one such rule, *weighted averaging*, which has proven to be of great utility both in person perception (Anderson, 1974; Kaplan, 1975) and juror judgment (Kaplan, 1977b; Kaplan & Kemmerick, 1974) tasks. According to the rule, judgments are an average of the weighted scale values of each piece of information ($w_i s_i$) and of the weighted initial initial impression ($w_0 s_0$). Initial impression is the scale value of the response based on no information, in other words, the preexisting bias. Equation 1 gives the algebraic expression of the weighted averaging model:

$$J = \frac{w_0 s_0}{\Sigma w_i + w_0} + \frac{\Sigma w_i s_i}{\Sigma w_i + w_0} . \qquad [1]$$

An immediate implication of Equation 1 is that the effective weight of any scale value component—information about the object or initial impression—is relative to the weight of the other components. Thus the effective importance of any given evidential fact is relative to the importance of other facts. Central to our inquiry, note also that the effective impact of initial impression is relative to the weight of information about the judged object. Thus to minimize biasing effects, two broad strategies emerge. First, one may *directly* reduce the weight of the bias by, for example, instructing jurors to ignore prejudgmental values. But such instructions are commonplace, and their failure to remove biasing in many existing studies sheds doubt on the effectiveness of a direct strategy. Second, one may *indirectly* reduce the impact of the first term on the right-hand side of Equation 1 by increasing the contribution of the second term, that is, by increasing the contribution of legally relevant information. Indeed, the strategy is implicit in the Sixth Amendment, which provides that decisions be governed by evidence fairly presented in court.

EXPERIMENTAL TREATMENT OF BIASES

The three experiments reported here explore several means of influencing the contribution of biases by varying the weight of trial evidence. In addition, the experiments examine different forms of prejudgmental biasing. *Biases* are defined here as tendencies to judge a defendant or issue on a basis apart from the qualities of the defendant, the case, or the issue. At least two sets of distinctions may be made in the sorts of biases that could affect trial outcome. First, biases may be specific to the defendant or plaintiff (e.g., racial, ethnic, or economic prejudice) or they may be general (e.g., conviction or acquittal proneness). General biases are investigated in the first two experiments, while the third experiment embodies bias induced specifically toward a defendant. Second, biases may be enduring and stable trait dispositions in the juror (e.g., leniency or harshness) or relatively transient, situational states in the individual (e.g., a temporally and situationally induced good or bad mood). Both provide an initial impression to be integrated with information about the object (see Kaplan, 1975, for a detailed discussion). Trait biases were manipulated in Experiments 1 and 2, and state biases were induced in Experiment 3.

EXPERIMENTS 1 AND 2

Method

Overview

Both experiments used similar procedures and subject populations but differed in the guilt appearance of trial descriptions. In both, simulated jurors identified as having either lenient or harsh attitudes toward punishment of criminals judged guilt, and recommended punishment, of defendants in hypothetical traffic felony cases. In Experiment 1, three case summaries contained evidence that was incriminating for the defendants, and three contained evidence that was exonerating. Subjects judged all six distinct cases. Subjects performed in one of three instructional conditions designed to affect the reliability of case evidence. *Unreliable*-condition subjects were told that the case summaries were provided by an unreliable and often inaccurate source and had raised contentions by opposing attorneys. *Reliable*-condition subjects were told that cases were summarized by a highly trustworthy source. *Control* subjects were told nothing of the source.

An independent sample of harsh or lenient subjects judged two traffic felony cases in Experiment 2. Cases were constructed so that a mixed, or ambiguous, level of guilt was normatively implied. Half of each type of subjects were told that some evidence might be inaccurate and might be safely disregarded (without specifying which evidence was unreliable), and the remainder were admonished that all evidence should be considered equally accurate and important, even if conflicting.

Trial Cases: Experiment 1

Case descriptions judged by subjects consisted of half-page summaries of events and circumstances in traffic felonies representing a variety of charges. These summaries constituted six of the eight described in Kaplan and Kemmerick (1974) and were constructed as follows: Eight summaries of traffic cases were abstracted from the *California Law Reports* and modified to produce two parallel versions of each—one that was moderately incriminating and one that was moderately exonerating. The final set of cases was obtained from a series of modifications, with independent groups of subjects judging both guilt and punishment after each modification. A final group of subjects (n = 15) gave mean guilt ratings for the incriminating and exonerating cases of 15.2 and 6.9, respectively, on a scale ranging from 0 to 20. Corresponding mean ratings for the two versions on the punishment scale ranging from 1 (minimum) to 7 (maximum) were 4.73 and 2.60, respectively.

Each subject judged the six different cases, but only the incriminating version for three cases and the exonerating version for the remainder. Systematic care was taken that each version of each case was judged by the same number of subjects by employment of a Latin square design of Case × Version allocation to subjects (see Table 1). Specifically, blocks of subjects were assigned the three incriminating and three exonerating cases in a given row of a 6 × 6, self-conjugate, standard Latin square constructed via a one-step cyclic permutation of rows (Kirk, 1968, p. 153). For a given cell of the between-subjects design (Juror Bias × Source Reliability), six blocks of four subjects constituted the rows, and the six basic cases constituted the columns. Since there were to be two levels of juror bias and three source reliability conditions, this basic Latin square was repeated six times, once for each cell of the between-subjects design. Columns were subsequently randomized within a block of jurors, so that each possible combination of case and incriminating version was read by 24 jurors (4 in each Bias × Reliability cell), and in a random order.

Trial Cases: Experiment 2

The two cases of the initial eight developed in Kaplan and Kemmerick (1974) that were not used in Experiment 1 were used here.

TABLE 6.1
Evidence and Traffic Case Combination (Experiment 1)

Subject replication	Traffic case					
	A	B	C	D	E	F
1	H	H	H	L	L	L
2	L	H	H	H	L	L
3	L	L	H	H	H	L
4	L	L	L	H	H	H
5	H	L	L	L	H	H
6	H	H	L	L	L	H

Note: H = incriminating version; L = exonerating version.

However, unlike Experiment 1, subjects were not given incriminating or exonerating versions. Instead, ambiguous or mixed-value cases were constructed by alternately combining facts from the two versions of a case into a single summary. Care was taken to exclude directly contradictory facts from the summaries. Order of presentation of the two resulting case summaries was counterbalanced across subjects.

Procedure: Experiment 1

Experimental booklets contained the six experimental cases, preceded by four practice cases. In addition to providing practice in using the rating scales, these practice cases served as scale anchors, two being extremely incriminating in content and two extremely exonerating. Practice cases were photocopied directly from the *California Law Reports* to promote authenticity. Written instructions described the experiment as a study of verdicts in real cases. Subjects were led to believe that comparison of the actual verdict with responses expressing degree of belief in guilt was the main purpose of the study. They were cautioned to judge each case independently and to avoid using the endpoints of the guilt scales except in cases of absolute certainty.

Weight of evidence was varied by inserting information about evidential reliability into the instructions. In the unreliable condition, subjects were told that the summaries had been prepared by an inexperienced clerk and in each case were disputed on certain points by both defense and prosecution attorneys. Segments of questionable accuracy were not identified and subjects were told to "do their best" with available evidence. Reliable-condition subjects were told that the court summaries had been prepared by a respected judge, known for his ability to prepare accurate summaries, and that both attorneys had attested to the accuracy of the presentation. Finally, control subjects received no information about the source or accuracy of the summaries. Twenty-four subjects with harsh dispositions and 24 subjects with lenient dispositions served in each reliability condition. Subjects were run in small groups, approximately 6-10 subjects per session.

For each case, subjects rated perceived degree of guilt from 0 (definitely not guilty) to 20 (definitely guilty). Then they were instructed to assume that the defendant had been found guilty and to rate the degree of punishment recommended, from minimum (1) to maximum (7) allowable by law for the given charge.

Procedure: Experiment 2

The procedures for Experiments 1 and 2 were similar, except for the substitution of the two cases of mixed incrimination value for the six experimental cases and a change in reliability instructions. In Experiment 2, half of the subjects of each bias type were told that some evidence might seem inconsistent, since witnesses differ in accuracy and opposing attorneys have different goals, so that it would be necessary to pay less attention to some points than to others (*discounting condition*). The other half of the subjects were told that some evidence in each case might seem inconsistent, since witnesses were acquainted with different aspects of the case, but that all evidence was equally accurate and should be treated as equally valid and important (*equal weighting condition*). The former condition was intended to reduce confidence in the evidence, although different positions might be discounted by differently biased subjects.

In addition to rating degree of guilt and recommended punishment for each case, subjects were asked to report, and then rank, the three items of evidence that were most influential in determining judgment.

Subjects

In both experiments, subjects with harsh or lenient beliefs about treatment of lawbreakers were identified by the Attitude Toward Punishment of Criminals Scale (APC; Wang & Thurstone, cited in Shaw & Wright, 1967). Higher scores represented harsher attitudes, with 34 being the maximum possible score. Subjects scoring 7 or below and 17 or above were considered lenient and harsh persons, respectively, and constituted the upper and lower 15% of mass-tested respondents (n $\simeq$ 1000). In all, 72 harsh and 72 lenient subjects participated in Experiment 1; 24 harsh and 24 lenient subjects served in Experiment 2.

Subjects were male and female introductory psychology students (equally distributed among experimental conditions) who received extra course credit for participation. Service was limited to registered voters, who were therefore potential jurors.

Results

Experiment 1

Defendant guilt. Figure 1 displays the mean ratings of defendant guilt, with higher ratings reflecting greater guilt attribution. A number of facts are immediately apparent. First, subjects' a priori bias toward criminals affected judgment of the six defendants, so that harsh subjects assigned greater guilt than did lenient subjects, $F(1, 138) = 10.96, p < .001$. Moreover, this biasing was independent of the guilt appearance of evidence; the Evidence $\times$ Bias interaction failed to reach statistical significance, $F(1, 138) = 1.18$. Reliability of evidence, however, did affect the magnitude of the biasing effect, as shown in the convergence of the curves for harsh and lenient subjects across reliability conditions, interaction $F(2, 138) = 2.55, p < .08$. Harsh subjects gave stronger guilt ratings than lenient subjects when information was characterized as unreliable or when no characterization was made, but not when the information was reliable. Except for the obvious effect of evidential incrimination, $F(1, 138) = 732.94$, no other effect reached significance.

One other observation is worth noting about the interaction between reliability instructions and dispositional biases. The reduction in biasing effects under reliable conditions was due largely to a shift (toward guilt) in lenient subjects. Across cases, the mean responses for lenient subjects in control, unreliable, and reliable conditions were 9.81, 9.69, and 11.02, respectively, while the parallel means for harsh subjects were 11.64, 11.55, and 11.07, respectively.

The Duncan multiple-range test was applied to the individual cells of the design, and significant differences were noted between harsh and lenient subjects under control and unreliable conditions for both cases ($p < .05$), but not under reliable evidence conditions. Moreover, lenient subjects significantly increased guilt ratings from unreliable to reliable conditions, but only for the incriminating case ($p < .05$). The increase in response for lenient subjects from control to reliable conditions was marginally significant ($p < .10$) for the exonerating case.

On a related note, observe that lenient subjects shifted toward stringency in both case types. In the incriminating cases, this result naturally follows from movement away from the initial bias and toward the incriminating nature of the evidence. In the exonerating case, however, movement should have been toward acquittal under reliable evidence conditions. But recall that the normative value of exonerating evidence was near 7 on the 21-point scale. Therefore, the

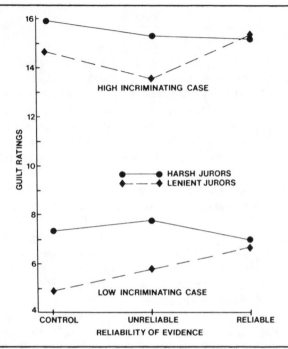

Figure 6.1   Guilt ratings as a function of juror bias, evidential incrimination value, and evidential reliability (Experiment 1).

upward slope of the curve for lenient subjects reflects, in both incrimination value instances, movement toward the normative evidential value.

Punishment recommendations. Similar analyses were performed on mean punishment recommendations (see Table 2), and the outcome was essentially similar to the guilt rating data in Figure 1. That is, harsh subjects were more punitive than lenient subjects, $F(1, 138) = 13.06$, $p < .001$, but the difference due to bias diminished when information was reliable, interaction $F(2, 138) = 3.22$, $p < .05$. Once again, biasing effects did not differ for different levels of evidential incrimination, interaction $F(1, 138) = .56$.

In summary, a priori disposition did bias both guilt attributions and punitiveness under control and unreliable evidence conditions, but biasing was absent, in the sense that disposition had no differential effect, when evidence was reliable. Reliability instructions, however, had no significant effect on harsh subjects; coverage of the biased

TABLE 6.2
Mean Rated Punishment as a Function of Juror Bias, Evidential
Incrimination, and Evidential Reliability (Experiment 1)

Subject bias	Evidence characterization		
	Control	Unreliable	Reliable
	Incriminatory cases		
Harsh	5.48	5.58	5.04
Lenient	4.58	4.33	4.95
	Exonerating Cases		
Harsh	2.84	2.82	2.75
Lenient	1.87	1.83	2.48

Note: Punishments were assigned on a scale of 1 (minimum) to 7 (maximum).

groups was effected through a reduction in the a priori tendencies of lenient subjects.

Experiment 2

Defendant guilt. Subjects rated guilt, and recommended punishment, for defendants in two cases containing mixed evidence with respect to incrimination, under either discounting or equal weighting instructions. Mean guilt ratings for the Instructions × Subject Bias design are found in Figure 2. For ease of presentation, these means are averaged across the two cases, but statistical analysis treated the cases as a replication factor, with two levels. Only two effects reached significance, and both are clearly seen in the figure. Persons with harsh attitudes toward criminals again gave higher guilt ratings, $F(1, 44) = 8.42, p < .01$, but only when instructions emphasized the potential unreliability of some information. When subjects were instructed that all evidence was equally important and reliable, dispositional effects were negligible, interaction $F(1, 44) = 4.37, p < .05$. Again, note that the convergence of the two subject groups was due largely to lenient subjects becoming more stringent under the latter condition. Duncan multiple-range comparisons showed significant differences ($p < .05$) between the disposition groups under unreliable evidence conditions and a significant increase in guilt ratings for the lenient subjects when evidence was reliable.

Punishment recommendations. Parallel data were obtained for punishment recommendations (see Table 3). Harsh-dispositioned subjects were more punitive than lenient subjects, $F(1, 44) = 7.74, p < .01$, but

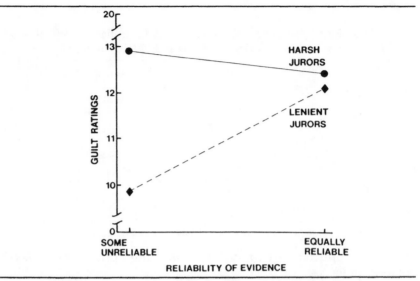

Figure 6.2   Guilt ratings as a function of juror bias and evidential reliability in cases of mixed evidential value (Experiment 2).

more so when encouraged to discount some elements of information, interaction $F(1, 44) = 5.76$, $p < .05$. Duncan multiple-range analyses showed that the condition in which lenient subjects responded to unreliable information produced significantly less punishment than the remaining conditions ($p < .05$).

Evidence reported as influential. Subjects were asked to list for each case the three items of evidence that they believed had most affected their response. These items were coded by two independent scorers as either incriminating or exonerating in value. The scoring was deemed to be reliable (interscorer coefficient of agreement = .95). Table 4 gives the mean proportion of exonerating evidence cited by each group of 12 subjects in the Bias × Instructions design. Harsh and lenient subjects cited about the same proportion of exonerating facts when told that the facts were equally reliable, but lenient subjects cited more exonerating facts when encouraged to discount some evidence. Separate chi-square analyses were performed comparing the number of incriminating versus exonerating facts cited by each subject group under each of the reliability instructions conditions. Harsh subjects cited more incriminating facts under both reliable and unreliable conditions, $\chi^2(1) = 10.88$. But lenient subjects did not cite significantly more incriminating facts when information was unreliable, $\chi^2(1) = 1.79$. It is noteworthy that retrospective reports of influential evidence

TABLE 6.3
Mean Rated Punishment in Cases of Mixed Evidential
Incrimination (Experiment 2)

Evidence characterization	Subject bias	
	Harsh	Lenient
Reliable	4.33	4.08
Unreliable	4.42	3.00

Note: 12 subjects per cell. Punishments were assigned on a scale of 1 (minimum) to 7 (maximum).

closely patterned the guilt judgments—lenient and harsh subjects were equally influenced by exonerating evidence when it was reliable, but lenient subjects were more influenced by exonerating considerations when evidence was cast as unreliable. A tenuous implication is that when evidence is questionable, persons (particularly those of the lenient persuasion) will discount information inconsistent with their bias. This explanation is tenuous because reports of importance were retrospective, and the relationship between cited information and judgments is correlational. It may be that subjects reported influential evidence to accord with their judgments of the defendant.

Discussion

Reduction of bias effects accrues when the weight of evidential information is maximized. This result is consistent with the general model of social judgment in which judgment is an algebraic combination of the value of information about the object and a predispositional impression, each weighted by its effective importance. That persons weight their predispositions relative to the importance of stimulus information suggests that the contribution of the former may be reduced by any situational factors that enhance consideration of the latter. For example, increased opportunity to contemplate stimulus information reduces the effect of the initial impression (Tesser & Conlee, 1975).

An analysis of variance in Experiment 1, omitting the reliable evidence condition, disclosed that effects of bias were not greater in the conditions in which evidence was characterized as unreliable than in the control conditions: Conditions × Subject Bias interaction $F(1, 92) = .001$. This equivalence implies that persons without being told

TABLE 6.4

Percentage of Exonerating Facts Cited as Influential in the
Judgment of Cases of Mixed Evidential Incrimination (Experiment 2)

	Subject bias			
	Harsh		Lenient	
Evidence characterization	%	No. of exonerating/ incriminatory facts	%	No. of exonerating/ incriminatory facts
Reliable	27	16/43	30	20/47
Unreliable	22	15/54	42	28/38

Note: 12 subjects per cell; a total of six facts was cited by each.

otherwise may assume some unreliability in the evidence, possibly a legacy of media courtroom dramas.

We have suggested that the source of biasing was localized in the initial impression. This assumption follows naturally from subject selection procedures. Subjects were classified by their preexisting responses to criminals in general—responses to others in the absence of concrete information about a defendant. Elsewhere, Ostrom, Werner, and Saks (1978) suggest that the effect of bias is largely in the relative weights assigned to bias-congruent and bias-incongruent evidence. While the possibility is not incompatible with locating bias in the judgmental value (initial impression) that one brings into the judgment equation (and indeed, there was the suggestion in Experiment 2 that some subjects do weight bias-incongruent information less under certain conditions), it is unlikely to account for the results of Experiment 1, since biasing effects were found for trial cases that contained homogeneous information. That is, lenient subjects were unable to elevate the weight of exonerating information in incriminating cases (there was none), and harsh subjects could not elevate the weight of incriminating evidence in exonerating cases (again, there was none). And yet the groups differed on the two types of cases, in the same direction and to the same extent. Our best course at this time, in considering the two viewpoints, is to say that prior attitudes affect both preexisting values and the importance placed on congruent and discrepant information.

Turning to the implications of these data for courtroom behavior, we find that two dilemmas seem to emerge. The first concerns the adversary principle on which our Anglo-American justice system is based. Facts emerge in the trial through the efforts of adversarial attorneys, who in the process attempt to discredit testimony favorable to the other side. Though this system may appear to serve the cause of fairness and truth (see e.g., Freedman, 1970; Thibaut, Walker, LaTour, & Houlden, 1974), it also increases the appearance of evidential contentiousness and unreliability. Our data show that such an appearance enhances the manifestation of predispositional bias. The problem is how to increase the reliability of trial testimony without severely restricting the adversarial principle. At the other end of the spectrum is the inquisitorial system, common in continental Europe. Here, the presentation of evidence is the responsibility of a skilled fact finder acting impartially. In this instance, information credibility would be enhanced, and conditions would favor bias reduction. We suggest that if an adversarial framework is to be followed, attacks on opposing evidence must be limited so as to keep juror bias effects to a minimum. To strike this delicate balance between maintaining evidential weight and fair opportunity for the defendant, the expanded use of pretrial conference techniques (e.g., Walker & Thibaut, 1971) may be desirable.

A second dilemma lies in the fact that it was the lenient subjects who laid their biases aside when evidence was reliable. Traditionally, lenience is a desirable bias; jurors are instructed to presume innocence. Similarly, if one is to err in a verdict, tradition has it that leniency is preferred ("It is better that ten guilty persons escape than one innocent suffer"; Blackstone, 1769/1962, p. 420). The problem for legal scholars and technicians, then, is to find ways to increase evidence credibility without seriously restricting the defendant's rights to a client-centered defense or the prominence of leniency biases.

EXPERIMENT 3

This experiment aimed at generalizing the conceptual basis of the first two experiments in two ways. First, the experiment was conducted in a more realistic setting: A mock trial was enacted in a real courtroom with older, non-college-student subjects, who had the opportunity to deliberate. Though aspects of the testimony, the response task, and the deliberation were controlled and limited, the enactment, setting, type of subjects, and presence of deliberation brought this experiment closer to real jury functioning.

Second, this experiment manipulated state, rather than trait, dispositional bias. Through varying the conduct of the defense or prosecuting attorney, or the judge and experimenter, the temporary mood of jurors was manipulated. These operations have their parallel in real courtrooms. A flamboyant or obnoxious attorney may prejudice the client's or state's case. Unsettling conditions in the courtroom such as heat or closeness (see Griffitt & Veitch, 1971) , undue delays, as well as personal woes and physical distress may also temporarily bias one's evaluative response to another. We ask, How is this extralegal but real factor of the juror's state combined with trial information in reaching a judgment? And, if annoying conditions do have a biasing effect, is there hope for mitigation in the normal course of events?

Method

Subjects

Eight juries were composed of 12 Caucasian jurors each. Sex composition (29 males, 67 females) was roughly proportional within juries.[1] The average age within juries ranged from 31-37 years, with a grand mean of 35.2 years. Occupations and education were diverse,[2] and all subjects were eligible for jury duty, though less than half had ever served on a jury. Subjects were recruited from the area surrounding Glen Ellyn, Illinois—a community of 20,000 inhabitants in the western suburbs of Chicago. Subjects responded to newspaper advertisements and notices in public places (libraries, supermarkets, etc.) and were paid $5 for participation.

Trial Content

Two parallel trials were contrived. Facts concerning a case of attempted manslaughter were obtained from materials described in Walker, Thibaut, and Andreoli(1972). These were rewritten in the form of trial transcripts. One trial was constructed to give a moderately strong appearance of guilt and the other to provide a moderately strong appearance of innocence. Mean normative ratings (1 = innocent; 20 = guilty) were 15.85 and 7.15, respectively (ns = 15). In order to yield the desired normative responses, the trials contained roughly 75% incriminating (or exonerating) facts and 25% exonerating (or incriminating) facts.

The charge was the same in both cases: The defendant was accused of stabbing a victim with broken glass in a tavern argument. In both cases the defendant pled self-defense, but in one trial the facts pointed toward an unprovoked assault, and in the other, toward a menacing victim.

Procedure

Trials were enacted in a courtroom provided by the Lewis University College of Law. When subjects had phoned for an appointment, they were told that the experiment would last 15 minutes, but to allot 2 hours in case they had to wait for other "trials" to finish. They initially met with the experimenter in a classroom, where preliminary instructions were given and personal data were taken. They were again told that once we entered the courtroom, the trial should not take more than 15 minutes. To describe the task and to engage their enthusiasm, we told subjects that they would be seeing an enactment of an actual trial that had taken place. Our purpose, we said, was to see whether mock jurors would return the same verdicts as the true jury if they had access to an abbreviated version of the trial, containing only the skeleton of the facts presented in court. A secondary purpose was to see what would happen if jurors reported verdicts on a continuous scale, rather than as a dichotomy, and if deliberation were limited to a distinct period. Spontaneous comments in all juries, both during preliminary briefing and during debriefing, suggested that the opportunity to compare responses with a true jury was highly motivating. In fact, during debriefing, it took several repetitions of the fact that the case was fictitious before jurors ceased demanding to know what the true jury had done. In preliminary briefing, subjects were advised that the best way to match the true jury was to act naturally and not try to guess what others had done. Again, their remarks, and the heatedness of deliberation later on, suggested that they took their roles seriously.

After briefing, juries were led to the courtroom and admonished not to speak to each other once the trial began. The trial was conducted in as authentic a manner as possible, with an older law student playing the judge. College students role played witnesses, and advanced law students acted as attorneys. All had been thoroughly rehearsed in their roles and elicited from a witness only the facts that the script attributed to that witness. Deviation from the script was allowed only for stylistic purposes; evidence was not spontaneously fabricated.

The experimental factors consisted of the two versions of the trial (incriminating or exonerating) and the manner in which the trial was conducted. There were four variations in trial conduct. One trial of each incriminating version was run on a "straight" basis. The facts were elicited as in the script, and the trials consumed 15 minutes. The other three variations were designed to prolong the trial to 50 minutes, to annoy the jurors, and to create bad feelings. One pair of trials was prolonged because of the obnoxious, repetitive, and badgering behavior of the defense attorney. In a dramatic manner, he established the same facts repetitively by means of redundant questions, expressed annoyance with witnesses and the other attorney, and was given to obnoxious asides to his audience. The third pair of trials had the prosecutor engaging in these annoyances and irrelevancies, and in the last pair of trials, the judge and experimenter were guilty of annoying the jurors. In this last variation, the judge interrupted the trial at predetermined intervals to ask pointless questions, to scold both attorneys, to give obscure points of law, and once to leave the room for a phone call. The experimenter experienced mysterious break-downs in recording equipment and misplaced his trial notes, necessi-tating annoying delays.

After the conclusion of the trial, jurors individually rated the degree of guilt on a 20-point (1 = definitely innocent; 20 = definitely guilty) scale. Then they retired to deliberate the case for 10 minutes, under instructions to discuss all aspects of the case. They were not required to reach consensus. After deliberation, ratings were again taken, and subjects were debriefed with respect to the nature of the trials and the purpose of the experiment. At the outset of the postrating interview, the experimenter elicited their reaction to the conduct of the experiment. In all but the control trials, extreme annoyance was expressed, even to the point of nasty comments about the experi-menter when he was the cause of annoyance. No subjects admitted to suspicion about the manipulations, either postexperimentally or during the deliberation (which was audiotaped).

Eight juries of 12 members participated, one jury to each Trial $\times$ Conduct condition.

Results

Defendant Guilt

Mean guilt ratings for each jury are displayed in Figure 3; higher ratings reflect stronger guilt attribution. Consider first the predelibera-tion judgments. In both types of cases (i.e., high or low appearance of defendant guilt), greatest guilt was attributed to the defendant when his attorney was the source of annoyance, and least guilt was assigned when the prosecutor was offensive or when there was no annoyance present. The condition in which the neutral parties—judge and experimenter—were at fault fell between these extremes in guilt ratings.

Now consider the postdeliberation ratings, shown in the right-hand data points in Figure 3. The biasing effects of courtroom conditions virtually disappear. The induction, and then reductions, of biasing effects is shown statistically by the overall analysis of variance, which obtained an interaction between predeliberation/postdeliberation

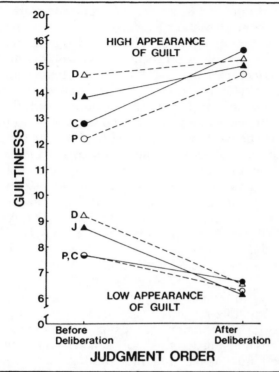

Figure 6.3 Guilt ratings as a function of courtroom behavior of attorneys and judge (Experiment 3). (The four sets of curves represent the different sources of annoyance: D = defense attorney; J = judge and experimenter; P = Prosecutor; and C = control [no annoyance].)

responses (within subjects) and trial conditions (between subjects), $F(3, 88) = 6.21$, $p < .01$.

In the overall analysis, besides the built-in effect for trial appearance, $F(1, 88) = 142.63$, $p < .001$, one other effect reached significance— the interaction between predeliberation/postdeliberation measures and trial appearances, $F(1, 88) = 97.46$, $p < .001$. This result represents the polarization of predeliberation responses toward greater extremes following discussion, a phenomenon that has been labeled the "polarization effect" (see Kaplan, 1977a). This shift in individuals' responses toward greater extremes following discussion has theoretical and practical implications for bias reduction that will be taken up in the next section.

In order to further explore the interactions, a Duncan multiple-range test was applied. In *predeliberation* ratings, subjects subjected to the misanthropic defense attorney reported greater certainty of guilt than did controls or those exposed to obnoxious prosecutors ($p <$ .05). Moreover, annoying judge behavior led to greater attributions of guilt than did the annoying prosecutor or control conditions when the evidence was incriminating ($p < .05$); a similar, though nonsignificant, tendency ($p < .10$) was noted for exonerating evidence. Within evidential incrimination levels, on the other hand, there were no significant differences between trial conditions in *postdeliberation* ratings. These comparisons, which show biasing effects in predeliberation but not postdeliberation ratings, receive further support from separate analyses of variance conducted for the two ratings. A trial condition effect was lacking in analysis of postdeliberation ratings, $F(3, 88) = 1.32$, as was the Trial Conditions $\times$ Trial Appearance interaction, $F(3, 88) = 1.07$. However, the trial conditions factor was marginally significant in the analysis of predeliberation ratings, $F(3, 88) = 2.42, p <$ .07. That this biasing effect was similar for both cases is shown by the negligible interaction between trial conditions and trial appearances, $F(3, 88) = .07$.

Turning now to the polarizing effect of deliberation, we find that the Duncan multiple-range test disclosed a significant shift toward extremeness for all treatment groups ($ps < .05$) except for subjects exposed to an annoying defense attorney and incriminating evidence, who showed no change due to deliberation. So the effect of deliberation was to polarize responses toward the dominant valence of the evidence and away from the bias induced by trial conditions.

Courtroom conditions *can* bias judgments of individual jurors. Specifically, conditions arousing negative feelings can hurt the defendant's case. However, the impact of the juror's state on his or her judgment was moderated by the relationship between the source of the state and the defendant; the stronger the relationship between source and defendant, the greater the impact (defense $>$ judge $>$ prosecutor). Apparently, there is a cognitive element mediating state effects.

Deliberation Content

Deliberations were taped and content analyzed. Counts were made of the number of references to judge, lawyer, or experimenter behavior and of references to testimonial evidence. Across all eight trials, only 10 references were made to courtroom behavior, and 204 separate statements referred to evidence. References to evidence consumed about 28 minutes of deliberation across the eight trials, compared to less than 1 minute (distributed across the four trials in which reference was made) spent on actions of trial principals. This suggests that the reduction of bias effects was not due to the airing of grievances or to peer pressure to ignore such an extralegal factor. In fact, there were no references at all to the behavior of the defense attorney, who was the source of the greatest biasing in predeliberation ratings and whose biasing effects were most ameliorated by discussion. Hence it appears that bias reduction was effected by straightforward discussion of the evidence.

GENERAL DISCUSSION

Theoretical Implications

Judgments by jurors are a joint function of existing predispositions toward the defendant (biases) and information pertinent to the judgment (evidence). Both components may be represented by a common parameter—scale value—and the method by which the two are integrated may then be determined. The common principle that emerges from these experiments is that the contribution of the bias component decreases as the importance of the evidence is increased. This principle implicates a particular integration strategy: The components are inversely weighted, as in the weighted averaging model given by Equation 1. Note also that although biasing effects vary with the *weight* of information, they are constant across variations in *scale value* of information (Experiments 1 and 3). Similar parallelism of effects has been found for the integration of defendant characterization and trial evidence (Kaplan & Kemmerick, 1974). Parallelism implies a linear integration function, whereby the contribution of bias is independent of the scale value of stimulus information and is in accord with studies of the integration of dispositions with stimulus person information in standard personality perception paradigms (Kaplan, 1975).

Deliberation had the dual effect of polarizing individual jurors' predeliberation responses and reducing reliance on biases. Both effects may be due to the same mechanism. Facts of the case are reiterated in discussion, and as a consequence, an individual juror may take more evidence into account in the postdeliberation judgment than in the predeliberation responses. If the predominant balance of the evidence under discussion is univalent (as was true in Experiment

3), according to Equation 1 the response will be pulled in the direction of the information value and away from the preinformation bias. Consequently, discussion of information that is more extreme in value than the preinformation bias will lead simultaneously to response polarization and bias reduction, because of an increase in amount and weight of information (see Kaplan, 1977a, and Kaplan & C. Miller, 1977, for a detailed treatment of polarization effects).

This same analysis can be applied to Izzett and Leginski's (1974) finding that the effects of a defendant's identity are reduced by deliberation. The contribution of extralegal factors is lessened when deliberation allows the integration of legally relevant information into the response. More generally, any conditions that permit the subject to consider and then integrate relevant information will reduce reliance on preexisting dispositions. When able to rehearse (or discuss) relevant information, one is better able to integrate the information and to draw the response away from the more neutral preexisting disposition. This result is shown in Tesser and Conlee's (1975) report of more extreme attitudinal responses when subjects have greater time and opportunity for thought.

The relative weighting of bias and evidence is demonstrated by the convergence of differently biased subject groups with increased weighting of information. But note in Figure 3 that this convergence accompanies a general polarization of response for all groups. This raises the possibility that convergence may be due to simple ceiling and floor effects and not to true reduction in the contribution of bias. This alternative possibility may be examined in Experiment 2. Here, convergence of biased groups required convergence toward a moderate scale point (see Figure 2), since the information was mixed in scale value. The fact that bias effect reduction can occur in the middle as well as at the extremes of the scale weakens a scale-endpoint interpretation.

Bias in the Courtroom

We have tried to achieve some generality in our treatment of bias; for example, we have examined trait and state biases and different means of increasing evidential weight. However, biases here have been of a general nature; that is, global feelings about defendants have been manipulated. More specific biases (e.g., toward sex, race, or particular issues) invite study by similar methods. Based on the observation that effects due to a defendant's identity are lessened by deliberation (Izzett & Leginski, 1974), it may be that defendant- or issue-specific biases can be mitigated by the same procedures employed here.

These findings refer to jurors' certainty of defendant guilt. In courtroom proceedings, the verdict is expressed in a dichotomous fashion, implicating the additional consideration of jurors' criteria for a guilty verdict (Thomas & Hogue, 1976). Although shifts were observed in *certainty* as a function of bias reduction, it remains to be seen whether dichotomous *verdicts* shift as well; that is, whether these demonstrated shifts pass jurors' criteria for conviction or acquittal.

Some general observations are in order regarding the role of bias in the courtroom. We have suggested that systems which encourage adversarial attacks on the trustworthiness or validity of evidence also encourage the manifestation of existing biases in subsequent judgments. Balancing this pessimistic observation is the suggestion that, given the ameliorating effects of deliberation and the hope that trials will usually be conducted in a decorous fashion wherein legally relevant evidence will not be totally denigrated, the effects of bias can be contained.

But does our judicial system want all biases to be contained? Historically, biases have been, and continue to be, sought. In the beginning, juries were composed of persons with knowledge of the case and were expected to apply this foreknowledge, as well as local customs, to their verdict. Impartiality as a value is only of recent vintage. Even so, certain biases are still encouraged. Juries are admonished to presume innocence. Furthermore, they are constituted to contain peers from the locale of the charged offense. This requirement is in keeping with the doctrine that juries act as the "conscience of the community" (cf. Brooks & Doob, 1975) in applying existing social mores to each case. While this discretionary power has the virtue of flexibility (Curtis, 1952) and responsiveness to changing societal views (Howe, 1939; Wigmore, 1929), it is also an invitation for bias and is legally encouraged (Brooks & Doob , 1975). The problem is not simply *how* to control the manifestation of bias in jurors' judgments, but *which* biases to control, and whether "desirable" biases can be preserved when minimizing "undesirable" effects.

NOTES

1. All juries contained four males and eight females, except for the jury exposed to exonerating evidence and an annoying prosecutor (two males) and the jury exposed to incriminating evidence and an annoying prosecutor (three males).

2. Forty-nine subjects had completed high school only, 47 had attended or completed college, and 13 had engaged in postgraduate work. Educational level did not appear to be systematically imbalanced among the juries.

REFERENCES

Anderson, N. H. Information integration theory: A brief survey. In D. Krantz, R. Atkinson, R. D. Luce, & P. Suppes (Eds.), *Contemporary developments in mathematical psychology* (Vol. 2). San Francisco: Freeman, 1974.

Blackstone, W. *Commentaries on the laws of England of public wrongs.* Boston: Beacon Press, 1962. (Originally published 1769)

Boehm, V. R. Mr. Prejudice, Miss Sympathy, and the authoritarian personality: An application of psychological measuring techniques to the problem of jury bias. *Wisconsin Law Review,* 1968, 734-750.

Brooks, W. N., & Doob, A. N. Justice and the jury. *Journal of Social Issues,* 1975, *31,* 171-182.

Curtis, C. P. The trial judge and the jury. *Vanderbilt Law Review,* 1952, *5,* 150-166

Freedman, M. H. Professional responsibility of the civil practitioner: Teaching legal ethics in the contracts course. In D. T. Weckstein (Ed), *Education in the professional responsibilities of the lawyer.* Charlottesville: University Press of Virginia, 1970.

Griffitt, W., & Veitch, R. Hot and crowded: Influences of population density and temperature on interpersonal active behavior. *Journal of Personality and Social Psychology,* 1971, *17,* 92-98.

Howe, M. de W. Juries as judges in criminal cases. *Harvard Law Review,* 1939, *52,* 582-616.

Izzett, R., & Leginski, W. Group discussion and the influence of defendant characteristics in a simulated jury setting. *Journal of Social Psychology,* 1974, *93,* 271-279.

Jurow, G. New data on the effect of a "death qualified" jury on the guilt determination process. *Harvard Law Review,* 1971, *84,* 567-611.

Kalven, H., Jr., & Zeisel, H. *The American jury.* Boston: Little, Brown, 1966.

Kaplan, M. F. Information integration in social judgment: Interaction of the judge and informational components. In M. F. Kaplan & S. Schwartz (Eds.), *Human judgment and decision processes.* New York: Academic Press, 1975.

Kaplan, M. F. Discussion polarization effects in a modified jury decision paradigm: Informational influences, *Sociometry,* 1977, *40,* 262-271 (a).

Kaplan, M. F. Judgments by juries. In M. Kaplan & S. Schwartz (Eds.), *Judgment and decision processes in applied settings.* New York: Academic Press, 1977 (b).

Kaplan, M. F., & Kemmerick, G. D. Juror judgment as information integration: Combining evidential and nonevidential information. *Journal of Personality and Social Psychology,* 1974, *30,* 493-499.

Kaplan, M. F., & Miller, C. E. Judgments and group discussion: Effect of presentation and memory factors on polarization. *Sociometry,* 1977, *40,* 337-343.

Kaplan, M. F., & Schersching, C. Reducing juror bias: An experimental approach. In P. Lipsitt & B. Sales (Eds.), *New directions in psycholegal research.* New York: Van Nostrand Reinhold, 1978.

Kirk, R. C. *Experimental design: Procedures of the behavioral sciences.* Monterey, CA: Brooks/Cole, 1968.

Mitchell, H. E., & Byrne, D. The defendant's dilemma: Effects of jurors' attitudes and authoritarianism on judicial decisions. *Journal of Personality and Social Psychology,* 1973, *25,* 123-129.

Nagel, S. S. *The legal process from a behavioral perspective.* Homewood, IL: Dorsey Press, 1969.

Ostrom, T. M., Werner, C., & Saks, M. J. An integration theory analysis of jurors' presumptions of guilt or innocence. *Journal of Personality and Social Psychology,* 1978, *36,* 436-450.

Shaw, M. E., & Wright, J. M. *Scales for the measurement of attitudes.* New York: McGraw-Hill, 1967.

Tesser, A., & Conlee, M. C. Some effects of time and thought on attitude polarization. *Journal of Personality and Social Psychology,* 1975, *31,* 262-270.

Thibaut, J., Walker, L., LaTour, S., & Houlden, P. Procedural justice as fairness. *Stanford Law Review,* 1974, *26,* 1271-1289.

Thomas, E. A. C., & Hogue, A. Apparent weight of evidence, decision criteria, and confidence ratings in juror decision making. *Psychological Review,* 1976, *83,* 442-465.

Walker, L., & Thibaut, J. An experimental examination of pretrial conference techniques. *Minnesota Law Review,* 1971, *55,* 1113-1137.

Walker, L., Thibaut, J., & Andreoli, V. Order of presentation at trial. *The Yale Law Journal,* 1972, *82,* 216-226.

Wigmore, J. A programme for the trial of jury trial. *Journal of the American Judicature Society,* 1929, *12,* 166-170.

SECTION II

SUMMARY

Critics of the jury system have charged that, compared to the dispassionate stance of a professional judge, a panel of average citizens is so riddled with personal sympathies and prejudices that jury decisions are hopelessly biased. In defense of the system, others maintain that, as jurors, people take their role seriously, rise to the occasion, and render justice in ways that are consistent with the evidence. Which of these images is the more accurate? The chapters in this section suggest that although there is support for both, juries—by and large—base their verdicts on a rational consideration of the evidence.

To be sure, there are personal traits that trial lawyers should look for during the voir dire. The experiment described in chapter 4 indicated that the authoritarian personality is someone to be reckoned with. Characterized as politically conservative, rigid, submissive to powerful figures, and punitive toward others who violate conventional values, people who are high rather than low on authoritarianism tend to favor the prosecution (or the defense, when the defendant represents the establishment) in a criminal case. Bray and Noble's study with mock juries in a murder trial demonstrates how this trait, and possibly others as well, can influence verdicts.

Myers's (1979) research, however, leads us to question whether nonevidentiary bias plays all that important a role in actual jury verdicts. In an archival study, Myers looked at 201 jury trials in Indianapolis. For each case, she obtained information about it from prosecutors' files, police arrest records, telephone interviews with the crime victims, and so on. By correlating jury verdicts with legally admissible evidence (such as whether a weapon had been recovered or whether the defendant had been identified by an eyewitness) and with nonevidentiary factors (such as the defendant's race or employment status), Myers found that, for the most part, juries' decisions were as they should be—based on the evidence.

Do jury verdicts conform to a rational or nonrational model of decision making? Kaplan and Miller (1978), in chapter 6, offer a qualified, "it depends" answer to this question. These investigators take as a starting point the idea that jurors approach their task as they do any other judgment situation. That is, they must integrate information from a variety of sources, including their own pretrial beliefs as well as the evidence introduced in court. Each piece of information varies in terms of (1) whether it makes the defendant appear guilty or not guilty and (2) how important it is to the final judgment. According to their theory, the impact of personal bias will be reduced to the extent that the evidence is perceived as clear and reliable. Their research generally supported that prediction.

Collectively, these chapters suggest that jurors may very well enter the courtroom biased in their predisposition. If the evidence is mixed or ambiguous, jurors' predispositions could affect their decisions. But when the available information clearly favors a particular outcome, then their verdicts are ultimately driven by that evidence. There are, we believe, significant exceptions to this rule. There are certain types of cases that, because of their subject matter, awaken deep-seated personal values over which people adamantly disagree. Rape, politics, racial prejudice, and capital punishment are among these emotional topics. At this point, research suggests that individual juror bias plays a uniquely prominent role in these kinds of cases. The best example, perhaps, can be found in the controversial practice of selecting juries in cases involving the death penalty.

In states that have capital juries decide on the defendant's guilt and then on a sentence, judges typically follow a procedure known as *death qualification,* whereby people are excluded if they state that they would not, under any circumstances, vote to impose the death penalty. By removing all prospective jurors who oppose capital punishment, is the final jury inherently biased toward the prosecution? In recent years, psychologists have investigated this question in great detail; and consistently the answer is, yes—death-qualified juries are more authoritarian in their predispositions and more likely to convict

than normally selected juries (Thompson, Cowan, Ellsworth, & Harrington, 1984). In the face of an impressive array of studies supporting this
conclusion, the U. S. Supreme Court, in *Lockhart v. McCree* (1986),
upheld the practice of death qualification. In his majority opinion, the
now Chief Justice William Rehnquist conceded that death-qualified
juries are somewhat more conviction prone but that this fact did not
violate the defendant's right to an impartial jury. As this reasoning
illustrates, biased decision making is not unique to jurors—judges,
too, are susceptible.

REFERENCES

Lockhart v. McCree (1986).
Thompson, W. C., Cowan, C. L., Ellsworth, P. C., & Harrington, J. C. (1984).
    Death penalty attitudes and conviction proneness: The translation of
    attitudes into verdicts. *Law and Human Behavior, 8,* 95-113.

SECTION III

JURY COMPETENCE
Introduction

Throughout its long history, the trial jury has been fraught with criticism and controversy. Most recently, juries have been portrayed as unrepresentative (see section I) and potentially biased (see section II). Furthermore, jurors' ability to process the masses of sophisticated, technical information in long trials has been questioned; in the last few years, a "complexity exception" to the Seventh Amendment has been proposed, reflecting the notion that the jury is not competent to decide complex civil suits (Sperlich, 1982). Even the recent U.S. Supreme Court Chief Justice Warren Burger has suggested that massive civil suits that involve thousands of exhibits and weeks of testimony by expert witnesses might be better decided by a single judge than by a jury. But others have affirmed their support for the jury system even in a complex litigation. This section explores this issue.

When discussing "jury competence" two aspects need to be differentiated. First, are jurors able to *comprehend* the material presented to them? Do they understand the judge's instructions on points of law, as well as the testimony and exhibits introduced in court? Second, are they able to *remember* the material they have learned? Especially if the trial runs for months, or even years (as a few have done), do jurors' abilities to remember fail? If so, what kinds of modifications in courtroom procedure are effective to increase comprehension and memory?

For due process to be achieved, it is necessary for a jury to understand its task. In every jury trial, the judge instructs the jury on points of law, including definitions of legal terms, elements of the crime (or dispute), and the standard of proof (beyond a reasonable doubt, if a criminal trial, or the preponderance of evidence, if a civil suit). Usually, judges can decide for themselves when to deliver these instructions, but most prefer to do so at the end of the trial, as the need for instructions on some aspects of the law may not be apparent at the beginning of the trial. The first chapter in this section, written by two of the editors of this book, illustrates the impact of the timing, during the course of the trial, of the reasonable doubt instruction. Kassin and Wrightsman describe its effects both on the verdicts of mock jurors and on the amount of information they retained about the evidence.

The second chapter, by Amiram Elwork, James J. Alfini, and Bruce D. Sales, deals with another aspect of the jury's comprehension of the judge's instructions. These are usually composed with concern for their technical accuracy at the forefront, but with little or no effort to improve their understandability. The psychologists who carried out this study produced rewritten and revised jury instructions, attempting to maintain their legal accuracy while improving their readability and comprehensibility.

Chapter 9, by David U. Strawn, a former judge, and G. Thomas Munsterman, of the Center for Jury Studies, is a brief but highly provocative set of suggestions for remedying many of the problems included under the stigma that "jurors don't understand and can't remember." A summary to this section discusses, among other matters, some recent efforts by trial judges to introduce innovations in courtroom procedures.

REFERENCE

Sperlich, P. W. (1982) The case for preserving trial by jury in complex civil litigation. *Judicature, 65*, 394-419.

7

ON THE REQUIREMENTS OF PROOF
The Timing of Judicial Instruction and Mock Juror Verdicts

SAUL M. KASSIN
Williams College
LAWRENCE S. WRIGHTSMAN
University of Kansas

In trials by jury, the judge is obligated to instruct jurors in both general and case-specific matters of law. These instructions serve a number of functions: The judge orients jurors in their task, outlines the undis-

Authors' Note, This research was conducted while the first author was on a postdoctoral fellowship at the University of Kansas and was supported in full by Faculty Research Grant 3401 to the second author. We would also like to thank Martin F. Kaplan and two anonymous reviewers for their helpful comments on the manuscript. Requests for

puted facts and issues of the case, explains the relevant law, and informs jurors about procedural matters (McBride, 1969). From the defendant's perspective, perhaps the most crucial of the mandatory instructions is that concerning the "requirements of proof" (LaBuy, 1963). Specifically, the accused is entitled to the instruction that he or she is presumed innocent, that the burden of proof is on the prosecution, and that all elements of the crime must be proven to a constitutional standard of "beyond a reasonable doubt."

Although the potential importance of the judge's charge is widely recognized (McCart, 1964), its actual effectiveness is a subject of controversy. On the one hand, the courts assume that jurors understand their instructions, use them in making decisions, and are acutely sensitive to even minor variations in wording. Thus attorneys often request specific instructions, appellate courts have occasionally reversed verdicts on the basis of an improperly worded instruction, and many states currently favor the practice of having judges recite a preapproved pattern instruction in order to ensure standardization. Experimental support for the effect of variations in instructional content has recently been obtained. Kerr et al. (1976) presented mock jurors with three definitions of reasonable doubt: one that described a lax criterion of reasonableness (i.e., "you need not be absolutely sure that the defendant is guilty to find him guilty." p. 286), one that described an extremely stringent criterion (i.e., "if you are not sure and certain of his guilt, you must find him not guilty," p. 286), and one in which reasonable doubt was not defined. As it turned out, these varying definitions significantly influenced both individual and group verdicts—a lax criterion resulted in a high conviction rate, whereas a stringent one produced a low rate of conviction. Subjects for whom reasonable doubt was not explicated fell between these extremes. This study thus demonstrated that verdicts are indeed influenced by the reasonable doubt element of the requirements-of-proof instruction.

On the other hand, it has been suggested by legal scholars (Frank, 1949) and researchers (Sealy & Cornish, 1973) that these instructions have little effect on jurors' verdicts. One common criticism is that because they are written in statutory language, the instructions are often confusing to laypersons untrained in the law (Elwork, Sales, &

reprints should be addressed to Saul M. Kassin, who is now at the Department of Psychology, Williams College, Williamstown, MA 01267.

From Journal of Personality and Social Psychology (1979), 37(10), 1877-1887. Copyright © 1979 by the American Psychological Association. Reprinted by permission of the publisher.

Alfini, 1977). In fact, one study revealed that 40% of 375 sampled jurors reported that they did not understand their judge's instruction (Hervey, 1947). A second criticism is aimed at the timing of the judge's charge. Although the procedure is not fixed by law, the jury is typically instructed at the close of the trial presentation, that is, after the evidence has been presented. Although it is possible that this sequence increases the salience of the instruction and its availability for recall during deliberation,[1] a number of sources (e.g., McBride, 1969) have questioned the utility of an instruction that is given at a stage when jurors might have already decided on a verdict. Kalven and Zeisel (1966) noted that jurors often form very definite opinions about a defendant's guilt or innocence before the close of the trial. Accordingly, Judge E. Barrett Prettyman (1960) argued the following:

> It makes no sense to have a juror listen to days of testimony only then to be told that he and his conferees are the sole judges of the facts, that the accused is presumed to be innocent, that the government must prove guilt beyond a reasonable doubt, etc. What manner of mind can go back over a stream of conflicting statements and alleged facts, recall the intonations, the demeanor, or even the existence of the witnesses, and retrospectively fit all these recollections into a pattern of evaluation and judgment given him for the first time after the events; the human mind cannot do so.... Why should not the judge, when the jury is sworn, then and there tell them the rules of the game. (p. 1066)

In view of the flexibility in courtroom procedure and the potential importance of a judge's charge to the jury, the absence of research on temporal factors associated with the instructions is surprising (Elwork, Sales & Alfini, 1977, is an exception). After all, order effects in the perception of unfolding behavior sequences have repeatedly been noted in both person perception (Jones et al., 1968) and jury contexts (Walker, Thibaut, & Andreoli, 1972). In the latter study, Walker et al. (1972) varied the order in which the prosecution and defense presented their cases but did not address the issue of judicial instruction.

The present study was designed to investigate the relationship between the timing of a judge's instructions and mock juror verdicts for a criminal case. In particular, the aims of the research were twofold. First, we sought to determine whether or not a prototypical, ecologically valid instruction on the requirements of proof influences jurors' decisions and whether the timing of that instruction mediates its efficacy. In order to achieve these goals, requirements-of-proof instructions were gleaned from those currently employed (DeVitt & Blackmar, 1977; LaBuy, 1963; McBride, 1969) and were introduced to subjects before testimony, after testimony, or not at all. At the conclusion of the trial presentation, subjects rendered their individual verdicts and answered a number of other case-related questions. Since the requirements of proof are defendant oriented, their effectiveness should be manifested in a lowered rate of conviction. Based on jurors' tendencies to make early decisions about guilt or innocence and Judge Prettyman's (1960) reasoning that instructions can have their intended effects only when they are delivered before jurors have made up their minds, a kind of primacy or inoculation effect was predicted. That is, the present instructions should produce fewer guilty verdicts when presented before the evidence than when presented after it.

The second general aim of the present study was to explore the mechanism or cognitive process that underlies the proposed order effect. Requirements-of-proof instructions may operate either by decreasing the belief that the defendant committed the crime (i.e., a lowered probability-of-commission estimate) or by increasing the standard or threshold to which that likelihood is compared (i.e., a stringent interpretation of reasonable doubt). Consequently, both were assessed. A collateral issue addressed here was whether or not subjects who are instructed prior to the presentation of evidence evaluate evidentiary information differently as it unfolds from those who do not receive prior instruction. Accordingly, half the subjects in each instruction group made judgments of guilt-innocence at various points during the trial. It was hypothesized that instructed subjects would set a higher standard by which to evaluate the case against the defendant and would therefore be less influenced by the prosecutor's case throughout the trial.

METHOD

Subjects and Design

A total of 107 introductory psychology students (47 male, 60 female) participated in the study. The experiment was conducted in 25 small groups ranging in size from 3 to 7 and took 1 hour and 20 minutes to complete. Each group was randomly assigned to one of six cells produced by the 3 (Judge's Instructions Before Evidence, Instructions After Evidence, No Instructions) $\times$ 2 (Multiple Judgments vs. Single Judgment Only) factorial design.

Procedure

Upon entering, subjects were told that they would observe a videotaped trial simulation, after which they would be asked to render a verdict. They were further instructed that as jurors they should be attentive but should not take notes and should not converse while the trial presentation was in progress.

All subjects were then told that in order to get the entire trial presentation on one reel of tape, a few pauses and meaningless exchanges had been deleted, but that all the testimony remained intact. Those groups who were to receive the judge's instruction, however, were informed that this instruction had inadvertently been deleted but would be read to them at the appropriate time from the original transcript. Finally, subjects in the multiple-judgment cells were informed of the fact that at certain points the tape would be stopped and their judgments would be assessed. The trial was then presented.

The Trial

The stimulus trial was one that had previously been employed (Juhnke et al., 1979). Stylistically, the simulation was presented on a 1-hour (black-and-white) videotape in which a number of law students retried a case in a realistic courtroom setting. It was filmed from a juror's perspective: The judge, attorneys, and witness stand were all in view.

Substantively, the trial was based on an actual criminal case in which the defendant, Ronald Oliver, was charged with stealing a car and with transporting it across state lines.[2] Though continuously presented, the trial consisted of the following three distinct phases: (1) opening statements by prosecutor and defense; (2) direct examination, cross-examination, and redirect examination of two prosecution witnesses (the salesman from whom the vehicle was stolen and the arresting officer) and one defense witness (the defendant); and (3) closing arguments of counsel (prosecution, defense, prosecution). The judge's instructions on the requirements of proof represented a fourth phase whose presence-absence and timing were varied.

In one condition, these instructions appeared prior to the introduction of evidence (i.e., between the first and second phases). In a second condition, they appeared after the closing arguments (i.e., after the third phase). In a third condition, no instruction was given. The specific instruction employed was neither strong nor weak. Rather, it was patterned after the approved instructions designed to convey each element of the requirements of proof: presumption of innocence, burden of proof, and reasonable doubt (see DeVitt & Blackmar, 1977; McBride, 1969). The instruction read as follows:

> Ladies and gentlemen of the jury—at this point I want to emphasize that the law presumes the defendant, Ronald Oliver, to be innocent unless proven otherwise. A defendant begins the trial with a "clean slate" with no evidence against him.
>
> This presumption places the burden not upon the defendant to prove his innocence but, on the contrary, the burden is on the prosecution to convince you beyond any reasonable doubt that the defendant, Ronald Oliver, committed the crime. That burden never shifts at any stage of the proceeding to the defendant. Ronald Oliver has no obligations of any kind to go forward and prove that he is innocent.
>
> You have now heard the term "reasonable doubt." What is it? It is a doubt based upon reason and common sense—the kind of doubt that would make a reasonable person hesitate to act in important matters. To summarize, the defendant is presumed innocent, so the prosecution must prove to your satisfaction beyond any reasonable doubt that Ronald Oliver is guilty. If two conclusions can reasonably be drawn from the evidence—one of innocence and one of guilt—the jury should adopt the one of innocence.

Dependent Measures

At the close of the trial, all subjects responded individually and without deliberation to a two-page questionnaire in which they first rendered a dichotomous judgment (guilty-not guilty) and indicated their confidence in that verdict on a 0- to 8-point scale. They then rated the strength of the evidence as well as their interest and involvement in the case (all on 0- to 8-point scales).

Since verdicts are a function of the perceived probability that the defendant committed the crime and of the standard of proof deemed necessary for conviction, both of these variables were also assessed. All subjects were thus asked, "What is the likelihood that the defendant committed the crime?" to which they responded by circling a number from 0 to 100 (in multiples of 5), and "A defendant should be found guilty if there is at least _____% chance that he committed the crime." Finally, subjects answered 16 short-answer recall questions that pertained to the major facts of the case (e.g., "On what highway was Ron Oliver stopped?"). The total number of correctly recalled items served as a measure of fact recall.

In addition to providing these outcome data, half the subjects indicated their judgments (guilty-not guilty), confidence values, and probability-of-commission estimates at six distinct points during the trial—after both the direct examination and cross-examination of each witness. Specifically, they were asked, "If the trial ended now, would you vote that the defendant is *guilty* or *not guilty?*" "How confident are you in this judgment?" (0-8) "What is the likelihood that the defendant committed the crime?" (0-100). It was thus possible to trace beliefs as the trial unfolded and to examine whether subjects who were already instructed on the requirements of proof (instructions before) evaluated the evidence differently from those who had not yet been instructed (instructions after and no instructions). Previous research employing these multiple judgments (e.g., Weld & Danzig, 1940) has been criticized on the ground that such a procedure may bias final verdicts (Davis, Bray, & Holt, 1977). For that reason, only half the subjects in the present study made these on-line responses. A comparison of their posttrial responses with those of single-judgment subjects thus provided a test for the (non)reactivity of the procedure.

RESULTS

Outcome Measures

Overall, 53% of the subjects voted guilty and 47% voted not guilty. The pattern of verdicts in each cell appears in Table 1.

In order to test for all main and interaction effects and to determine which model best fits these categorical data, these dichotomous judgments were analyzed with a likelihood ratio (goodness of fit) chi-square (Fienberg, 1977). Results indicated that the simplest model that described the observed frequencies was the two-way interaction between instructional set and verdicts, $\chi^2(6) = 1.21, p > .97$. None of the more complicated models (i.e., those involving the multiple vs. single judgments factor) contributed any explanatory power to this Instructional Set $\times$ Verdict model. Put another way, the pattern of verdicts was accounted for by the main effect for timing instruction. Table 1 shows that the instructions-before condition produced 37% guilty verdicts, compared to 59% in the instructions-after and 63% in the no-instructions conditions.

A scalar variable was defined by combining subjects' verdicts with their confidence ratings (confidence itself was unaffected by the independent variables). Specifically, positive confidence values were assigned to guilty verdicts and negative values to verdicts of not guilty. Scores could thus range from –8 (maximum confidence in not-guilty verdict) to 8 (maximum confidence in guilty verdict). A 2 $\times$ 3 analysis of

TABLE 7.1
Pattern of Final Verdicts in Each of the Six Cells

Instruction and verdict	Multiple judgments		Single judgments	
	No.	%	No.	%
Before				
Guilty	7	39	6	35
Not guilty	11	61	11	65
After				
Guilty	12	63	10	56
Not guilty	7	37	8	44
None				
Guilty	12	71	10	56
Not guilty	5	29	8	44

variance on this measure revealed one marginally significant effect for timing of instruction, $F(2, 101) = 2.90, p < .06$. Duncan's multiple-range test further indicated that subjects in the instructions-before condition were less likely ($p < .05$) to convict the defendant than were noninstructed subjects (means of $-.94$ and 2.35, respectively). Instructions-after ($M = 1.79$) and noninstructed conditions did not so differ. An analysis of variance on the probability-of-commission estimates yielded results that closely paralleled those for the verdict-confidence measure—the only significant effect was for timing of the judge's instruction $F(2, 101) = 2.92, p < .06$. Only subjects who received instructions before the evidence viewed the defendant as less likely to have committed the crime ($p <. 05$) than did the noninstructed subjects (mean percentage estimates of 64% and 77.6%, respectively); those who were instructed after the reception of evidence ($M = 73.1\%$) did not lower their probability-of-commission estimates.

Contrary to predictions, no significant differences were obtained on evaluations of evidence strength, interpretations of reasonable doubt, or self-ratings of interest and involvement. Interestingly, a close look at the reasonable-doubt data indicates that the overall estimate of reasonable doubt ($M = 86.07$) was almost identical to that previously reported for college students (Simon & Mahan, 1971, obtained a general estimate of 87% and an estimate of 85% when the crime was auto theft). Subjects thus believed that there should be at least an 86% chance that the defendant committed the crime in order to vote for conviction.

Finally, subjects demonstrated a moderately high level of recall, averaging 12.15 correctly recalled items from a total of 16.[3] Further analysis indicated that a main effect was obtained for timing of instruction on the number of case-related facts recalled, $F(2, 101) = 3.26, p < .05$. Surprisingly, subjects in the instructions-after condition recalled fewer items ($M = 11.30$) than those in either the instructions-before ($M = 12.51$) or noninstructed ($M = 12.69$) conditions. The presence of the instruction between the evidence and response assessment apparently inhibited recall.

In sum, the mere timing of instructions had an impact on jurors' final judgments. Results for the verdict-confidence measure tended to support the major hypothesis that instructions on the requirements of proof would reduce subjects' tendencies to convict (i.e., relative to no instructions) only when delivered prior to the introduction of testimony. Although the timing variable had no significant effect on interpretations of reasonable doubt, preinstructed subjects actually viewed the defendant as less likely to have committed the crime than either the instructions-after or no-instructions subjects. Those who received instructions at the end of the trial did not respond differently on the verdict and probability-of-commission measures from those who were never instructed. In fact, they even recalled fewer of the case-related facts than all other subjects did. Finally, whether or not subjects made midtrial judgments did not affect any of the above variables. The nonreactive nature of this multiple-judgment procedure was thus confirmed.

Process (Midtrial) Measures

Overall, 68% of the midtrial responses were guilty verdicts. For the 54 subjects who made these judgments, the pattern of verdicts is presented in Table 2. As with the outcome data, these verdicts were analyzed with a likelihood ratio goodness-of-fit chi-square. Again, the simplest model that explained the observed frequencies was the two-way interaction between instructional set and verdicts, $\chi^2(3) = 6.50, p = 1.0$. Although a higher order model composed of both Instruction $\times$ Verdict and Decision Point $\times$ Verdict interactions also fits the data, $\chi^2(20) = 3.13, p = 1.0$, it did not contribute significantly to the predictions made by the simpler model. Midtrial verdicts were thus accounted for by the effect for instructional set. Table 2 shows that across all decision points the instructions-before group yielded 41% guilty verdicts, compared to 82% in both the instructions-after and no-instructions groups.

TABLE 7.2

Pattern of Midtrial Verdicts for the Three Instruction Groups
at Each of the Six Decision Points

Instruction and verdict	Decision point					
	1	2	3	4	5	6
Before						
Guilty	8	8	8	7	5	8
Not guilty	10	10	10	11	13	10
After						
Guilty	16	16	17	16	13	15
Not guilty	3	3	2	3	6	4
None						
Guilty	15	14	15	14	14	12
Not guilty	2	3	2	3	3	5

Note: Decision points 1-6 immediately follow the direct examination and cross-examination of the prosecution's two witnesses and the defendant.

A verdict-confidence measure was again created and was this time submitted to a 3 (Instructions) $\times$ 6 (Decision Point) analysis of variance. Figure 1 illustrates the strong main effect for the instruction factor, $F(2, 51) = 10.15$, $p < .001$, on these verdict scores. As before, this analysis clearly indicated that subjects who were instructed before the evidence ($M = -1.14$) were consistently less likely to convict the accused ($p < .001$) than were either the instructions-after or non-instructed subjects ($Ms = 3.91$ and 3.65, respectively). These latter groups did not differ. An additional main effect for the decision point factor, $F(5, 255) = 4.26$, $p < .001$, indicated, as expected, that verdict scores fluctuated widely as the trial progressed. As might be anticipated, the conviction rate was highest at the third point—right after the prosecutor examined his second witness ($p < .01$). The interaction between instructional set and decision point did not approach significance ($F < .1$).

On the question of whether jurors' early impressions were predictive of their final predeliberation verdicts, Table 3 represents the correlations between subjects' midtrial and final verdict-confidence scores. It can be seen that over all multiple-judgment groups the average correlation between midtrial and posttrial verdict scores was .44 ($p < .01$). In fact, the average correlation between the verdict scores rendered at even the first decision point and those given at the end of the trial was .28 ($p < .05$). To some extent, then, subjects' decisions were substantially formed very early in the trial presentation.

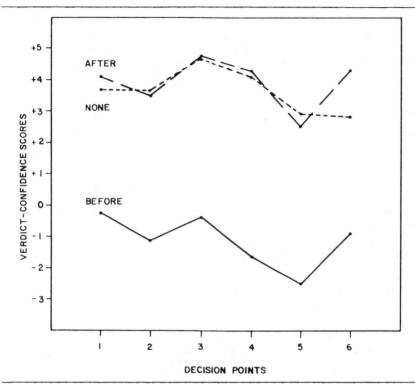

Figure 7.1   The pattern of verdict-confidence scores for the three groups at each of six decision points. (Higher scores indicate confidence in guilt.)

Results for the repeated probability-of-commission measures followed a similar pattern (see Figure 2). A main effect for timing of instruction, $F(2, 5) = 6.58$, $p < .005$, revealed that during the trial, the instructions-before group ($M = 52.5\%$) viewed the defendant as less likely to have committed the crime ($p < .01$) than either the instructions-after or no-instructions group (68.16% and 71.67%, respectively), who again did not differ from each other. Moreover, a main effect for the decision point factor, $F(5, 255) = 3.08$, $p < .01$, indicated that the perceived probability of commission was lowest at the fifth point—right after the defendant testified in his own behalf.

In sum, subjects' midtrial judgments fluctuated in the predicted directions (i.e., guilty judgments after the prosecutor's examination and not-guilty judgments after the defense's examination). More important, these judgments were influenced largely by whether or not subjects had been instructed on the requirements of proof. That is,

TABLE 7.3

Correlation Coefficients of Midtrial and Final Verdict-Confidence
Scores in Each Group and Across All Groups

Group	Verdict–confidence score					
	1	2	3	4	5	6
Before	.14	.42	.57**	.46**	.42	.54*
After	.22	.22	.18	.15	−.03	−.15
None	.31	.30	.37	.42	.45	.86***
Overall	.28*	.41**	.47***	.44**	.36**	.52***

Note: Correlations are based on ns of 18, 19, and 17 (N = 54).
*p < .05; **p < .01; ***p < .001.

although instructional set and decision point did not interact (i.e., their curves were almost perfectly parallel, thereby indicating that preinstructed subjects were neither less influenced by the prosecutor's testimony nor more influenced by the defendant's testimony), subjects who had been instructed before the evidence immediately and continually viewed the defendant as less likely to have committed the crime.

DISCUSSION

The present study demonstrated what might be described as a primacy effect. A judge's instruction to the jury was effective when delivered prior to but not after the presentation of evidence. That is, mock jurors who were instructed on the presumption of innocence, burden of proof, and reasonable doubt before observing the testimony were ultimately less likely to vote for conviction. It was noted earlier that verdicts are a function of the perceived likelihood that the defendant committed the crime and of the standard or threshold to which that likelihood is compared. In the present experiment, variations in the timing of the instruction affected estimates of the probability of commission but not interpretations of reasonable doubt. Subjects who received the instructions before the evidence thus demonstrated a low rate of conviction because they actually viewed the defendant as less likely to have committed the crime.

Although the present experiment was not theoretically guided, it now appears that an information integration model of juror judgments (Kaplan & Kemmerick, 1974) might well describe the results. Briefly, each piece of evidentiary and nonevidentiary information possesses

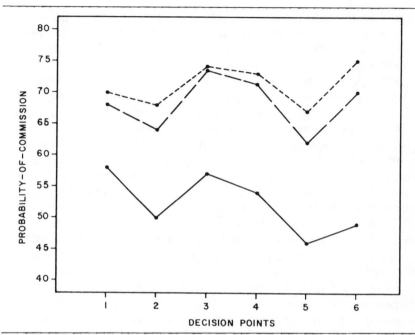

Figure 7.2 The pattern of probability-of-commission estimates for the three groups at each of six decision points.

some scale value along a dimension of guilt-innocence and a weight that determines the importance of that information. A trial judgment is then formed on the basis of a weighted-average combination of stimulus components. In the context of the present study, subjects received two global categories of information: the trial presentation and judicial instruction. From the probability-of-commission responses of noninstructed subjects, the scale value of the trial information may be estimated at .78 (i.e., .78 is the marginal mean for noninstructed subjects) Although the scale value of the requirements of proof instruction was not assessed in the present study, it should— by legal ideal—have implied a scale value or initial probability of commission of 0 (Ostrom, Werner, & Saks, 1978). On the assumption that the scale values of the instruction and trial presentation remained constant (these assumptions are supported indirectly by the lack of timing effect on interpretations of reasonable doubt and ratings of evidence strength, respectively), to what do we attribute the effects for the timing manipulation? Within an impression formation paradigm, Anderson (1965) found that later adjectives keep a fixed scale value but decrease in their weight. This mechanism describes the present results—the prodefendant instruction received a greater weight when delivered before than when delivered after the evidence.[4]

What *process* underlies these findings? At least two plausible mechanisms are worth evaluating. It was hypothesized that prein-structed subjects would demand a greater burden of proof when evaluating the strength of the prosecutor's case as it unfolds during the trial. This critical, evaluative "schema" was expected to manifest itself in different fluctuating patterns in the responses of the instructed (instructions-before) and noninstructed (instructions-after and no-instruction) midtrial judgment groups. However, the absence of an Instruction × Decision Point interaction on verdicts and probability-of-commission ratings ruled out this hypothesis. In fact, the three instruction groups demonstrated remarkably similar midtrial shifts in judgment (see Figure 1). Those who had been instructed were neither more influenced by the defense nor less influenced by the prosecutor than the others were. Instructed subjects thus did not reject or distort the prosecutor's evidence to fit an initial impression or presumption of innocence. And why should they? Luchins (1957) had demonstrated that by forewarning observers of the imminence of additional infor-mation, the proactive effects of early information on subsequent information are suppressed. Subjects in the present study and jurors in general *expect* to be confronted with inconsistent information. Early information in this setting (i.e., judicial instruction) is thus unlikely to produce the strong bias that would stimulate the processes of discounting or assimilation.

The process that did appear to operate was considerably less complex. Subjects who were instructed before the evidence were more likely than the others were to vote for acquittal and indicated a lower probability of commission *even from the first decision point*. Although they responded similarly to testimony that followed, their initial leanings resulted in fewer guilty verdicts at the conclusion of the trial. The impact of this initial reaction is reflected in the significant correlation between first and final verdict scores. Simply put, most preinstructed subjects "presumed innocent," whereas the others "presumed guilty."

The *practical* implications of the present study are straightforward. Mandatory code provisions do not forbid or discourage judges from using their discretion in instructing the jury before the trial. A number of states (e.g., Indiana, 1966), individual judges (e.g., Prettyman, 1960), and legal scholars (e.g., McBride, 1969) have thus adopted or advocated delivery of preliminary instructions prior to the presentation of evidence. In Missouri (1964), for example, the Supreme Court Committee on Jury Instructions recommended that "the jury be instructed before the trial begins. . . . The committee believes that it is better to draw the jury's attention to these matters before the trial rather than waiting until after the jurors may have reached a decision" (quoted in McBride, 1969, p. 62). This latter example is unfortunately an exception rather than the rule, which is that preliminary instructions are vastly underutilized (DeVitt & Blackmar, 1977). Viewed in this context, the present study provides firm support for proponents of procedural reform in the courtroom. The Anglo-American system of justice has traditionally favored the accused on the philosophy that acquitting a truly guilty person is better than convicting a truly innocent one (Ploscowe, 1935). Yet the present results suggest that the accused may not benefit from this protective instruction unless it is delivered to jurors before the trial. In this regard, perhaps the requirements of proof might well be included in the currently popular "juror handbooks" that are distributed to jurors as part of a pretrial orientation (National Institute of Law Enforcement and Criminal Justice, 1975) and might perhaps be presented at both the beginning and the end of the proceedings (Elwork et al., 1977).

From a methodological standpoint, the multiple-judgment procedure initially employed by Weld and Danzig (1940) merits increased consideration in future research. The present study confirmed that it does not bias jurors' ultimate verdicts or any other posttrial measures (also see Pyszczynski, Note 1). Moreover, it appears to be valuable for examining jurors' reactions to the trial as it unfolds. Questions concerning the relative impact of different trial phases (e.g., opening statements and closing arguments, direct examination vs. cross-examination) and different kinds of evidence (e.g., tangible exhibits, expert or eyewitness testimony) may be fruitfully investigated through the midtrial assessment of verdicts.

Finally, some of the limitations of the present results deserve mention. As with other nonevidentiary factors, the timing of an instruction cannot be expected to influence the outcome of a one-sided case (i.e., an extremely strong or weak case against the defendant). Rather, the effects should be considered limited to close, ambiguous cases. Note also that the present experiment assessed the verdicts of nondeliberating jurors. Whether or not deliberation provides enough of a corrective strategy to erase the timing effect upon juries remains open to question. Finally, the trial used in the present study was much shorter than the average criminal case.

Whether or not the timing manipulation would affect jurors' responses in realistically longer trials remains to be seen.

NOTES

1. Jones and Goethals (1971) have termed this the "recall readiness" hypothesis for recency effects.

2. A transcript taken verbatim from the videotape and a summary of the trial are available upon request.

3. Only the major facts in the case were tested. Moreover, these facts were typically repeated throughout the trial proceedings (e.g., the highway on which Ron Oliver was stopped was first mentioned during the prosecutor's opening statement and was reiterated during the examination of both the arresting officer and the defendant and during the closing arguments). As a result, the facts tested could not be classified for further analysis as proprosecution or prodefense, nor could they by located at a single point in the trial.

4. Note that although the present analysis treats judge's instructions as information that has a scale value and weight, Kaplan and his colleagues are quick to point out that strictly speaking, because instructions do not pertain to the specific defendant or crime, they do not relate to information scale value (S_1). Instead, instructions should affect an initial impression of the defendant that exists prior to jurors' receiving information about him or her (S_0), that is, the impression of defendants in general (see Kaplan & Miller, 1978).

REFERENCE NOTE

1. Pyszczynski, T. A. The effects of opening statements on liability judgments at various points in a simulated jury trial. Unpublished master's thesis, University of Kansas, 1978.

REFERENCES

Anderson, N. H. Primacy effects in personality impression formation using a generalized order effect paradigm. Journal of Personality and Social Psychology, 1965, 2, 1-9.

Davis, J. H., Bray, R. M., & Holt, R. W. The empirical study of decision processes in juries: A critical review. In J. L. Tapp & F. J. Levine (Eds.), Law, justice, and the individual in society: Psychological and legal issues. New York: Holt, Rinehart & Winston, 1977.

DeVitt, E. J., & Blackmar, C. B. *Federal jury practice and instructions* (Vols. 1-3). St. Paul, MN: West Publishing, 1977.

Elwork, A., Sales, B. D., & Alfini, J. J. Juridic decisions: In ignorance of the law or in light of it? *Law and Human Behavior,* 1977, *1,* 163-189.

Fienberg, S. E. *The analysis of cross-classified data.* Cambridge, MA: MIT Press, 1977.

Frank, J. *Courts on trial: Myth and reality in American justice.* Princeton, NJ: Princeton University Press, 1949.

Hervey, J. C. Jurors look at our judges. *Oklahoma Bar Association Journal,* 1947, *25,* 1508-1513.

Indiana pattern jury instructions. Indianapolis, IN: Bobbs-Merrill, 1966.

Jones, E. E., & Goethals, G. R. *Order effects in impression formation: Attribution context and the nature of the entity.* Morristown, NJ: General Learning Press, 1971.

Jones, E. E., Rock, L., Shaver, K. G., Goethals, G. R., & Ward, L. M. Pattern of performance and ability attribution: An unexpected primacy effect. *Journal of Personality and Social Psychology,* 1968, *10,* 317-340.

Juhnke, R., Vought, C., Pyszczynski, T. A., Dane, F. C., Losure, B. D., & Wrightsman, L. S. Effects of presentation mode upon mock jurors' reactions to a trial. *Personality and Social Psychology Bulletin,* 1979, *5,* 36-39.

Kalven, H., & Zeisel. H. *The American jury.* Boston: Little, Brown, 1966.

Kaplan, M. F., & Kemmerick, E. D. Juror judgment as information integration: Combining evidential and nonevidential information. *Journal of Personality and Social Psychology,* 1974, *30,* 493-499.

Kaplan, M. F., & Miller, L. E. Reducing the effects of juror bias. *Journal of Personality and Social Psychology,* 1978, *36,* 1443-1455.

Kerr, N. L., Atkin, R. S., Stasser, G., Meek, D., Holt, R. W., & Davis, J. H. Guilt beyond a reasonable doubt: Effects of concept definition and assigned decision rule on the judgments of mock jurors. *Journal of Personality and Social Psychology,* 1976, *34,* 282-294.

LaBuy, W. J. *Jury instructions in federal criminal cases.* St. Paul, MN: West Publishing, 1963.

Luchins, A. S. Primacy-recency in impression formation, In C. I. Hovland (Ed.), *The order of presentation and persuasion.* New Haven, CN: Yale University Press, 1957.

McBride, R. L. *The art of instructing the jury.* Cincinnati, OH: W. H. Anderson, 1969.

McCart, S. W. *Trial by jury.* Philadelphia: Chilton Books, 1964.

Missouri Supreme Court Committee on Jury Instructions. *Missouri approved jury instructions.* New York: Vernon Law Book Company, 1964.

National Institute of Law Enforcement and Criminal Justice. *A guide to jury system management.* Washington, DC: U.S. Department of Justice, 1975.

Ostrom, T. M., Werner, C., & Saks, M. J. An integration theory analysis of jurors' presumption of guilt or innocence. *Journal of Personality and Social Psychology,* 1978, *36,* 436-450.

Ploscowe, M. The development of present-day criminal procedures in Europe and America. *Harvard Law Review,* 1935, *48,* 433-473.

Prettyman, E. B. Jury instructions—First or last? *American Bar Association Journal,* 1960, *46,* 1066.

Sealy, A. P., & Cornish, W. R. Juries and the rules of evidence. *Criminal Law Review,* April 1973, 208-223.

Simon, R. J., & Mahan, L. Quantifying burdens of proof: A view from the bench, the jury, and the classroom. *Law and Society Review,* February 1971, 319-330.

Walker, L., Thibaut, J., & Andreoli, V. Order of presentation at trial. *Yale Law Review,* 1972, *82,* 216-226.

Weld, H. P., & Danzig, E. R. A study of the way in which a verdict is reached by a jury. *American Journal of Psychology,* 1940, *53,* 518-536.

8

TOWARD UNDERSTANDABLE JURY INSTRUCTIONS

AMIRAM ELWORK
Hahnemann University
JAMES J. ALFINI
American Judicature Society
BRUCE D. SALES
University of Arizona

The considerable time and effort that lawyers and judges generally expend in drafting and debating jury instructions is premised on the notion that jurors will listen attentively and attempt to follow the law as

Authors' Note, For a detailed account of the recommended procedures for writing understandable jury instructions that resulted from this study, see Elwork, Sales and Alfini, WRITING UNDERSTANDABLE JURY INSTRUCTIONS (Charlottesville, VA.: Michie/Bobbs-Merrill, 1982). This study was funded by Grant MN31355-01102 from the National Institute of Mental Health, Center for the Studies of Crime and Delinquency, and Grant 78-NI-AX-0600 from the National Institute of Justice, U.S. Department of Justice to the Law-Psychology Graduate Training Program of the University of Nebraska and the enunciated in the judge's instructions. If jurors are to decide cases according to law, the jury instructions become critical to justice. Yet some legal commentators have referred to the jury instruction process as a meaningless "ritual".[1] Perhaps the most forceful criticism comes from Jerome Frank:

> What a crop of subsidiary semi-myths and mythical practices the jury system yields! Time and money and lives are consumed in debating the precise words which the judge may address to the jury, although everyone who stops to see and think knows that those words might as well be spoken in a foreign language. Yet, every day, cases which have taken weeks to try are reversed by upper courts because a phrase or sentence, meaningless to the jury, has been included in, or omitted from the judge's charge.[2]

Such criticisms have prompted a movement during the past two decades to develop "pattern," "standard," or "uniform" jury instructions.[3] Proponents believe that pattern instructions conserve lawyer and judge time (by eliminating the need to draft instructions from scratch), reduce the number of appeals and reversals based on legally erroneous instructions, and increase juror comprehension of the applicable law (by using simple language).[4] Although there is some indication that the widespread use of such instructions has accomplished the first two objectives,[5] recent studies suggest that the third objective—juror comprehension—has not been realized. In general, these studies have demonstrated that patterns still result in low juror comprehension levels.[6]

Such findings present us with an important question: Are the low comprehension rates due to the incompetence of the jurors or the incomprehensibility of the judge's charge? If low comprehension rates persist regardless of the wording of the instructions, then arguments to abolish or limit the use of the jury on the grounds of juror incompetence[7] would be strengthened. On the other hand, if juror comprehension improves significantly by rewriting pattern instructions, committees drafting pattern instructions would do well to devote more attention and resources to drafting instructions in understandable language.[8]

American Judicature Society. The analyses, conclusions, and opinions expressed are those of the authors and not necessarily those of the sponsoring organizations and funding agencies.

From *Judicature* (1982, March-April), 65, 432-443. Reprinted with permission of the authors.

This article reports research that addresses this policy dilemma. We sought to develop standardized procedures that jurisdictions using pattern instructions could follow to increase the instructions' comprehensibility, and to test the efficacy of these procedures on sets of instructions from two criminal cases.

METHODOLOGY

We decided that it would be best to use one relatively complex set of jury instructions and one simple set. Such a combination would give us a chance to test the efficacy of our procedures under the worst and best conditions. After much searching, we acquired videotapes of two trials containing appropriate jury instructions.

The first set of videotapes came from an actual criminal trial in Nevada that had been televised by a local station.[9] The charge was attempted murder and included several lesser offenses. The defendant made alternative pleas of not guilty and not guilty by reason of insanity. Not only were the legal issues involved complex,[10] but the way the instructions were written was also complex. Judges in Nevada do not have a set of standard jury instructions and often must rely on quotes from supreme court decisions. We felt from the beginning that this set of instructions would require complete rewriting, and it did. This set of instructions will be referred to as the "Smith instructions," after the alias we adopted for the defendant.

The second set of videotapes was of a mock (but completely realistic) burglary trial produced in Florida for other research.[11] The jury instructions for this trial were modified to conform to an updated version of the Florida pattern jury instructions.[12] Compared to the Smith instructions, these were considerably simpler both in terms of the legal issues involved and the language. This set of instructions will be referred to as the "Walker instructions," named after the fictitious defendant.

We decided to measure the effectiveness of our procedures in three different ways. First, we hoped to demonstrate that our standardized procedures would improve comprehension substantially. Second, we wanted to demonstrate that our procedures would ultimately result in a "sufficient" level of comprehensibility. Third, we sought to demonstrate the "external validity" of our results. That is, we hoped to show that our rewritten jury instructions would be as comprehensible in real life as they were in our testing sessions.

Project participants were paid volunteers randomly drawn from voter registration lists in Lincoln, Nebraska—paralleling the jury selection procedure used by the local federal district court. The jurors were sent letters signed by the federal district judges asking them to come to the federal courthouse to participate in the study.

Although approximately 500 volunteer jurors participated, the number for whom we report data in this article is 314. The remaining jurors were used in pretest and external validating testing phases of the project.

The initial groups of jurors were given a brief summary of either the Smith or the Walker case.[13] They were then shown a videotape of one of the authors of this article reading the original instructions for the case. After each rewriting cycle, subsequent jurors, of course, were presented with a videotape presentation of the instructions rewritten for that cycle.

After viewing the videotaped instructions, each juror was escorted to a room with an examiner and asked a series of short-answer questions in personal interviews. We decided to use personal interviews after several pretests indicated that the volunteer jurors did not exert enough effort when tested in groups and with a pencil-and-paper format. The Smith jurors were asked a series of questions from an 89-item questionnaire, while the Walker jurors received questions from a 30-item questionnaire. Both questionnaires were aimed at testing jury understanding of their duties and responsibilities as jurors, as well as points of law relating to the case.[14]

The testing sessions were audiotaped and subsequently transcribed. Two trained examiners independently reviewed each transcription to determine the correctness of each response. Interexaminer reliability was extremely high (91 percent agreement).

Before discussing our results, two caveats are in order. First, even though we intended to test equally the efficacy of our procedures on both sets of instructions, we ran out of sufficient time and money. Faced with the choice of having to sacrifice thoroughness with one of the sets of instruction, we decided to modify our plans, for the simpler Walker instructions.

With the Walker instructions we tested half the original points of law once, then rewrote that half and tested them again. With the Smith instructions, however, we tested all the original points once and rewrote them all twice, testing them for the second and then third time after each rewriting. Furthermore, whereas we retested the Smith instructions in the context of mock trials, we did not do so with the Walker instructions. Fortunately, the results were so dramatic with both sets of instructions that our unequal treatment of the sets does not weaken our conclusions.

Second, the juror comprehension rates that we reported are based on the test that we devised and administered to the jurors. The validity of the content of the questions and the correctness of the responses is, of necessity, based on rational rather than empirical methods.[15] Other researchers might have devised different questions to conduct the same study or may have worded the questions differently, thereby possibly generating different comprehension rates. Thus the comprehension rates are most meaningful when compared across rewriting cycles.

IMPROVING COMPREHENSION

In summary, significant improvements in juror comprehension resulted after each successive rewriting effort for both the Smith (complex) and Walker (simple) instructions. This conclusion is based on several convergent measures used to analyze the jurors' responses to the questionnaires. For example, with the original Smith instructions, the average (mean) percentage of right answers on our questionnaires per juror was 51 percent.[16] After our first rewriting, this average increased to 66 percent,[17] and after our second rewriting effort it increased to 80 percent.[18] Each of these increases was statistically significant.[19]

Jurors receiving the original Walker instructions, on the average, got 65 percent[20] of the questions asked right. After one rewriting this average increased to 80 percent.[21] This was a statistically significant increase.[22] For reasons explained in the preceding section, we did not rewrite the Walker instructions a second time.

Another measure of improvements through rewriting is to compare the average (mean) percentage of correct answers per question (not per juror). With the original Smith instructions, the average (mean) percentage of right answers per question asked was 59 percent.[23] (In other words, on the average, each question asked was answered correctly 59 percent of the time). After our second rewriting effort with these instructions, the average rose to 81 percent.[24] With the original Walker instructions, the average proportion of right answers per question was 65 percent.[25] After one rewriting this average rose to 80 percent.[26]

The above measures do not indicate whether comprehension improved on a wide and varied number of legal points or on just a few, because the measures report only the average levels of comprehension and require summing across questions and jurors. Thus we also measured the proportion of questions that showed improved comprehension as a function of our rewritten instructions.

The Smith questionnaire contained 86 questions,[27] each testing a separate point of law. After our first rewriting, improvements in comprehension were evident in 72 percent (62) of the questions (a statistically significant result).[28] Of the remaining 28 percent (24) for which the rewritten instructions did not increase comprehension, 67 percent (16) were already at a minimum of 80 percent comprehension under the original instructions. Thus part of the reason why changes had not occurred for these questions was that there was little room for improvement.

After our *second* rewriting of the Smith instructions, improvements in comprehension, when compared to the *original* instructions, were evident in 85 percent (73) of the questions (a statistically significant result).[29] Of the remaining 15 percent (13) of the questions for which there were no increases in comprehension, 69 percent (9) were already at a minimum of 80 percent comprehension under the original instructions. We also found that our *second* rewriting improved comprehension over the *first* on 69 percent (59) of the questions (again, this is a statistically significant result).[30] Of the remaining 31 percent (27), for which there were no increases in comprehension, 59 percent (16) were already at a minimum of 80 percent comprehension.

Similar results were achieved with our simpler instructions from the Walker trial. The Walker questionnaire contained 30 questions. After one rewriting, improvements in comprehension were evident in 83 percent (25) of the questions; this is a statistically significant result.[31] Three of the remaining five questions were already at 80 percent comprehension or higher with the original instructions.

Even if rewriting had improved comprehension in 100 percent of the questions but with only small increases, then there might be some question about the practical value of our procedures. For example, if 40 percent of the jurors understood a specific point of law with the original instructions, and 45 percent of jurors understood this same point of law with the rewritten instructions, the increase certainly would not be worth the effort. Thus we decided to measure the sizes of the improvements cited above.

Of the questions that showed comprehension improvements after the first rewrite of the Smith instructions, 29 percent were improvements of more than 20 percentage points. The average (mean) increase in comprehension per question asked was 16 percentage points.[32] After the second rewriting, 49 percent of the improvements were above 20 percentage points. The average increase in comprehension per question after the second rewrite was 27 percentage points.[33] With the Walker instructions, 40 percent of the improvements were above 20 percentage points. The average increase in comprehension per question for the Walker instructions was 19 percentage points.[34]

Finally, it's of interest to know whether the questions that resulted in the greatest improvements were crucial to the case or nonessential. We believe that the questions yielding highest improvements in comprehension did contain some of the most crucial points of law for our two trials. However, the reader will have to make his or her own judgment. In Table 1, we have reproduced the 10 Smith (these were the complex instructions) questions achieving the highest improvements in comprehension, along with the actual comprehension figures after our final (second) rewriting effort.

The original jury in the Smith trial found the defendant guilty of the lesser included offense of battery with the intent to kill. Yet, only *one* out of 34 (3 percent) of our volunteer jurors (see question 38 in Table 1) was able to tell us the difference between the lesser offense and the original charge, in the context of the original Smith instructions. Thus it is doubtful that the original jurors understood this distinction either.

"SUFFICIENT" COMPREHENSION

Ultimately, the definition of what is *sufficiently* comprehensible will depend on the judgments of the legal community. Yet, to be able to calculate and meaningfully report the efficacy of our procedures for ensuring minimal levels of comprehension within individual juries, we were forced to assume certain exemplary standards. That is, we decided to assume two possible standards of sufficient comprehensibility and judge our results against them. The first standard contained the following two explicit criteria (for cut-off points); (1) that any given point of law "should" be understood by *at least two-thirds* of a 12-member jury (or eight out of 12 jurors) and (2) that this level of comprehension should be achieved in *at least eight out of 10 juries.*

The second standard we used was more stringent and contained the following two explicit criteria: (1) that any given point of law "should"

TABLE 8.1

Ten "Smith" Questions Showing Most Improved Comprehensibility

	Proportion of right answers	
	Original instructions	After second rewrite
22. There are four rules (or qualities) that a juror should remember (or look for) in deciding whether something that Mr. Smith did was an act in an attempt to murder his wife. Please name what these are. (Define act in an attempt to murder.)	.03	.68
25. Before a jury can decide that Mr. Smith's intentions were to attempt to murder his wife, the jury must make sure that he had four specific types of thoughts. Please name these four types of thoughts. (Define intent to murder.)	.14	.77
26. What can cause a person to have malice?	.08	.77
28. What are the two general ways that malice can be shown to exist? In other words, how does a jury decide whether a defendant had malice?	.08	.85
35. There are three parts to the crime called "battery with a deadly weapon." Please name these three parts.	.35	.97
38. What is the difference between the definitions of battery with intent to kill and attempted murder?	.03	.80
58. What is the difference between being convinced beyond a reasonable doubt versus being convinced by a preponderance of the evidence? If there is a difference, please explain what the difference is.	.11	.73
69. As has already been stated, it is the jury's duty to judge the evidence. Please explain what two types of judgments they have to make about the evidence.	.22	.91
70. There are seven types of information that a jury can use in deciding whether to believe a witness's testimony. What are they?	.17	.96
74. When someone who is an expert testifies, what types of information can such a witness use to reach an opinion?	.23	.91
Average	.14	.84

Note: The wording of some of the questions and answers here differs from that in the appendixes to Elwork et al., *Writing Understandable Jury Instructions* (Charlottesville, VA: Michie/Bobbs-Merrill, 1982) in order to conform with the present study's rewritten version of the instructions.

be understood by at least three-fourths of a 12-member jury (or nine out of 12 jurors) and (2) that this level of comprehension should be achieved *in at least nine out of 10 juries.*

We found that with the original Smith instructions, the above-mentioned lower standard of sufficient comprehensibility was achieved with only 16 percent (14) of the 86 total questions asked. That is, we found that only 14 questions would be understood by at least two-thirds of the jury members in at least 80 percent of 12-member juries. Put another way, with the original Smith instructions the remaining 84 percent (72) of the questions did not reach the above-mentioned standard of minimum sufficiency. After our two efforts at rewriting the Smith instructions, we were able to achieve our above-mentioned standard with 53 percent (46) of the questions.[35]

Using the more stringent second standard, we found that it was achieved with only 7 percent (6) of the questions in the context of the original Smith instructions. After rewriting these instructions twice we were able to achieve our more stringent standard with 26 percent (22) of the questions.[36] Using only the more stringent standard with the original Walker instructions, we found that it would be achieved with 10 percent (3) out of the 30 total questions asked. After one rewriting of the Walker instructions, we were able to increase this level of comprehensibility to 27 percent (8) of the questions.[37]

In looking for an explanation of why we had not achieved our standard of sufficiency with all of the questions in each of our questionnaires, we first tried to identify what characteristic(s) of a question tended to be highly correlated with its final level of comprehensibility. Not surprisingly, we found that the questions least likely to reach our minimum standard of sufficiency were the ones least comprehensible at the start.

With the Smith instructions, for example, 75 percent (30/40) of the questions that did *not* reach our standard of sufficiency were among those achieving the lowest comprehension scores initially (below the median score). In other words, because these points of law needed the most improvement, they were less likely to reach our criterion than easier ones, given the same amount of rewriting. Whereas this finding suggests that the more difficult items require more rewriting, it does not suggest that it is impossible to reach our standards.

Indeed, two aspects of our results suggest that even the most difficult of our points of law could have reached standards of sufficiency had we been able to spend more time on them. First, as already exemplified in Table 1 above, the least comprehensible points of law under the original Smith instructions tended to improve the most after rewriting. Second, 28 percent (13) of the questions on the Smith questionnaire that *did* reach our minimum criterion, were among the half on the questionnaire with the lowest comprehension levels initially (below the median). Thus it is possible to take the points of law with the lowest comprehensibility and rewrite them until they reach our minimum standards, though it may take more effort than for points of law that are clearer at the start.

RELEVANCE FOR REAL LIFE

Another objective was to demonstrate that our methodology produced jury instructions just as effective in real life as they were in our testing sessions. Social scientists refer to this as external validity. We had to demonstrate external validity for two aspects of our methodology. First, we had to show that our recruitment procedures resulted in samples of volunteer jurors representative of actual jurors in our jurisdiction. Second, the comprehension levels measured in our testing sessions had to be representative of comprehension levels that jurors would have in the context of trials and deliberations.

Representativeness of Our Volunteer Jurors

Unless our volunteer jurors were representative of real jurors in ways relevant to the comprehension of jury instructions, then arguably all of the data presented above cannot be assumed as externally valid. If we cannot generalize our data to real jurors, then the procedures themselves become useless for practical application.

For example, our recruitment procedures and the nature of the tasks for which we asked people to volunteer might have tended to attract *only* the most intellectual members of our community, who would tend to get atypically high scores on our questionnaires. If this were so, then our results would tend to give more optimistic estimates of comprehensibility than might be the case among real jurors. To ensure that our recruitment procedures were not subject to such criticism, we compared our volunteers with the 150 jurors who had served immediately prior to our study in actual trials at the local federal district court where we had conducted our study. The jurors were compared by education, age, and sex.

As can be seen from Table 2, on average the higher a juror's education was, the more likely he or she was to answer more of our questions correctly,[38] regardless of whether the juror had received the original or the rewritten instructions. Thus it became even more important for us to determine whether our recruitment procedures might have attracted more highly educated people than would be expected among real jurors. Table 3 presents a comparison between the educational levels of our volunteer jurors and those of real jurors at our local federal district court.

Though the figures appear to reveal a small bias toward higher education in our sample of volunteer jurors, the differences were *not* statistically significant. It is possible that our sample sizes were not large enough to demonstrate statistical significance for the very small differences that may have in fact existed between our volunteers and real jurors.[39] Even if this were true, however, the fact that the differences were very small make them unworthy of concern.

With regard to age, we found that among our volunteer jurors, those above age 59 tended not to do as well on our questionnaires

TABLE 8.2

Comparison Between Level of Education and
Performance on Questionnaires

Education level	Average proportion of right answers*
Under 12 years of education	49%
12th grade education (high school grads)	65
13 to 15 years (some college or technical training beyond high school)	67
16 years of education (college graduates)	73
Above 16 years (graduate or professional training beyond college)	78

*Computed by averaging across results obtained in the original and rewritten versions for Smith and Walker instructions.

(including both original and rewritten versions for both Smith and Walker instructions, see Table 4).[40] If our recruitment procedures tended to draw an unrepresentatively large proportion of retired-older people, then the results presented above arguably were more pessimistic than would be expected with real jurors. Table 5 compares the age and gender of our volunteer jurors and those of real jurors. There were *no* statistically significant differences found. In fact, our recruitment procedures drew a proportion of jurors aged 60 and older that was remarkably similar to the proportion in our real juror sample.

Finally, we looked at gender in the same way that we looked at the other two demographic variables. On the average, our male volunteer jurors answered correctly 70 percent of the questions asked of them, while our female jurors answered 67 percent correctly. This difference was not statistically significant.[41] Give the above mentioned nonsignificant result, it makes no difference to the validity of our conclusions whether our recruitment procedures were biased toward one sex. Ironically, this was the one demographic variable for which our recruitment procedures were biased. As can be seen from Table 5, there was a greater proportion of females in our sample of volunteer jurors than in the sample of real jurors.[42]

In summary, these analyses suggest that our recruitment procedures did draw volunteer jurors similar to real jurors along dimensions relevant to the comprehension of jury instructions (e.g., education and age). Thus the comprehension levels measured through our

TABLE 8.3
Education Levels of Volunteer and Real Jurors

Education level	Percentage of 269 volunteer jurors*	Percentage of 150 real jurors
Under 12 years of education	6%	16%
12th grade education (high school grads)	36	35
13 to 15 years (some college or technical training beyond high school)	22	29
16 years of education (college graduates)	18	12
Above 16 years (graduate or professional training beyond college)	17	8

*Does not total 100 percent due to rounding.

procedures are not invalid as a result of the unrepresentativeness of our samples. They are representative where it matters.

The above analyses of the effects of demographic characteristics on comprehensibility also empirically illustrated another point, which we had already concluded on the basis of our subjective experience. That is, differences between individual jurors had an effect on the comprehensibility of jury instructions.

Representativeness of Our Testing Sessions

It could be that the reported superiority of our rewritten instructions may not be valid because our statistics are based on jurors' comprehension of instructions presented outside the context of a trial. That is, perhaps the jurors who received our original instructions would have done much better during a real trial, where they would

TABLE 8.4

Comparison Between Age and Performance on Questionnaires

	Average proportion of right answers*
Under 40 years	75%
40 to 59 years	72
60 and older	56

*Computed by averaging across results obtained in the original and rewritten versions for Smith and Walker instructions.

have listened to the evidence, the arguments and comments of counsel and deliberated with other jurors.

After all, it is possible that the specific context of evidence makes legal instructions more understandable. Furthermore, lawyers and judges do often make comments during a trial that clarify the legal instructions. Finally, where individual jurors may not understand certain points of law, the deliberation process may correct this problem. One of the purposes for allowing jurors to deliberate is to give them more time to think about the legal instructions and consult with one another on points they do not understand.

We decided to test the above hypothesis using our videotaped Smith trial, the real trial that had been televised in Nevada. As we have indicated, paid volunteer jurors were asked to come to a local federal district courthouse to view our videotaped trial and to deliberate and reach a verdict. They were randomly assigned to one of 18 juries consisting of about six jurors each. (Depending on the number of volunteers who kept their appointment on any given day, the number of jurors per jury varied from five to seven.)

Since we could only keep jurors from 9 a.m. to 5:30 p.m., with an hour off for lunch, we were forced to edit our videotaped trial down to five hours. More specifically, we cut seven hours of testimony down to four hours, and more than two hours of closing arguments down to one hour. In doing so, two considerations remained foremost: preserving the content of the trial as much as possible and developing a tape that did not appear edited. With regard to the evidence, for example, we simply cut out much of the repetitive evidence and some of the questions and answers designed to lay the foundation for the witnesses.

Because we wanted our jurors to receive one of two versions (original and rewritten) of jury instructions that differed only in the way they were written, the portion of the original videotape with the

TABLE 8.5
Age and Gender of Volunteer and Real Jurors

	Percentage of 269 volunteer jurors	Percentage of 150 real jurors
Age		
Under 40 years	32%	37%
40 to 59 years	41	38
60 and older	27	25
Sex		
Male	34	48
Female	66	52

judge's final instructions was also cut out. Instead the instructions were read via videotape by one of the authors of this article. Half of the juries received the original Smith instructions, and the other half received the final rewritten version of these instructions. Jurors were given copies of the instructions to read along with the videotaped presentation and to take them into the deliberation rooms.

After viewing the trial and the instructions, our volunteer jurors were asked to retire to a deliberation room and reach a verdict. Upon reaching a verdict or running out of time, two or three (depending on the number of staff available) members of each jury were randomly chosen and asked to stay on to answer some questions; the rest were dismissed. Jurors were not told about this last procedure in advance. In other words, while watching the trial and deliberating they were not aware that some of them would be later questioned on the jury instructions. The total number of jurors questioned about the original instructions was 23, whereas with the rewritten instructions the total was 22.

After the deliberation, there was simply not enough time to ask jurors as many questions as we had asked our volunteers in previously described testing sessions. Thus we decided to present each with a mini-questionnaire of 10 randomly chosen questions from among the half which had been the most difficult (those below the median level of difficulty) in previous testing sessions.

As can be seen from Table 6, even in the context of a trial and after deliberating, the original Smith instructions resulted in our questions being answered correctly only 40 percent of the time, on the average. In contrast, the rewritten set of instructions resulted in our questions being answered correctly 78 percent of the time, on the average.[43] The dramatic difference between these two levels of comprehensibility

TABLE 8.6

Proportions of Correct Responses to Questions on Original and
Rewritten Instructions: The Effect of Trial and Deliberation

	Original Instructions		Rewritten Instructions	
	Without trial or deliberation	With trial and deliberation	Without trial or deliberation	With trial and deliberation
8. What is the purpose of (or reason for having) jury instructions?	.39	.63	.89	.78
18. There are two parts to every crime. Name them and describe what each means.	.33	.57	.91	1.00
25. Before a jury can decide that Mr. Smith's intentions were to attempt to murder his wife, the jury must make sure that he had four specific types of thoughts. Please name these four types of thoughts. (Define intent to murder.)	.14	.45	.77	.79
35. There are three parts to the crime called "battery with a deadly weapon." Please name these three parts.	.35	.65	.97	.95
38. What is the difference between the definitions of battery with intent to kill and attempted murder?	.03	.06	.80	.88
48. Define what is mean by "a reasonable doubt."	.27	.22	.55	.50
56. How convinced should the jury be before deciding that Mr. Smith was or is insane?	.05	.09	.56	.40
69. As has already been stated, it is the jury's duty to judge the evidence. Please explain what two types of judgments they have to make about the evidence.	.22	.40	.91	.79
74. When someone who is an expert testifies, what types of information can such a witness use to reach an opinion?	.23	.10	.91	.85
94. How should the opinions of other jurors affect a juror's own decisionmaking?	.31	.78	.86	.84
Averages (Means)	.23	.40	.81	.78

belies the notion that the original Smith instructions could be shown to be as comprehensible as the rewritten instructions if tested in the context of a trial.

We also examined how these jurors compared with those who had been tested earlier outside the context of a trial. The presentation of the *original* Smith instructions in the context of a trial, when compared to their presentation without a trial, did result in higher levels of comprehensibility (40 percent versus 23 percent correct answers per question, on the average).[44]

However, the comprehension levels, by any standard, were still unacceptable. The presentation of the *rewritten* instructions in the context of a trial, when compared to their presentation without a trial, did not affect comprehension levels in either practical or statistical terms. This would appear to suggest that the trial and deliberative processes may have some corrective effect on poorly drafted instructions, but not enough to raise the instructions to an acceptable level of comprehensibility.

CONCLUSION

This study suggests that juror comprehension of judicial instructions can be increased significantly. The use of relatively simple, practical procedures to demonstrate this also suggests that attempts to increase comprehension levels are well worth the effort.[45] However, it remains to be seen whether pattern instruction drafting committees will adopt such procedures. Although drafting committees in certain states have shown an interest in increasing the understandability of their instructions, most committees apparently have been content to develop legally accurate instructions without regard for, and sometimes at the expense of, juror understandability.[46]

It is unlikely that most drafting committees will initiate serious attempts to increase comprehensibility unless the comprehensibility issue is more closely tied to the interests of the legal profession. As Brenda Danet has pointed out, "Legal language is precise only when it is in the draftsperson's interest to be precise."[47]

Ironically, the original justification for focusing on accuracy provides a clue to one possible development along those lines. The drafting committees' preoccupation with legal accuracy has been justified, in large part, by pointing to the need to reduce challenges to the legal correctness of the instructions on appeal. As research revealing low comprehension levels of currently used instructions comes to the attention of the legal profession, however, lawyers may be encouraged to shift their focus to the comprehensibility issue as a new ground for appeal.

Even then, however, policy decisions will have to be made about the level of comprehensibility that is to be considered "sufficient" to ensure a just and fair result. If studies indicate that 75 percent of jurors can generally be expected to understand a particular instruction, should this be deemed acceptable from a policy standpoint? Should this decision depend on the nature of the instruction? Should we insist, for example, on higher comprehensibility levels for burden of proof instructions than for seemingly less important preliminary instructions? Should the relative costs of linguistic reform be considered in reaching these decisions? These and other policy questions will become increasingly important as efforts escalate to make jury instructions more understandable.

NOTES

1. Winslow, The Instructions Ritual, 13 HASTINGS L. J. 456 (1962).

2. Frank, LAW AND THE MODERN MIND 181 (Magnolia, MA: Peter Smith Publisher, Inc. 1930).

3. In 1979, it was reported that 38 states had published sets of pattern instructions for civil cases and 38 states had developed sets of patterns for criminal cases. Nieland, PATTERN JURY INSTRUCTIONS: A CRITICAL LOOK AT A MODERN MOVEMENT TO IMPROVE THE JURY SYSTEM (Chicago: American Judicature Society, 1979).

4. McBride, THE ART OF INSTRUCTING THE JURY (Cincinnati: W. H. Anderson, 1969 (1978 Supplement).

5. Close, *Theory and Practice of Standardized Jury Instructions* 31 INS. COUNSEL. J. 490 (1964): Comment, *The Jury Instruction Process-Apathy or Aggressive Reform?* 49 MARQ. L. REV. 137 (1965); Beasley, *Pattern Charges* 27 ALA. LAW 181 (1966). For a study that questions the accuracy of these assumptions see Nieland, Assessing the Impact of Pattern Jury Instructions 62 JUDICATURE 185 (1978).

6. Buchanan, Pryor, Taylor and Strawn. *Legal Communication: An Investigation of Juror Comprehension of Pattern Instructions,* 26 COM. Q. 31 (1978); Charrow and Charrow, *Making Legal Language Understandable: A Psycholinguistic Study of Jury Instructions,* 79 COLUM. L. REV. 1306 (1979); Elwork, Sales and Alfini, *Juridic Decisions: In Ignorance of the Law or In Light of It?* 1 L. AND HUMAN BEHAVIOR 163 (1977); and Sigworth and Henze, "Jurors' Comprehension of Jury Instructions in Southern Arizona" (Unpublished, 1973).

7. See e.g., Frank, COURTS ON TRIAL (Princeton, N.J.: Princeton University Press, 1949); Gleisser, JURIES AND JUSTICE (New York: Barnes, 1968).

8. Pattern jury instructions drafting committees have been criticized for paying insufficient attention to the goal of juror comprehensibility. As Nieland points out, most drafting committees are composed solely of members of the legal profession: "While these individuals communicate very well with each other in the special language of the law, few are well enough versed in semantics to communicate legal concepts to jurors. . . . The primary objective of most drafting committees is likely to be in the area with which they are particularly familiar—the technical accuracy of instructions." Nieland, *supra* n. 3, at 23.

9. For a description of the televising experiences with this trial see Goldman and Larson, *News Camera in the Courtroom during State v. Solorzano: End of Estes Mandate?* 10 SW. NEV. L. REV. 2001 (1978). For ethical reasons, we have referred to the defendant as "Smith" in all textual references.

10. For a discussion of research indicating juror difficulty in comprehending the insanity defense see James, *Juror's Assessment of Criminal Responsibility,* 7 SOC. PROB. 58 (1959); and Arens, Granfield and Susman, *Jurors, Jury Charges and Insanity* 14 CATHOLIC UNIV. L. REV. 1 (1965).

11. Taylor, Buchanan, Pryor and Strawn. "How Do Jurors Reach a Verdict? A Field Experiment" (1979). (Unpublished manuscript, available from second author at Department of Communication, University of Central Florida).

12. Florida Supreme Court Committee on Standard Jury Instructions in Criminal cases. FLORIDA STANDARD JURY INSTRUCTIONS IN CRIMINAL CASES, 3rd ed. rev. (Tallahassee, FL: The Florida Bar, 1978).

13. It should be noted at this point that a primary purpose of this study was to develop comprehension-testing procedures that could be used by pattern instruction

drafting committees if our attempt at rewriting proved successful. With this in mind only a sample of the experimental jurors, toward the end of the study, were shown the videotaped trials and asked to deliberate before being tested on the instructions. Such a procedure would prove too costly to drafting committees and was adopted by us only to demonstrate the external validity of our results (the procedures used to test external validity are explained in detail at a subsequent point in this article).

14. The original set of instructions for the Smith case, together with the rewritten instructions and the lengthy questionnaires used to evaluate comprehensibility, can be found in the appendixes to Elwork, Sales and Alfini, WRITING UNDERSTANDABLE JURY INSTRUCTIONS (Charlottesville, VA: Michie/Bobbs-Merrill, 1982).

15. For an expanded discussion of this and other issues relating to our methodology see Elwork, Sales and Alfini, *id.*, ch. 3.

16. S.D. = 20 percent, N = 60.

17. S.D. = 19 percent, N = 50.

18. S.D. = 19 percent, N = 79.

19. Original vs. first rewrite yielded t(108) = 3.87, p < .001; first rewrite vs. second rewrite yielded t(127) = 3.98, p < .001.

20. S.D. = 14 percent, N = 43.

21. S.D. = 19 percent, N = 37.

22. Original vs. first rewrite yielded t(78) = 4.03, p < .001.

23. S.D. = 29 percent.

24. S.D. = 20 percent.

25. S.D. = 26 percent.

26. S.D. = 15 percent.

27. The questionnaire for the original instructions is actually composed of 89 questions. Three of these questions were found to be unnecessary for the questionnaire on the rewritten instructions. Thus comparisons can be made on 86 questions only.

28. Assuming that by chance alone we could expect half or 43/86 of the questions to increase in comprehension, $\chi^2(1) = 16.79$, p < .001.

29. Assuming that by chance alone we could expect half or 43/86 of the questions to increase in comprehension, $\chi^2(1) = 41.86$, p < .001.

30. Assuming that by chance alone we could expect half or 43/86 of the questions to increase in comprehension, $\chi^2(1) = 11.91$, p < .001.

31. Assuming that by chance alone we could expect half or 15/30 of the questions to increase in comprehension, $\chi^2(1) = 13.33$, p < .001.

32. S.D. = 13 percent.

33. S.D. = 22 percent.

34. S.D. = 15 percent.

35. This is a statistically significant increase, $\chi^2(1) = 26.20$, p < .001.

36. This is a statistically significant increase, $\chi^2(1) = 10.92$, p < .001.

37. This is a statistically significant increase, $\chi^2(1) = 2.76$, p < .04, one-tailed.

38. $F(4, 20) = 3.74$, p < .05; note that because of low frequencies in the extreme cells, the trend presented in Table 2 was clearly evident only after the data from all of our testing sessions with the Walker and Smith instructions were combined—this included a total of 269 jurors.

39. With sample sizes of 269 and 150, our chi-square tests had a power of .95 (at the .05 alpha level) to be sensitive to at least medium size differences, but no such differences were revealed. See Table 7.64 in Cohen, STATISTICAL POWER ANALYSIS FOR THE BEHAVIORAL SCIENCES (New York: Academic Press, 1977).

40. That age affected comprehension was evident and statistically significant with each of our questionnaires (Walker original, Walker rewritten, Smith, original, Smith first rewrite, Smith, second rewrite); $F_{(2,40)} = 5.53$, $p < .05$, $F_{(2,34)} = 8.71$, $p < .05$, $F_{(2,57)} = 5.53$, $p < .05$, $F_{(2,47)} = 4.65$, $p < .05$, $F_{(2,76)} = 6.49$, $p < .05$; Post hoc comparisons between the eldest jurors and the other two groups using the Sheffé method, all proved to be statistically significant at .05 level. Other comparisons were not statistically significant.

41. With our sample of 269 jurors, a test had a power of .95 (at a .05 alpha level to be sensitive to at least a medium size difference, but was not found. See Table 2.4.1 in Cohen, *supra* n. 39.

42. $\chi^2(1) = 9.62$, $p < .01$.

43. The difference between these two levels of comprehensibility is statistically significant, $t(18) = 3.52$, $p < .001$.

44. $5(18) = 1.77$, $.05 < p < .10$.

45. Brenda Danet raises this question in the broader context of linguistic reform in the legal process, See, Danet, *Language in the Legal Process* 14 L. AND SOC'Y REV. 445(1980).

46. In his forward to *Missouri Bar Committee Comments on Missouri Approved Instructions—Criminal* (1974), Richardson states: "The Committee steadfastly insisted that above all else its proposed forms must be accurate, complete and impartial, even if some sacrifice of conciseness and simplicity must be made."

47. Danet, *supra* n. 45, at 541.

9

HELPING JURIES HANDLE
COMPLEX CASES

DAVID U. STRAWN
Attorney, Orlando, Florida
G. THOMAS MUNSTERMAN
Center for Jury Studies

The jury trial evolved as a linear, chronological event during a leisurely time in our history. There was time to think and deliberate. Communities were small enough that jurors might know something about a subject being disputed. In fact, it was expected. Technology was far simpler, and it was reasonable to expect many men and women to understand all of the pertinent technology of the day.

The same institution today is being used without serious deliberate change in its procedures, in a culture which is intensively technological, and in which legal concepts and factual concerns have become far

From *Judicator* (1982, March-April), 65, 444-447, Reprinted with permission of the authors.

more refined and difficult. Obviously, the jury trial's inertia is straining against the new tides of a culture that it aided in creating, and is vital to preserving.

While the jury's fact-finding function has not changed, the law has become more convoluted, and the facts-to-be-found more complex. When a complex case arises—civil or criminal—judges are often specially selected by the bench, counsel are among the bar's finest, a special venire may be brought in (often warned of the probable length of the trial), experts on jury selection are consulted. Voir dire is often done individually and at great length, pretrial is more intense and pretrial motions may challenge everything from jury selection to the jurisdiction of the court. Although *pretrial* procedures have become specialized for such complex cases, it is business as usual in the courtroom after selection of the jury. The trial proceeds much as it would 100 years ago.

It is naive to think that the format for presentation of information that resolves a one-day burglary case can intelligently and defensibly resolve a three-month patent infringement or antitrust case. The jury who can recall all witnesses in the burglary case cannot be expected to resolve conflicts in the testimony of 100 witnesses in an antitrust case. The lawyers in this latter case may well be relying on computers to "remember" what they cannot expect to recall as humans. Yet, the jury may not even be permitted to take notes in many courtrooms.

We expect miraculous performances of today's juries in complex cases, but we don't need miracles. Instead, procedural changes could permit juries to continue to handle complex cases more effectively. Some possibilities are suggested in this article.

A STEP-BY-STEP APPROACH

Why do trials have to take place, "all at once?" There is a hierarchy of decisions in every jury trial. Freshman law students learn this quickly in order to survive the onslaught of information from texts and faculty. They then learn to use the hierarchies in answering examination questions. Juries could do the same

The most complex legal problem can be outlined, and an algorithm or "logic tree" created that will permit orderly discussion and resolution of the problem. For example, the first question in an algorithm for a burglary case might be, "Was the defendant in the store on the date and at the time of the burglary?" The "first question" to be answered by juries in more complex litigation will be nothing more than the first question the advocate knows he or she must answer in evaluating the litigation. Jury instructions using this sort of plain language algorithm have been successfully used, and have demonstrated that they do not alter outcomes while they do reduce deliberation times and increase jury focus on the evidence, showing a potential over traditional instructions for juror comprehension.[1]

The levels of decision suggested by these contemporary jury instructions may also suggest time dimensions for the judge's conduct of the case. For example, in a products liability case, where there are cross-claims and third-party claims, the claims of the original plaintiff against the original array of defendants potentially liable to the plaintiff might be litigated first. By having a jury verdict returned on these issues alone, the necessity for all defendants to provide evidence and argument on the cross-claims and third-party claims for indemnity or the like will possibly by eliminated or reduced by the verdict determining which defendants are liable to plaintiff. The jury's answers to special interrogatories will dictate any necessary further litigation between defendants and tiers of defendants.

Rather than litigating everything at once, the only matters litigated are those logically dictated by the order effects of the law. The same jury can serve throughout this progressive process in successive deliberations.

The idea of sequentially litigating issues has been applied on some courts.[2] For instance, in Seattle counsel asked the court to try the case issue by issue with the decision on the first issue given after presentation of evidence restricted to that issue.[3] Via this method, the parties hoped to narrow the discovery required. In addition, having the case terminated early by one of the first issue verdicts or by settlement would reduce the added expense to the clients, already high due to the complex nature of the case. When applied to the jury trial, there is the added potential of reduced counsel preparation time.

EXPERT PANELS AND "HOW TO" TRAINING

Since juror comprehension is considered the root of the problem in the complex case, why not have portions of the case requiring minor value judgments tried by the judge only, or expert panels, and other portions tried by the jury? For example, a suit involving patient violation in a complex process might have the engineering issues decided by a panel of experts or the court alone. If a violation is found, the balance of the case, including damages, would be decided by a jury.

Communication scientists and psychologists have long known that simple training exercises can greatly aid groups in avoiding deadlock and efficiently resolving conflicts. How about giving the jury some special training in how to be a jury? Such training could aid juries in avoiding "debate" and encourage "deliberation." Perhaps the jury selected for trial of a complex case should have instructions not only on the law but on the deliberation process. Simple training could help prepare them for the problems that groups predictably encounter in resolving conflicts. Very elementary rules have already been published and hang in many deliberation rooms.[4] For example, avoiding a "straw vote" [a commitment] before discussing the evidence.

Jury forepersons could be trained to aid the jury as facilitators of full deliberation. In those courts where the judge selects the foreperson, judges tend to look for persons having leadership qualities to strengthen deliberation. Perhaps the jury foreperson should receive special training, even if only concise written suggestions.

VIDEOTAPED TESTIMONY AND INSTRUCTIONS

Why don't we videotape testimony so that, instead of "reading back" with all of its inherent dullness and differences in communication from actual witnesses' testimony, the jury could call for and receive an actual recreation of the testimony of any witness, at any time, in the jury room. It is unnecessary to parade everyone into the courtroom to have a reporter flatly intone once-live testimony. The TV screen could be placed in the jury room to facilitate this.

We should also videotape the judge's instructions. This could be done quickly and easily in a simple courthouse studio. Before they are actually given to a jury, the judge could edit and correct errors. Trial counsel would be given an opportunity to preview the instructions, although ideally a charge conference would have occurred before the taping. These instructions can be replayed by the jury as many times as necessary to assure comprehension of important legal points.

If we have an audio or video recording of the judge's instructions, why not create a written transcript of the sound track and give it to the jury? Research has demonstrated that juror comprehension of instructions for a burglary case increased as much as 14 percent by letting jurors read the instructions along with the judge, as opposed to merely listening to him.[5]

JUDICIOUS LAW GIVING

When instructions are given at the beginning of the trial or throughout the trial as is now done in some courts,[6] juror comprehension of legal ideas is enhanced. The inadequacy, in the complex case, of the traditional method of waiting until the end of the trial to tell the jurors what they should have been looking for throughout the trial is obvious. In complex cases, the judge's teaching function needs much greater emphasis. A day or two of judicially conducted "classroom" instruction on the law, after jury selection but before the trial begins, should be the norm in complicated cases. This instruction should not be mistaken as day-long lectures on the lineage of the trial from the Magna Carta to the present as some courts still feel is necessary.

Trial counsel's opening statements should be expanded to encourage use of visual aids and demonstrative devices. Judges should consider allowing counsel brief introductory statements to the jury before the testimony of expert witnesses to aid the jury in listening for those points counsel believes are vital. A "day's end" summary by counsel of the testimony and evidence produced that day should be encouraged. An appropriate time limit will discourage a series of "closing arguments" resulting from these procedures.

Communication science literature indicates that the first information obtained by the jury about the case is probably the information around which they will form their preliminary hypotheses. It is therefore desirable that the first information the jury hears about the law be from the judge, not from the lawyers during voir dire.

Lawyers protest that they cannot test for bias about the case unless jurors know about the case and the law's requirements. Why not have the judge instruct the entire venire about the law as the first event of the trial? Then, have counsel making opening statements, at length, to the entire venire. And, only then, proceed with voir dire. The likelihood of selection of a well-informed jury, capable of trying the complex case, should be greatly improved by these procedures.

ANSWERING JURORS' QUESTIONS

If we are even to learn what the jury understands and does not understand about the law and the issues in the case, it will only be from listening to jurors as they ask questions. What lawyer could imagine going through law school and never asking a question of a professor? And what judge can imagine a confident understanding of complex appellate arguments without an opportunity to question the attorneys?

We do not encourage feedback from jurors because we are frightened of "prejudice." Why don't we find a way to encourage juror questioning and therefore juror comprehension, avoiding prejudice at the same time? Several judges have found ways.[7] For example, a routine could be developed in which jurors would be encouraged to write their questions out as they have them, submit them to the bailiff at each recess or more often if they think the question is highly pertinent at the time. The bailiff will deliver the questions to the court, who will then determine an appropriate answer with the aid of counsel, or ask the witness the question. If the juror has asked an objectionable question, then the juror can be told simply that such evidence is not permissible in the case, and the case must be decided on the evidence that the law allows.

Experience indicates that jurors' questions do not, per se, transform the American trial process from its adversarial model to an inquisitorial one. It is still the adversaries who will provide information deemed necessary by the fact finder, where the evidence is admissible. If the evidence is not admissible, then it will be the judge's responsibility to explain this fact to the juror.

A tactic for making such explanations more palatable to the juror would be to explain in advance of trial the theory of the rules of evidence, such as using "hearsay" as an example of a "rule against rumors." Many judges who permit juror questioning tell the jury at the beginning of the trial that their questions will be considered as are questions from the attorneys, and the same standards will apply. The judge should also promise to explain the rejection or denial of any question after deliberations are completed to assure each juror that all will be clarified.

CONCLUSION

We offer these suggestions to show that means for aiding the American jury's continued evolution are at hand. Some are simple and demonstrated, others costly and in need of verification. The bench and bar should not assume that the jury cannot address the complex case. Trial procedure should now receive the attention and effort lavished upon pretrial procedures in the past three decades.

Rather than let the uninitiated examine the issue, a commission, including former jurors, appellate and trial judges, trial attorneys, social scientists, and experts in communications and information processing should study the problem. The commission would examine the ideas advanced in this article and elsewhere and other proposals that it would no doubt generate to provide unique perspectives about the proper presentation of complex cases to juries.

Current trial procedures do not help jurors comprehend and properly resolve complex cases. Many feel the jury is not being given a fair trial by the members of the bench and bar who would trim its importance. The American jury is the embodiment of much of our constitutional ideal. It has become an engineer of our democratic republic—a focal point of participatory government. We should not be so easily persuaded to adopt the English way, after struggling so resolutely to be free of it and to be assured of participation in government through the jury.

NOTES

1. Strawn, Taylor and Buchannan, *Finding a Verdict Step by Step*, 60 JUDICATURE 383 (March, 1977); Pryor, Buchannan and Strawn, "Communication In The Courtroom: The Effect of Process Instructions on Jury Deliberation," paper presented at April, 1978 meeting of the Southern Speech Communication Association.

Other research has demonstrated that careful attention to vocabulary and structure of jury instructions can yield significant gains in juror comprehension. *See,* Alfini, Elwork and Sales, *Juridic Decision, L. and Contemp Probl, 1979, and their article in this issue* (page 432) [*Editors' note:* The second article has been included as chapter 8 in this book].

2. Withrow and Suggs, *Procedures for Improving Jury Trial of Complex Litigation,* 25 ANTITRUST BULL. 493 (Fall, 1980).

3. Private communication with Judge James A. Noe, Seattle Superior Court, November, 1980

4. Center for Jury Studies Newsletter, No. 2-5, September 1980.

5. Strawn and Buchanan, *Jury Confusion. A Threat to Justice,* 59 JUDICATURE 478 (May, 1976).

6. *Let's Learn to Instruct the Jury,* 18 JUDGE'S J. 40 (Summer, 1979)

7. Center for Jury Studies Newsletter, No. 3-1, January 1981.

SECTION III

SUMMARY

An overriding theme in the preceding chapters seems to be the distinction between comprehension and comprehensibility. Critics of jury decision making lay blame at the feet of jurors, claiming they are inherently unable to comprehend the proceedings. But defenders of the system—and the editors include themselves in this category—find fault with the comprehensibility of the process. Two aspects stand out in the articles reprinted here: Jurors are presented the mass of factual evidence before they even know what the rules of the game are (chapter 7), and when they are given instructions as to how to proceed, these are riddled with obscure and technical terms embedded in complex clauses and compound sentences (chapter 8). This is not to say that the courts are entirely at fault either; as Sperlich (1982), a defender of juries in complex civil litigation notes, "Surely, some jurors do not comprehend some of the evidence and, therefore, are not good finders of fact. But some of the cases brought to our courts are so vast and intricate that it is doubtful that anyone could comprehend and decide them" (p. 396).

Sperlich's comment raises an interesting question. If we do away with the traditional jury as the decision maker in complex and prolonged cases, what mechanism replaces it? Nordenberg and Luneburg (1982) suggest, as one device, requiring college-educated jurors in highly complex litigation. Such a suggestion is clearly inconsistent with the requirements of the Jury Selection and Service Act of 1968, prescribing that juries be selected at random from a cross-section of the community. (The Supreme Court has, however, been more vigilant in imposing this requirement in criminal cases than in civil cases.)

Another alternative is, of course, a bench trial; in fact, litigants already have this option. But is that necessarily an improvement? Sperlich (1982) notes, there is much reason to doubt that "judges are... the superior triers of fact, even in complex cases" (p. 413). Kalven and Zeisel's (1966) massive study of 3,500 jury trials, in which the trial judges were asked to evaluate the jury's performance, reported high rates of agreement between the jury's verdict and what the judge's would have been. And when we compare jury effectiveness with that of the judge's, we note the relevance of the empirical finding of safety in numbers, that group decisions made by interacting individuals are better than those made by solitary individuals (Forsyth, 1983).

As chapter 9 notes, changes in the court system's procedures have not been consistent with changes in the nature of trial process that have evolved over the last century. The procedural changes advocated by Strawn and Munsterman in chapter 9 include the following:

(1) sequentially litigating issues
(2) using expert panels to judge specific, complex aspects of a case
(3) providing juries with special training on how to deliberate
(4) videotaping the testimony and instructions
(5) giving judicial instructions, early in (or even throughout) the trial
(6) permitting a brief "day's end" summary by attorneys of the evidence presented that day
(7) permitting jurors to ask questions

All of these suggestions seem eminently reasonable and effective to us. On the few occasions that judges have permitted some of the more "radical" of these interventions, both they and the jurors have been more satisfied with the process. Still another modification to increase jurors' comprehension is jurors' note taking. If the trial were video-taped and the tape given to the jury at the beginning of deliberations, note taking would not be as necessary.

REFERENCES

Forsyth, D. R. (1983). *An introduction to group dynamics.* Monterey, CA: Brooks/Cole.
Kalven, H., Jr., & Zeisel, H. (1966). *The American Jury.* Boston: Little, Brown.

Nordenberg, M. A. & Luneburg, W. V. (1982) Decision-making in complex federal civil cases: Two alternatives to the traditional jury. *Judicature, 65,* 420-431.

Sperlich, P. W. (1982). The case for preserving trial by jury in complex civil litigation. *Judicature, 65,* 394-419.

SECTION IV

JURY SIZE
AND DECISION RULE
Introduction

More than 20 years ago, the distinguished civil rights lawyer and political scientist, James Marshall (1966), tested the American trial system and found it guilty of the charge of being woefully ignorant of elementary psychology. Marshall's book was titled *Law and Psychology in Conflict*; as the chapters in this section reveal, there are still grounds for such a label.

Marshall had little to say about the psychological validity of the jury system and the issues raised in the early sections of this book; his primary criticism dealt with the inaccuracies in the testimony of witnesses and the hindrances to the determination of truth that result from direct and cross-examination. But in the interim the courts have revised the jury system; these "reforms" include the acceptance of juries as small as six in number, as well as a nonunanimous decision rule. Do these judicial decisions reflect solid scientific findings? Or are they another example, to use Marshall's terms, of psychology and law in conflict?

The first chapter in this section, by Hans Zeisel of the University of Chicago and Shari Seidman Diamond of the University of Illinois at Chicago Circle, takes the U.S. Supreme Court to task for its claim that its "reforms" regarding jury size are based on solid "empirical data."

The authors suggest better research designs that would permit more credible conclusions about the impact of a smaller jury.

Chapter 11, by Norbert L. Kerr and Robert J. MacCoun of Michigan State University, is a more recent review of the issue of reduced jury size. The study compares the effects of simulated juries of sizes 3, 6, and 12, not only on their verdicts but also on the group process.

Chapter 12, by Charlan Nemeth, now of the University of California at Berkeley, reports several empirical studies of the other "reform," the shift toward a majority decision rule. Again, both outcome and process effects are evaluated.

In two of its more recent decisions, the U.S. Supreme Court has been somewhat more responsive to improved social science research. These developments are described in the summary to this section.

REFERENCES

Marshall, J. (1966). *Law and psychology in conflict.* New York: Bobbs-Merrill.

10

"CONVINCING EMPIRICAL EVIDENCE" ON THE SIX-MEMBER JURY

HANS ZEISEL
University of Chicago
SHARI SEIDMAN DIAMOND
University of Illinois at Chicago Circle

The United States Supreme Court has recently been increasing its references to what it likes to call "empirical" data. A genuine issue is occasionally documented by such data, for example the "unusual" character of capital punishment in *Furman v. Georgia.*[1] In some cases, however, the intent of such references is merely to ornament an

Authors' Note, The authors thank Nathan Leites for his critical reading of this paper.

From *University of Chicago Law Review* (1974), *41*, 281-295. Reprinted with permission of the publisher and authors.

already determined result; the famous footnote 11 in *Brown v. Board of Education*[2] is an example. The Court generally cites "empirical" studies as lawyers cite cases, treating their summary conclusions as if they were holdings in prior cases. Applied to empirical research, this treatment encourages the notion that empirical findings, like case law, are infinitely mutable. The courts are thus diverted from using empirical studies for their intended purpose: to shed light on hitherto unknown facts.

A more critical use of empirical data would better inform the courts and force them to face openly those instances in which their decisions are based on theory and merely ornamented by the "facts." Assurance of critical examination in the courts would also force researchers more carefully to connect their summary conclusions with the results of their studies.

In two recent decisions concerned with replacing the traditional twelve-member jury with the six-member jury, the Supreme Court admitted that there was a crucial empirical issue: whether the reduction in jury size would affect trial results. In both opinions the Court cited empirical data as proof that there was no such effect. In *Williams v. Florida*,[3] which upheld the use of the six-member jury in criminal cases in state courts, the Court, as we have shown elsewhere,[4] was misled in believing that there was such evidence.

The Court compounded its error in *Colgrove v. Battin*,[5] which sanctioned the use of the six-member jury in federal civil litigation. After claiming retrospective support from the "empirical evidence" in *Williams*,[6] the Court asserted that "four very recent studies have provided convincing empirical evidence of the correctness of the *Williams* conclusion that 'there is no discernible difference between the results reached by the two different sized juries.'"[7] Again the Court was misled; the four studies do not support this proposition. This failure to evaluate empirical research properly raises serious questions. To put these questions into sharper focus, this article will analyze the four studies cited in *Colgrove*[8] and suggest several study designs that would produce the needed evidence.[9]

I. THE FOUR STUDIES

On the surface all four studies do what their summaries claim: They compare the performance of twelve-member and six-member juries. Two of the studies, in Washington[10] and New Jersey,[11] compare jury trials within a system that allows litigants to choose between the two jury sizes. A third study, in Michigan,[12] also used actual trial results in what is called a before-and-after study. Until July 1970, civil cases in Michigan were tried before juries of twelve; after that date jury size was reduced to six. The fourth study[13] was a laboratory study in which experimental juries viewed the same videotaped trial, and jury size was randomly varied by the experimenter. Each of these approaches has shortcomings that can lead to erroneous conclusions if not properly handled. Unfortunately, all four studies failed to deal with these shortcomings and thus fail to provide reliable conclusions.

A. The Washington Study

Civil jury trials in the state of Washington are held before six-member juries, unless one of the litigating parties requests a twelve-member jury.[14] The authors of this study tried to determine whether there is any difference between six- and twelve-member juries by comparing the results of 128 workmen's compensation trials.

Where an attorney is presented with the opportunity to demand a twelve-member jury, he or she is likely to do so only for a reason. The jury fee is usually twice that for a six-member jury, and the attorney knows that the court may view the larger jury as an added burden. Whenever the studied attribute is present for a reason, rather than after random distribution by chance, surface comparisons between results become meaningless. For example, in a recent examination our students were asked to comment on the following statement: "Convicted defendants who were given probation have lower recidivism rates than defendants who were sent to prison. It has been argued that this is proof of the beneficial effect of probation." Clearly, the defendants who received probation were different from those imprisoned; the overall comparison is bound to be meaningless. Similarly, if the cases brought before twelve-member juries differed from the cases brought before six-member juries, any subsequent comparison is meaningless.

The Washington investigators recognized this problem, but thought it could be circumvented by words, stating "if we may properly assume that the assignment of jury size was essentially random . . . then we may conclude that the use of the smaller jury introduced no systematic bias into the trial outcomes."[15] Later, they try to justify such an assumption by observing, "[W]e cannot provide assurance that there was no systematic interaction between particular kinds of cases and the agreement between attorneys to use the small jury, but our survey of the records reveals no obvious interaction of this sort."[16] Thus, without basis, the study is presented as one of the few "quantitative comparisons of the performances of . . . six- and twelve-member juries in comparable cases."[17]

The investigators have ignored the fact that "random assignment" does not describe a selection result; it is a characteristic of the selection procedure, namely, one that leaves the selection to chance. Lawyer stipulations, however, are anything but random events; there is good evidence that lawyers are more likely to opt for the larger jury if the amount in controversy is larger.[18] It is therefore irrelevant to report the Washington finding that, in these workmen's compensation trials, six- and twelve-member juries found in equal proportions for the plaintiff,[19] because not only the jury size, but also probably the amount in controversy, was different.

B. The New Jersey Study

The New Jersey study, also conducted in a system in which the litigants had a choice of jury size, recognized the possibility that different types of cases might be presented to the two types of juries and documented the impossibility of direct comparison. Yet the study failed to deal with this difficulty and, in its summary conclusion, thereby misled the unwary reader.

The study leaves no doubt as to the major differences between the cases tried before the two types of juries. Both settlements and verdicts of twelve-member juries are, on the average, three times as great as for the six-member jury cases. Twelve-member jury cases also tended to be more complex. Twelve-member juries tried relatively few (twenty-three percent) of the total automobile negligence cases, but more (thirty-five percent) of the contract cases; eleven percent of the cases tried by twelve-member juries were "consolidated cases with verdicts for more than one party," while only six percent of the cases tried by six-member juries fell into that category.[21]

The study perceived the significance of these differences, noting that "the 'bigger' cases are tried before twelve jurors"[22] and that "the cases tend to be more complicated,"[23] but it goes on to make invalid comparisons and merely adds a caveat to each conclusion. That such a qualification is not enough is easily demonstrated.

The study's finding on trial time was that "cases before twelve-

TABLE 10.1
Average Settlement and Verdict[20]

	Six-member juries	Twelve-member juries
Average Settlement	$5,800	$15,800
Average Verdict	$8,600	$24,300

member juries take approximately twice as much trial time as those tried before six (11 hours compared to 5.6). One important reason . . . is that the cases tend to be more complicated."[24] There is nothing wrong with this statement: There is no hint that smaller jury size has anything to do with reducing trial time. Yet the summary begins with the statement that "[u]se of six-member juries in civil cases can result in substantial savings in trial time."[25] There is not a shred of evidence to support this claim. Indeed a reasonable conclusion would be that the trial time difference was caused by the decreased complexity of the cases, and not by a decrease in jury size.

Consider the following assumptions, each consistent with the evidence presented in the New Jersey study, about the relationship between trial time, complexity of cases, and size of juries:

(1) 25 percent of the cases tried before six-member juries are "complex;" 75 percent are "simple." The ratio is reversed for twelve-member juries.
(2) Average trial time for all "complex" cases is 15 hours; average trial for all "simple" cases is 3 hours.

Under these circumstances, as Table 2 shows, the average trial time for all six-member jury cases is 6 hours and the average trial time for all twelve-member jury cases is 12 hours, as found in the New Jersey study.[26] In our assumed data, however, complex cases tried before six-member juries take as long as complex cases before twelve-member juries, and the average trial time of simple cases is similarly unaffected by the size of the jury.

Perhaps the most disconcerting aspect of the study is that the authors apparently knew what analysis was required by the data. When they found that the average deliberation time of six-member juries was 1.2 hours, compared to 1.8 hours for the twelve-member juries, they became concerned.[27] Afraid that this difference might be interpreted as less diligent deliberation, and thus reflect poorly on the six-member jury, the authors suddenly improve their mode of analysis for this one result. They reported "that six-member juries deliberate as long as twelve-member juries *when the verdicts are for damages above $10,000.*"[28] At no other point is this method of comparing only

TABLE 10.2

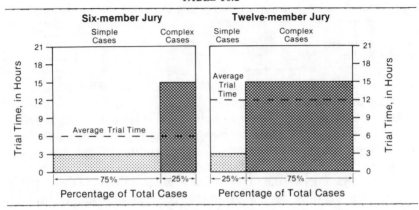

comparable groups of cases repeated. For this reason, none of the other findings is valid.

Whatever differences or nondifferences were observed, the data do not indicate that they can be attributed to the difference in jury size with one exception: There will be savings in juror manpower.[29] To come to that conclusion, however, no study is required.

C. The Michigan Laboratory Experiment

The Michigan laboratory study avoided the difficulties of comparability of cases by showing just one videotaped case to a series of six-and twelve-member juries.[30] A price must be paid for such experimental cleanliness; for instance, since the trial is not real, the validity of drawing inferences to real trials is uncertain. That problem will be by-passed for present purposes, and the study will be discussed as if the laboratory trials had been real ones.[31]

The experiment also had a more serious drawback. The use of only one trial had the disadvantage of narrowing the experimental experience and increasing the difficulties of drawing general conclusions. This drawback was aggravated by the fact that this trial was very special. The evidence in the case overwhelmingly favored the defendant; of sixteen juries, not one found for the plaintiff. This overpowering bias makes the experiment irrelevant. On the facts of this case, any jury under any rules would probably have arrived at the same verdict. Hence, to conclude from this experiment that jury size generally has no effect on the verdict is impermissible.[32]

TABLE 10.3
Jury Size, Predeliberation Vote, and Deliberation Outcome

Six-member			Twelve-member		
In predeliberation vote, jurors favoring:			In predeliberation vote, jurors favoring:		
Plaintiff	Defendant	Final Verdict	Plaintiff	Defendant	Final Verdict
0	6*	Def.	1	11*	Def.
0	6*	Def.	1	11*	Def.
1	5*	Def.	1	11*	Def.
1	5*	Def.	1	11*	Def.
2	4	Def.	2	10*	Def.
2	4	Hung	2	10*	Def.
2	4	Hung	5	7	Def.
3	3	Def.	7	5	Hung

*Sufficient majority for verdict existed before deliberation began.

These difficulties are exacerbated by a third circumstance. The experimental juries were instructed according to Michigan law, in which agreement by five out of six, or ten out of twelve jurors constitutes a verdict. Before deliberations began, each juror was asked to record privately which party he or she favored at that time. This predeliberation vote[33] revealed that six of the twelve-member juries and four of the six-member juries had reached the required majority before deliberation began. For these ten juries, deliberation was a mere formality, as shown in Table 4. Thus because the experimenter had selected a case that was heavily slanted in favor of the defendant, only six juries engaged in meaningful deliberations. Since three of those juries never reached a verdict, the experiment had only three successful jury deliberations. Such a small sample is in itself an inadequate basis for any inferences.

Nevertheless, one alleged finding should be more specifically discussed here, because on the surface it tends to support the Court's notion that the smaller jury may result in more open discussion among the jurors.[34] The laboratory study found "a tendency for six-member minority jurors to participate more than twelve-member minority jurors."[35] The minority juror in six-member juries occupied an average of twenty-one percent of the total deliberation time, compared to an average of thirteen percent for the minority juror in the twelve-member juries. The numbers are accurate, but the comparison is invalid; the juror's participation time in one case is divided by six, in the other by twelve. If a juror in a six-member jury talks for the same amount of time as a juror in a twelve-member jury, this method of

TABLE 10.4
Average Deliberation Time of Juries

Predeliberation Vote	Six-member jury	Twelve-member jury
Sufficient majority for verdict existed before deliberation	7 minutes (4 juries)	8 minutes (6 juries)
Sufficient majority did not exist before deliberation	38 minutes (4 juries)	36 minutes (2 juries)

computation will prove that the juror on the six-member jury participated twice as much. An appropriate method to compare individual participation would be to double the twelve-member average (or halve the six-member average) to allow for the differences in jury size.[36] If the study's error is corrected, the difference shifts slightly in favor of the twelve-member jury.

D. The Michigan Before-and-After Study

The twelve-member jury was replaced in Michigan on July 23, 1970, by the six-member jury. If nothing but jury size had changed at that time, it would be sensible to compare trial results before the change with results after it. The trouble is that unknown simultaneous changes may have also affected the trial results, and it is difficult to exclude such a possibility.[37] In this study the situation is worse, because two important changes are known to have occurred at the crucial point in time. A mediation board was instituted, and procedural rules were modified to allow discovery of insurance policy limits.[38] Under these circumstances it is difficult, if not impossible, to say whether any observed change or part of a change is due to the reduction in jury size or the other changes. If the various causes operate in opposite directions, a finding of no difference might be equally spurious.

To illustrate this point, consider the study's data that the average award in automobile negligence cases in which the jury found for the plaintiff was $11,147 with twelve-member juries and $23,768 with six-member juries.[39] The probability of settling a particular case without trial is related to the size of that case; the largest cases are least likely to be settled.[40] If the creation of the mediation board and better discovery procedures increased the proportion of settled cases, the average size of cases reaching trial would be increased. The data therefore could not be used to support a conclusion that six-member juries give higher damage awards. It is equally improper, however, for the author of the study to treat this difference as "not statistically significant"[41] and thereby claim support for his hypothesis that "the six-member jury's damage awards are identical to the twelve-member jury's awards."[42]

Other data in the study are similarly questionable. A wider variation in amounts awarded by six-member juries is indicated by the data for automobile negligence cases; they show a standard deviation—the statistical measure of variation—of $58,335 for the six-member jury awards and a standard deviation of $24,834 for the awards of twelve-member juries.[43] We like this data, because we predicted it:

> A result of this reduction in [jury] size is an increase in the gamble which litigants or defendants take in going before a jury; reduction of their size will reduce the predictability of jury verdicts. . . . An elementary statistical calculation again reveals that these averages of juror evaluations in comparable cases will fluctuate more in 6-member juries than they do in 12-member juries.[44]

Unfortunately, we cannot claim support from this data, for it is flawed by the same weaknesses that render the study's comparison of average awards suspect.

Since the investigator had no such methodological scruples, however, it is surprising that these data showing a "difference" are not mentioned in the crucial conclusions of the study: "this study provides empirical statistical evidence which tends to support Justice White's statement in *Williams v. Florida* that 'there is no discernible difference between the results reached by the two different-sized juries.'"[45] Such last sentences have a special attraction to those who like the conclusion and hence tend to disregard the hedging that comes earlier. The statement of conclusions was particularly improper because the Michigan study dealt only with civil trials, while *Williams* dealt with criminal juries.

These four studies, plus the nonexistent evidence in *Williams*[46], moved the Supreme Court to conclude in *Colgrove* that there is no discernible difference between twelve- and six-member juries either in criminal or in civil cases. It is a disconcerting picture.

II. SATISFACTORY EXPERIMENTS

Although no study has produced satisfactory evidence regarding the impact of six-member juries, there are strategies for studying this question that would produce the needed information.

The ideal research design would test the effects of jury size in a jurisdiction in which six-member juries are optional. A series of cases could be tried simultaneously before two juries, one composed of six members and the other of twelve. The parties' counsel would select eighteen jurors to form the two juries; before the trial, without the knowledge of either jury,[47] the attorneys and the court would decide which jury would decide the case. The jurors would not learn whether their jury made the real decision until deliberations were completed. This design would permit a comparison of jury reactions to the same trial and would allow a direct assessment of the effect of jury size. While this design would not violate the essential rights of the litigants or the integrity of the trial, it would require the consent of the trial court and the litigants.

In the next best design, comparable sets of cases would be tried before six-and twelve-member juries. Again, one would choose a jurisdiction in which jury size is optional. The study would exclude all cases in which a party insisted on a twelve-member jury or chose a six-member jury for reasons other than the lower fee. In the remaining cases, the parties would be indifferent about jury size, and the attorneys would be asked to agree to a lottery to determine whether their case would be tried before a six-member or twelve-member jury. In these cases, all litigants would pay only the six-member jury fee.[48] This random assignment of cases would provide a properly controlled experiment in which comparable sets of cases are tried by six- and twelve-member juries.

Two other possible experimental designs are suggested by the laboratory and before-and-after studies discussed above. A before-and-after design could conceivably develop useful data if the underlying assumption of such studies—no concomitant changes except the experimental one—could be verified. The trouble is that there can never be any assurance that nothing else changes; no method other than random assignment of cases provides such assurance.

Competently designed laboratory experiments, on the other hand, can put a microscope to details of the deliberation process that cannot be properly observed in an actual court. In the Michigan laboratory study, it was discovered too late that most jurors favored the defendant before deliberations began. Better pilot testing would have identified this difficulty, and a case could have been selected that offered more choice to the "jurors." Such balance will suffice if the number of "trials" is sufficiently large. If the sample is small, however, it will be advisable to equalize the initial vote distributions by assigning members to juries based on their initial ballots. This technique allows the experimenter to have all experimental juries begin with a vote distribution that requires meaningful deliberation.[49] Such juror assignment presupposes that the initial vote is a function of individual juror characteristics, not a function of jury size. In addition, it would be preferable to have more than a single case on tape.

Since each of the discussed designs has particular advantages and insufficiencies, an approach that combines a variety of research designs will provide the best results.[50]

CONCLUSION

The flaws in these studies are, as we have shown, not complex and surely not beyond the reach of modest expertise. It would be unfair, however, to place the blame for accepting unsatisfactory evidence entirely on the Supreme Court. If lawyers and social scientists write poor studies, and if legal journals publish them, the courts should be entitled to cite them. Yet the courts know how to consider critically traditional types of evidence presented in adversary proceedings.

The danger in asking for critical evaluation is that the courts might decide to ignore all such evidence. This turn, however, is not likely; there are too many issues in which such evidence is clearly needed. What is required is not simply judicial accessibility to such evidence through journals, but critical presentation in trial courts by experts under cross-examination. The real problem may be that too few trial lawyers appreciate the potential of such evidence and are content with citing studies in briefs. The citations thus reach the courts without the needed scrutiny. If the evidence has not been presented at trial, but the appellate court feels the need for it, there is ample precedent for the court to inform itself through informal inquiries directed at experts. In *People v. Collins*,[51] where proof was attempted through statistical calculus, the California Supreme Court appended to its opinion a statistical essay that clearly came from informal consultation.[52]

Perhaps the ultimate solution lies in eliminating a misleading label. "Empirical evidence" is a pleonasm; all evidence is, or ought to be, empirical. The term has come to distinguish systematically gathered facts from the facts in the individual case as they are traditionally defined. Perhaps the time has come when "empirical" legal studies should simply be called legal studies. Such working would reflect a desire for critical and intelligent use of these studies as an integral part of legal analysis.

In the meantime, the "convincing empirical evidence" discussed above has had a more immediate practical effect. After *Williams* several federal district courts, encouraged by the Chief Justice, promulgated rules making the six-member jury mandatory in civil cases. When this effort was upheld in *Colgrove,* the movement spread; today over sixty of the ninety-four district courts have made the six-member civil jury mandatory. The courts have now asked Congress to bring the remaining districts into line with legislation requiring the six-member jury in civil cases throughout the federal system.[53]

The truth is that a reduction in jury size is bound to affect both the composition and the verdicts of civil juries.[54] There will be less frequent representation of minorities on juries. The American Civil Liberties Union and the National Association for the Advancement of Colored People have pointed out the undesirability of this development at a time when minority grievances have been rechanneled from political forums into the courts.[55] In addition to this change in the quality of the jury, the mere reduction of its size must increase the variability of the jury's verdicts. Greater fluctuation in verdicts results in a lower degree of predictability and thus an increase in the gamble that litigants take in going before a jury.[56] There is elegant proof of trial lawyers' perception of this predicament. In some district courts, the six-member rule has been circumvented by a stipulation that allows the two alternate jurors to participate in the deliberations, resulting in the novelty of an eight-member jury.

The surface argument for the proposed reduction in size is economy. The federal court system would save about four million dollars annually if all civil juries were composed of six members. This amount is not negligible, but neither is it formidable; it represents two percent of the judicial budget and only about one-thousandth of one percent of the total federal budget.[57]

Moreover, it would be a mistake to regard the size of the federal civil jury as an isolated question. Some district court judges are already trying criminal cases—albeit by stipulation of counsel—before juries of six members. State legislatures across the country are teeming with bills, some already enacted, to reduce civil and criminal juries and to abandon the unanimity requirement. The movement to reduce the size of the federal civil jury must be seen in this context. If the country wants to reconsider the desirability of the civil jury, it should be done in open and direct debate. Perhaps such a debate should begin. But to pare the jury down and allow it to decay from the insufficiencies we impose is shabby treatment for an institution that has served the nation well.

At this point in the development only Congress can save the twelve-member jury. There is much talk now about reestablishing the authority of the Congress vis-à-vis the Executive. If the Congress also cares to reestablish its authority vis-à-vis the judiciary, it can undo this unseemly whittling down of the jury by simply reestablishing the twelve-member jury for all federal trials.

At a time when much of our justice system is under suspicion and public mistrust has reached the highest officer in the land, the integrity of the jury has survived. This would seem to be an inappropriate moment to punish it, even if money could be saved. Four million dollars might not be the right price for abandoning half of the American jury.

NOTES

1. 408 U.S. 238, 314, 345-54, 364-65 (1972) (Marshall, J., concurring).

2. 347 U.S. 483, 494, n.11 (1954) The note referred to an experiment conducted by the distinguished psychologist Kenneth Clark dealing with black and white children and black and white dolls. K. CLARK, EFFECTS OF PREJUDICE AND DISCRIMINATION ON PERSONALITY DEVELOPMENT (1950). The significance of this footnote became the topic of a debate in which Edmond Cahn undoubtedly had the upper hand. See Cahn, Jurisprudence, 30 N.Y.U.L. REV. 150 (1955).

3. 399 U.S. 78 (1970).

4. Zeisel, . . . And Then There Were None: The Diminution of the Federal Jury, 38 U. CHI. L. REV. 710, 712-15 (1971).

5. 413 U.S. 149 (1973).

6. See 399 U.S. at 101.

7. 413 U.S. at 159 n.15 (emphasis added).

8. See text and notes at notes 10-46 infra.

9. See text and notes at notes 47-50 infra.

10. Bermant & Coppock, Outcomes of Six- and Twelve-Member Jury Trials: An Analysis of 128 Civil Cases in the State of Washington, 48 WASH. L. REV. 593 (1973) [hereinafter cited as Washington Study].

11. INSTITUTE OF JUDICIAL ADMINISTRATION, A COMPARISON OF SIX- AND TWELVE-MEMBER JURIES IN NEW JERSEY SUPERIOR AND COUNTY COURTS (1972) [hereinafter cited as NEW JERSEY STUDY].

12. Note, Six-Member and Twelve-Member Juries: An Empirical Study of Trial Results, 6 U. MICH. J.L. REFORM 671 (1973) [hereinafter cited as Michigan Study].

13. Note, An Empirical Study of Six- and Twelve-Member Jury Decision-Making Processes, 6 U. MICH. J.L. REFORM 712 (1973) [hereinafter cited as Laboratory Study].

14. Washington Superior Court Rule 38 provides that, unless a party requests a twelve-member jury, all cases shall be tried before a six-member jury; the agreement of five-sixths of the jurors constitutes a verdict. WASH. SUPER. CT. R. 38.

15. Washington Study, supra note 10. at 595.

16. Id. at 596.

17. Id. at 594.

18. *See* Table 1 *infra*. To document this fact in the instant case, we asked a prominent Seattle attorney, specializing in workmen's compensation cases, about this matter. While he was uncertain about the impact of the six-member jury on verdicts, he said he requested a twelve-member jury whenever he had a "big" case.

19. Forty-five percent of the six-member juries found for the plaintiff, while forty-six percent of the twelve-member juries did the same. *Washington Study, supra* note 10, at 595.

20. The data shown in Table 1 are from NEW JERSEY STUDY, *supra* note 11, at 24.

21. *Id.* at 16.

22. *Id.* at 24.

23. *Id.* at 25.

24. *Id.* at 26.

25. *Id.* at 5.

26. The actual findings were 5.6 hours and 11 hours. *Id.* at 26.

27. *Id.* at 28-29.

28. *Id.* at 29 (emphasis added).

29. *Id.* at 8, 33-34.

30. *Laboratory Study, supra* note 13, at 719.

31. For a discussion of the problems of simulation and generalization, *see* Zeisel, *Experimental Techniques in the Law*, 2 J. LEGAL STUDIES 113 (1973).

32. The mistake of concluding that no difference exists between two institutions, such as six- and twelve-member juries, when a difference does in fact exist is called a Type II error. A major approach to reducing the risk of such errors is to increase the sample size.

33. This data and that reported in Table 3 were not reported in the original study; the author was kind enough to provide the details that allowed reanalysis of some of the data.

34. Colgrove v. Battin, 413 U.S. 149, 159 n.15 (1973) The Court referred to Note, *Reducing the Size of Juries*, 5 U. MICH. J.L. REFORM 87 (1971), which uses experience from small group research, primarily game playing to show that smaller groups lead to wider participation.

35. *Laboratory Study, supra* note 13, at 734.

36. The researchers could also have compared the participation by minority jurors as a group, rather than individually. The respective percentages for minority jurors in each jury could be aggregated, and a comparison of the totals would indicate the relative magnitude of minority participation.

37. *See Michigan Study, supra* note 12, at 675.

38. *Id.* at 679-81.

39. *Id.* at 691. Another before-and-after study, in Rhode Island, showed a similar increase in the average size of awards—from $33,000 for twelve-member juries to $52,000 for six-member juries. E. Beisner & R. Varrin, The Impact of the Six-Man Jury, Brown University 1973 (mimeograph).

40. Franklin, Chanin, & Mark, *Accidents, Money, and the Law. A Study of the Economics of Personal Injury Litigation*, 61 COLUM. L. REV. 1, 18 (1961) (Table 2).

41. *Michigan Study, supra* note 12 at 705. The author reaches this result primarily by reducing the apparent increase by a factor of ten percent, the decline in the purchasing power of the dollar as measured by the Consumer Price Index. One might require proof that inflation actually affected the jury. In any event, one must admire the author's ingenuity in removing an unwanted finding to reach a result that he seems to have sought from the start.

To determine whether the increased awards were produced by changes other than the jury size, the study might have compared settlements and awards in bench trials before and after the procedural modifications. If the bench trials showed the same pattern as the jury trials, it would be likely that the institution of a mediation board and changes in discovery rules, rather than a reduction in jury size, were the cause of the increase in awards.

42. *Id.* at 704.

43. *Id.* at 689.

44. Zeisel, Six-Man Juries, Majority Verdicts—What Difference Do They Make? March 15, 1973 (Occasional Papers from the University of Chicago Law School, No. 5) *See also* Zeisel, *supra* note 4, at 717-18.

45. Michigan Study, *supra* note 12, at 711.

46. This evidence consisted of the following:

(1) Judge Wiehl cited with approval C. Joiner, *Civil Justice and the Jury* (1962) in which Joiner states that "it could easily be argued that a six-man jury would deliberate equally as well as one of twelve." Joiner offered no evidence, hence Judge Wiehl had none either.

(2) Judge Tamm had presided over five-member juries in condemnation trials in the District of Columbia and found the juries satisfactory.

(3) Cronin reported on a run of forty-three six-member juries, obtained by stipulation of counsel, on one court of limited jurisdiction in Massachusetts; the highest verdict there was $2,500. The court clerk is said to have found these verdicts "about the same as those returned by regular twelve-member juries." Three lawyers (given preferential calendar treatment for their consent to the six-member jury) also could see no particular reason why the verdicts should be different.

(4) The Monmouth New Jersey County Court had tried one negligence case with a six-member jury, seemingly without any deleterious effect. See Zeisel, *supra* note 4, at 714-15.

47. Evidence from an ongoing and not yet reported experiment suggests the wisdom of keeping this knowledge from the jury. That experiment conducted by the authors with the cooperation of judges in the District Court for the Northern District of Illinois, suggests that, despite all precautions, a real jury in a criminal case is less likely to convict than a mock jury of the same size sitting in the courtroom with the real jury. It would seem that the real jury has a more demanding concept of "proof beyond a reasonable doubt" Cf. H. KALVEN, JR. & H. ZEISEL, THE AMERICAN JURY 182-90 (1966).

48. In the cases actually tried before a twelve-member jury, the difference between the six- and twelve-member jury fee could be made up by state subsidy or a research grant.

49. In a jurisdiction that allows majority decisions, all juries should include more than one out of six jurors who initially disagree with the majority. Ideally, the initial vote distribution should cover the entire range of possibilities including, for example, 4 to 2 (8 to 4) and 2 to 4 (4 to 8) to control for the possibility that the course of deliberations is determined by the particular position of the majority.

50. *See* H. ZEISEL, SAY IT WITH FIGURES 190-99 (5th ed. 1968).

51. 68 Cal. 2d. 319, 438 P.2d 33, 66 Cal. Rptr. 497 (1968); *see* Fairley & Mosteller, *A Conversation About Collins, supra.*

52. Occasionally the lack of standards for evaluating empirical evidence will lead not to the citation of a study but to its rejection. Thus an appellate court could excuse rejection by the trial court of such evidence as follows:

The judge determined that the elaborate statistical tables prepared from published lists by an expert for the defendants and designed to compare the compositions of the 1963 jury list, the 1963 registered voter list, and the 1963 police list did not present sufficient evidence on which to base any findings on this point. It was within his discretion not to be convinced by these tables no matter how carefully and accurately they may have been drawn as a matter of statistical analysis. In light of his extensive discussion of them in his rulings, we are unable to discern any substance to the argument that the judge dismissed them peremptorily.

Likewise, the judge acted within his discretion in refusing to admit similar tables based on interviews with persons not before the court. The defendants concede that the tables were based on hearsay evidence and can point to no statute or case in this Commonwealth requiring their admission. The fact that some commentators have recommended admission of properly conducted surveys, and that some courts in other jurisdictions have admitted them, does not mean that the judge here was in error in excluding tables based on data from a private survey specifically conducted in behalf of the defendants.

Commonwealth v. Beneficial Finance Co., 275 N.E.2d 33, 50 (Mass. 1971). I like to think that these surveys were competent evidence: I conducted them. [H.Z.]

53. *Hearings on H.R. 8285 Before the Subcomm. on Courts, Civil Liberties, and the Administration of Justice of the House Comm. on the Judiciary*, 92d Cong., 2d Sess. (January 23, 1974) [hereinafter cited as *Hearings*].

54. *See* Ziesel, *supra* note 4 at 715-20.

55. *Hearings, supra* note 53 (testimony of Charles Morgan, Jr., Executive Director, ACLU, and Nathaniel Jones, General Counsel, NAACP).

56. *See* Zeisel, *supra* note 4, at 717-18; text at notes 37-38 *supra*.

57. The claim for saving a considerable amount of time, in addition to saving juror fees, has never been substantiated or even made plausible. With voir-dire proceedings in the federal courts largely conducted by the trial judge, who addresses all jurors at the same time, there is little room for further savings. See Zeisel, *supra* note 4, at 711. The desperation of the supporters of the time-saving argument may be seen from testimony of Judge Edward T. Devitt, Chief Judge, United States District Court for Minnesota. He felt impelled to report: "Six jurors move in and out of a jury box in a shorter time than twelve." *Hearings, supra* note 53 (October 10, 1973).

11

THE EFFECTS OF JURY SIZE AND POLLING METHOD ON THE PROCESS AND PRODUCT OF JURY DELIBERATION

NORBERT L. KERR
ROBERT J. MacCOUN
Michigan State University

A number of Supreme Court rulings have focused the attention of social scientists and legal scholars on the issue of jury size. Although juries traditionally have 12 members, economic considerations have

Authors' Note: Portions of this article were presented at the annual convention of the Law and Society Association, Toronto, Canada, June 5, 1982, and the Third International Conference on Small Group Processes, Nags Head, North Carolina, June 1983. Support for this research was provided by National Institute of Mental Health Grant MH29919-01 to the first author. We would like to thank Richard Lempert, Sam Gaertner, and two anonymous reviewers for their helpful comments on an earlier draft. Requests for encouraged the use of smaller juries. In *Williams v. Florida* (1970), the Supreme Court held that there was no constitutional barrier to the use of juries with fewer than 12 members. The Court's explicit reliance on psychological reasoning had led to a number of studies to check the Court's assumptions of functional equivalence of different-sized juries (Beiser & Varrin, 1975; Bermant & Coppock, 1973; Buckhout, Weg, Reilly, & Frohboese, 1977; Davis, Kerr, Atkin, Holt, & Meek, 1975; Friedman & Shaver, 1975; Institute of Judicial Administration, 1972; Kessler, 1973; Mills, 1973; Padawer-Singer, Singer, & Singer, 1977; Roper, 1980; Saks, 1977; Valenti & Downing, 1975). Nearly all of these researchers have compared juries of 12 and 6 persons. The nearly universal finding is one of no reliable jury size effects on jury verdicts (see Hastie, Penrod, & Pennington, 1984, for a recent comprehensive review). However, some of these studies have documented several other interesting effects that were due to jury size (e.g., in participation rates, length of deliberations, recall of evidence). In addition, several theoretical analyses based on sampling theory (e.g., Lempert, 1975) have demonstrated that a reduction of jury size has an adverse effect on jury representativeness. Such findings and the vigorous objections of legal scholars (e.g., Lempert, 1975) to jury size reduction were cited by the Court in a subsequent ruling that proscribed juries with fewer than 6 persons in criminal trials (*Ballew v. Georgia*, 1978; see Saks, 1982, for an analysis of the *Ballew* ruling).

There are, however, reasons to believe that variations in jury size should have small but reliable effects on juries' verdicts. A number of formal models of jury decision making that are intuitively plausible (e.g., Grofman, 1976; Lempert, 1975; Tanford & Penrod, 1983) and have been empirically validated (e.g., Davis et al., 1975; Hastie et al., 1984) have all led to the prediction that larger juries should hang more often. With these models, one does not generally assume differences in the decision-making process for different group sizes; rather, one assumes with all models that unanimity is more likely when there is a preponderance of support in the group for one of the verdict alternatives at the beginning of deliberation, and sampling theory indicates that this is relatively more likely in smaller groups. There is some weak empirical support for the model's prediction. Zeisel (1971)

reprints should be sent to Norbert L. Kerr, Department of Psychology, Michigan State University, East Lansing, Michigan 48824-1117.

From *Journal of Personality and Social Psychology* (1985), *48*(2), 349-363. Copyright © 1985 by the American Psychological Assocation. Reprinted by permission of the publisher and authors.

reported a hung jury rate of 2.4% in a sample of 290 six-person criminal juries, slightly lower than the 5% rate observed in his national sample of 12-person juries. However, it is difficult to determine how comparable the cases and groups in these two samples really are. Padawer-Singer et al. (1977) reported that 8.7% of their 6-person mock juries hung, whereas 21.7% of their 12-person groups hung. However, these results were due entirely to the absence of any hung juries in their 6-person groups operating under a nonunanimous rule; there were no differences between the 6- and 12-person groups that were required to agree unanimously. Roper (1980) also reported a strong trend for more hung juries in 12- than in 6-person mock juries, but again the effect was not significant. None of the researchers in several other studies who examined jury size reported a reliable effect of jury size on hung jury rate (see Hastie et al., 1984, for a review). In summary, there is currently no firm empirical support for the models' prediction.

Fortunately, these models also suggest reasons why the existing research may have failed to obtain the effect. First, the effect is only predicted when cases are "close" ones—that is, when the individual juror conviction rate is near 50% (see Davis et al., 1975, Figure 1, or Tanford & Penrod, 1983, Table 1). A number of the researchers testing for jury size effects have used rather lopsided cases (e.g., Davis et al., 1975; Kessler, 1973). Second, even when the cases are very close ones, the predicted differences in hung juries tend to be fairly small. Although in a few studies reasonably large samples have been used (e.g., Davis et al., 1975), the enormous cost of using 6- and 12-person groups as replicates has generally resulted in sample sizes that are too small to test the models' prediction adequately.

A second prediction made with some of these models (e.g., Davis et al., 1975; Grofman, 1976; Tanford & Penrod, 1983) is that when cases are not close, the larger the group is, the more group deliberation will tend to polarize opinion (cf. Myers & Lamm, 1976). In general, these predicted effects are even smaller than those involving hung juries, and can be further obscured by ceiling and floor effects. Thus it is not surprising that, like the prediction on hung juries, this prediction has not been empirically confirmed.

The first objective of the present study was to provide a clearer test of these formal model predictions involving jury size. The verdicts (and especially the rate of hung juries) of 12-, 6-, and 3-person mock juries were compared.[1] The stimulus cases used in this study were carefully developed to be very close ones. The overall sample size was also quite large. We further increased the power of our tests by having each group consider several different cases, thereby increasing the reliability of the estimate of each group's tendency to hang.[2] An experimental simulation methodology was used to help avoid the confounds that have plagued field and archival studies of jury size (e.g., Institute of Judicial Administration, 1972). However, it should also be noted at the outset that statistical power and experimental control were purchased at a cost of realism. We attempted to confirm a theoretical prediction under conditions that were experimentally ideal, but highly artificial.

The use of a highly controlled method was also crucial to the study's second and chief objective: to examine certain features of the group deliberation process. We were particularly interested in examining a process issue that has figured heavily in the Court's and in modelers' reasoning about the jury size issue: How does the absolute and relative size of a faction affect its likelihood of maintaining or increasing that size? In *Williams v. Florida* (1970), the Court explicitly assumed a proportionality model, as have certain modelers. For example, according to Klevorick and Rothschild's (1979) model, juries with identical ratios of opposing factions are functionally equivalent. For example, a minority of one in a 6-person group is assumed to have the same chance of yielding to the majority as a member of a 2-person minority in a 12-person group. However, conformity research (e.g., Asch, 1956) tends to contradict such a proportionality model. Asch has shown that having some social support strongly attenuates the power of a majority. Latané's social impact theory (Latané, 1981; Latané & Wolf, 1981) makes a similar prediction. Asch's findings suggest, for example, that a minority of one in a 3-person group should be more easily influenced than a member of a 2-person minority faction in a 6-person group. Although there is much social influence research bearing indirectly on such issues (cf. Allen, 1965; Tanford & Penrod, 1984), there is very little in which these questions have been examined in the context of interacting, decision-making groups of different sizes. A study by Godwin and Restle (1974) is a noteworthy exception. They found that a model that took account of both the absolute and relative size of a faction better accounted for observed shifts in position than a model in which only the faction's relative size (i.e., relative to the opposing faction) was considered. They also found that minorities of one were particularly vulnerable to the influence of a unanimous majority. However, Godwin and Restle's task (estimating which of several stimuli another group had judged as "most out-standing") is a rather poor facsimile of the jury's task or any other common group decision task (e.g., it is unclear how persuasion might occur on Godwin and Restle's task).

Our second objective, therefore, was to examine the effect of factions' relative and absolute size on social influence in different-sized mock juries. The unit of analysis in our process analyses was the distribution or "split" of verdict preferences in the group. We examined both the likelihood of movements from initial split to final verdict (i.e., we estimated the D matrices of the Social Decision Scheme model; Davis, 1973, 1980) and the probabilities of movement between possible splits during deliberation (i.e., we estimated the T matrix transition probabilities of the Social Transition Scheme model; Kerr, 1981, 1982). Besides the validity and generality of the proportion-ality model, these analyses also allowed us to examine in the context of an interacting group a social influence question of longstanding interest (e.g., Asch, 1951; Gerard, Wilhelmy, & Conolley, 1968; Latané & Wolfe, 1981; Tanford & Penrod, 1984): the effect of the size of a unanimous majority on yielding by a minority of one. In summary, our process analyses sought to determine whether and how a group's size affects its decision-making process. Although this is an issue of particular relevance to the debate on jury size, it clearly has broader theoretical significance.

A third and final objective of this research was to examine the effect of the method a group used to poll its members on the group's final decision. Hawkins (1960) reported an association between the polling method freely chosen by his mock juries and the likelihood that the jury would hang; juries that had used a secret ballot technique were found to be more likely to hang than groups that had used public forms of polling (e.g., a show of hands). One explanation for this finding is that secret balloting made it more difficult for the majority to identify and hence pressure or persuade minority faction members. There are indications, though, that jurors are expected to state and defend their positions (e.g., Lempert, 1975), particularly when the jury is operating under a unanimity requirement. Another explanation is that the relationship is a spurious one; juries composed of or led by jurors who prefer to use a secret ballot may also act in other ways that make agreement less likely (e.g., avoiding direct and open conflict that may be necessary to achieve unanimity). This interpretation would suggest that secret polling is merely a symptom, not a cause of ineffective jury deliberation. One could even argue that open polling tends to publicly identify a juror with a particular position and to foster early and strong commitment to what may have initially been only a weak preference. This argument suggests that secret polling should lead to fewer, not more, hung juries. In any case, we would expect the effect of the method of polling to be most pronounced for larger juries deliberating close cases. In small juries considering lopsided cases, minority factions will necessarily be very small and should be easily identified, regardless of the method of polling. Because a number of close cases were considered by different-sized mock juries in this study, it was possible to test the latter prediction.

METHOD

Subjects

The subjects were 612 undergraduate students at Michigan State University who participated to earn extra credit in an introductory psychology course. Subjects were scheduled in same-sex groups approximately 20% larger than the scheduled jury size to allow for no-shows. If too many subjects came, the surplus subjects were excused; if too few subjects came, the group was run in the next smaller group-size condition. In addition, there were several regularly scheduled 6- and 3-person sessions.

Design

The basic experimental design was a 3 × 2 (3- vs. 6- vs. 12-Person Mock Juries × Open vs. Secret Polling Method) factorial. There were approximately 15 same-sex groups in each of the experimental conditions.

Materials and Equipment

Each group considered a set of nine one-page summaries of armed robbery cases, purportedly tried in San Diego, California, within the last 5 years. In fact, the cases were fictional ones that had been developed to produce nearly equal rates of conviction and acquittal by individual mock jurors from this population. Prior research with these cases (e.g., Kerr, 1981, 1982) has established that the cases are indeed close ones. Each summary consisted of two paragraphs, one summarizing the evidence for the prosecution and the other summarizing the evidence for the defense. Immediately before the start of deliberations, each group member received a folder containing all nine cases. On a cover sheet there was a summary of instructions typically provided by a judge to juries considering armed-robbery cases (e.g., a definition of armed robbery, a reminder of the presumption of innocence, a definition of the reasonable-doubt concept). The order of cases in the folder was randomized separately for each group.

Subjects recorded their predeliberation verdict preferences and any change in verdict preference occurring during deliberation by pressing one of two buttons (for guilty and not guilty) on a response panel. Each subject had one panel, and the foreperson had a second panel to indicate the group's verdict. The buttons on the response panels were interlocking: When a button was pressed it lit up as the light for the last response was extinguished; hence group members could always check their own last response with a glance at their panels. When a subject made a response, the response and the time it was made were automatically encoded and stored in the memory of a microcomputer. Because of some chronic hardware and software problems, these deliberation process data were not encoded for several groups (viz., for 7 of the 28 twelve-person groups, for 12 of the 31 six-person groups, and for 8 of the 30 three-person groups).

Subjects were seated around a large rectangular table. One seat was arbitrarily designated as the foreperson's and whichever subject took this seat served as foreperson. Low partitions separated the seating positions. They permitted group members to see and to talk to one another without obstruction but prevented observation of one another's response panels.

Procedure

Each group of 3, 6, or 12 subjects was asked to take on the role of a jury and deliberate each of the nine armed robbery cases. The use of the response panels and the procedure to be followed was then explained. After reading a case summary, subjects were to individually and privately decide how they would vote if they were on the actual jury that tried the case, and to indicate this preference on their response panels. When everyone had recorded their predeliberation verdicts for the case, the group was to begin deliberating. To enable each group to deliberate all nine cases, the groups had a maximum of 10 min to deliberate each case. The foreperson was to note the time at which deliberations began and ended and was to record these times on a supplied form. The group was to keep track of the deliberation time: A digital clock was visible to all members of the group. In addition, the experimenter would signal when 10 min had elapsed. If the group was unable to agree unanimously on a verdict within the time limit, the foreperson was to enter a verdict of hung and the group was to proceed to the next case.

The foreperson was advised to take a poll of the jury whenever necessary to check the group's progress toward unanimity. The manipulation of polling method was introduced at this point. In the open-polling groups, the foreperson was instructed to use only a show-of-hands method to poll the group. In the secret-polling condition, the foreperson was instructed to use secret written ballots for every poll of the group; ballots were supplied for this purpose.

If the group reached a unanimous verdict, the foreperson was to record it on the jury's panel, and the group was to proceed to the next case. After giving the foreperson a sheet that summarized the procedure and after answering all questions, the experimenter gave subjects their case folders and told them to read the cover sheet carefully and then to begin reading the first case. The experimenter then left and remained in a nearby room until the end of the session (except when it was necessary to tell a group that its time had elapsed on a case). When either a group had completed all nine cases or the time for the 2-hour experimental session had elapsed, groups were debriefed, thanked, and excused.

RESULTS

Deliberation Products: Verdicts

We hypothesized that the variables of jury size and polling method would exert their strongest effects when the cases were very close ones. Although the cases used here have been developed to produce individual conviction rates near 50%, in any particular experimental situation some of the cases come closer than others in achieving this (see Davis & Nagao, 1980, for an illustration of temporal drift in such parameters). In the present instance, when subjects' predeliberation verdict preferences were tallied for each case, four cases were found to have conviction rates between 35% and 65%. This set of cases were designated as the close set. The remaining five cases were designated as the clear set (although it may be noted that none of them resulted in highly lopsided conviction rates; the range in the clear set was between 32%-35% and 65%-74% guilty). In all the following product analyses, the group was the unit of analysis.

Because we were most interested in the likelihood of a hung jury, we first examined the rate at which the mock juries hung. The proportion of cases for which the group hung was computed for each mock jury for the close and clear case sets. These proportions were entered into a 3 × 2 × 2 (Group Size × Polling Condition × Case Set) least-squares repeated measures analysis of variance (ANOVA; see

Woodward & Overall, 1976).[3] Two effects were significant. First, and most important, there was a strong main effect for size, $F(2, 76) = 28.94$, $p < .001$. As the groups became smaller, the proportion of hung juries declined; the means were 12-person = 45% hung, 6-person = 28% hung, and 3-person = 9% hung. Newman-Keuls post hoc comparisons indicated that all pairwise comparisons of size conditions were significant ($p < .01$). There was also a tendency for the size effect to be stronger for the close cases than for the clear cases (e.g., the difference between 3- and 12-person groups was 44% for the close cases, but only 28% for the clear cases), but the Case Set × Size interaction was not statistically significant, $F(2, 76) = 2.72$, $p < .08$. The other significant effect was the Polling × Case Set × Group Size interaction effect, $F(2, 76) = 4.36$, $p < .025$. The means for this effect are presented in Table 1. Tests of the polling simple main effects indicated that when the cases were clear, there were no significant polling simple effects at any group size. However, when the cases were close, the polling simple effect was significant ($p < .05$) at every group size. For these cases, the 3-person groups revealed an effect similar to that obtained by Hawkins (1960): Hanging was less likely when polling was public. However, when the groups were larger the direction of the polling effect was opposite to that obtained by Hawkins: Public polling tended to increase rather than decrease the likelihood of a hung jury.

To examine the effect of jury size and polling method on the verdict reached by those juries that did not hang, we considered only the cases in which a group reached a verdict. For each group the conviction rates among close and among clear cases were computed. The few groups that failed to reach a verdict on any case within a case set were dropped from this analysis. These data were analyzed in a 3 × 2 × 2 (Group Size × Polling Method × Case Set) least-squares repeated measures ANOVA. The only significant effect was the main effect for case set, $F(1, 72) = 6.7$, $p < .05$; convictions were more likely in the clear (58%) than the close set (47%). Because four of the five clear cases tended to favor conviction (i.e., individual conviction rates $> 65\%$), this effect is neither surprising nor especially interesting. It is interesting to note, however, that mock jury size did not affect the relative likelihood of conviction versus acquittal, a pattern obtained in nearly all previous work.[4]

We also checked to see whether jury size or polling method had any effect on the degree of polarization produced by group deliberation (cf. Myers & Lamm, 1976). Again, certain formal models (e.g., Davis et al., 1975; Grofman, 1976; Tanford & Penrod, 1983) predict that the larger the group is, the more the initially preferred alternative will gain

TABLE 11.1
Effect of Polling × Size × Case Set on Hung Juries

Case set/Jury size	Polling method	
	Open	Secret
Close		
12	.56	.45
6	.42	.17
3	.02	.13
Clear		
12	.40	.42
6	.27	.21
3	.13	.08

Note: Values represent the mean proportion of deliberations resulting in a hung jury, averaged within groups.

in popularity as a result of group deliberation. This means, for example, that for a case on which individual jurors tended to favor conviction, the larger the jury is, the stronger this tendency to convict should be among juries. In order to test this conjecture, group verdicts were reclassified as either the same or opposite from the modal individual verdict preference; a group verdict that agreed with the individual preference was classified as a "polarized" verdict. Within each case set and group we calculated the proportion of all reached verdicts that were polarized verdicts. This variable was entered into a 3 × 2 × 2 (Group Size × Polling Method × Case Set) least-squares repeated measures ANOVA. Unsurprisingly, the clear cases were less likely to result in a reversal of the normative preference, $F(1, 72) = 46.6, p < .001$. There were no other significant effects. In particular, jury size was not significantly associated with this index of group polarization: Size, $F(2, 72) = 1.2, ns$; Size × Case Set, $F(2, 72) = 1.9, p > .10$.

In summary, the results were consistent with most previous research: When the mock jury was able to reach a verdict, the group's size had no significant effect on what that verdict was, nor did the method of polling. The analyses of the verdict product data clearly confirm the prediction that jury size and polling method do not materially affect what verdict is reached but can affect the likelihood that any unanimous decision will be reached. The latter finding represents the strongest empirical evidence to date that reductions in group size will increase the likelihood that the group will reach consensus.

Deliberation Products: Deliberation Time

We first computed the mean time each group spent per close case and per clear case, regardless of the initial split or jury verdict. A $3 \times 2 \times 2$ (Group Size $\times$ Polling Method $\times$ Case Set) least-squares repeated measures ANOVA yielded three significant effects. Unsurprisingly, it took significantly more time for groups to agree on the close cases than on the clear cases, $F(1, 71) = 6.5$, $p < .001$. There was also a significant three-way interaction effect, $F(2, 71) = 4.0$, $p < .05$. The polling effect was negligible in every condition but the 6-person clear-case condition, in which secretly polled groups took considerably longer to reach their verdicts. The result of primary interest was the group size main effect, $F(2, 71) = 22.45$, $p < .001$. As the hung jury data suggests, the larger the group was, the longer the group tended to take. Means were 3-persons = 167.2 s, 6-person = 321.8 s, and 12-person = 350.3 s. When interpreting these means, one should keep in mind that they reflect all deliberations, including initially unanimous groups that should have taken only a few seconds to reach a verdict. If the groups that were initially unanimous are dropped from the preceding analysis, the mean deliberation times naturally increase (3-person = 238.8 s, 6-person = 357.0 s, 12-person = 366.3 s). In this subsample, only the main effects were significant. Larger (i.e., 6- and 12-person) groups deliberated longer ($p < .001$); groups took longer to deliberate the close cases ($p < .05$); and groups deliberated longer under secret polling ($p < .01$). The latter effect may just reflect the extra time required to collect secret written ballots.

Deliberation Process: Initial Split
to Final Outcome Frequencies

One way of concisely summarizing the deliberation process is to determine the likelihood of groups moving from each possible beginning distribution of opinion to each possible outcome (viz., convict, acquit, or hung jury). In effect, this estimates the applicable social decision scheme matrix, D; see Davis (1973, 1980) and Kerr, Stasser, and Davis (1979). These data are presented in Table 2. The one pattern that is immediately evident is that, as sampling theory requires, the smaller the group is, the greater is the proportion of groups beginning deliberation at or near unanimity. For example, there were no 12-person groups beginning deliberation with a 0-guilty-to-12-not-guilty split, whereas there were 4 six-person and 24 three-person groups with initial unanimity for acquittal.

Several log-linear analyses were performed on these data.[5] First, the comparable rows (viz., those with initial ratios of convictors to

TABLE 11.2

Preliberation Distribution to Final Outcome Frequencies

% for conviction	12-person jury				6-person jury				3-person jury			
	Initial split	Outcome			Initial split	Outcome			Initial split	Outcome		
		C	A	H		C	A	H		C	A	H
100	12–0	14	0	0	6–0	16	0	0	3–0	49	0	0
92	11–1	16	0	0								
83	10–2	6	0	5	5–1	26	0	6				
75	9–3	10	0	15								
67	8–4	5	3	9	4–2	12	10	16	2–1	38	11	11
58	7–5	2	4	16								
50	6–6	1	9	13	3–3	3	13	12				
42	5–7	1	9	5								
33	4–8	0	7	5	2–4	0	21	4	1–2	5	38	6
25	3–9	0	3	0								
17	2–10	0	5	0	1–5	0	17	2				
8	1–11	0	4	0								
0	0–12	—	—	—	0–6	0	3	0	0–3	0	24	0

Note: C = convict, A = acquit, H = hung jury. In the "initial split" columns the first number in each pair = number of votes for conviction; second number = number of votes for acquittal.

acquitters of 2:1 and 1:2) were contrasted across the three group size conditions; that is, a $2 \times 3 \times 3$ (Ratio $\times$ Outcome $\times$ Group Size) contingency table was analyzed. There was a strong association of size with verdict, $\chi^2(4, N = 201) = 21.9, p < .01, \tau = .07$.[6] This effect was due to differences between the 3-person groups and the larger groups; analyses in which we compared the 6- and 12-person groups only produced no such effect, $\chi^2(2, N = 92) = 3.1, ns$. Inspection of Table 2 suggests that the 3-person groups were both less likely to hang and more likely to convict than the larger groups. Collapsing the convict and acquit categories resulted in a $2 \times 2 \times 3$ (Ratio $\times$ Outcome $\times$ Group Size) contingency table. Log-linear analysis resulted in a significant Size $\times$ Outcome association, $\chi^2(2, N = 201) = 14.1, p < .01, \tau = .08$, confirming that the overall effect was due, at least in part, to the lower probability of a hung jury in the 3-person groups. Dropping the hung-jury outcomes from the original contingency table resulted in a $2 \times 2 \times 3$ (Ratio $\times$ Outcome $\times$ Size) table. Analysis of this table also produced a significant Size $\times$ Outcome association, $\chi^2(2, N = 150) = 7.0, p < .05, \tau = .05$. Thus part of the overall effect was also attributable to the greater likelihood of conviction in the 3-person groups.

The near equivalence of 6- and 12-person groups' initial split to final outcome probabilities was corroborated by an analysis of the five rows for which the (nonunanimous) initial splits are in the same ratios (viz., 5:1, 4:2, 3:3, 2:4, 1:5). Although there was a tendency for the 12-person groups to be more likely to hang, the Size $\times$ Outcome association was not significant, $\chi^2(2, N = 210) = 4.99$, $p < .10$. None of the separate comparisons within each row yielded a significant size effect.

The earlier analyses of the verdict data showed a steady increase in the likelihood of a hung jury as group size increased. The present analysis suggests that this effect does not reflect process differences between the 6- and 12-person groups. Twelve- and 6-person groups beginning with comparable distributions of verdict preferences (i.e., in the same ratio) had statistically indistinguishable outcome probabilities. Thus the substantial difference in hung-jury rates for 6- and 12-person groups was due to differences in the distribution of starting splits, not to differences in their decision-making processes.

This equivalence breaks down, though, when we include 3-person groups in the analysis. Three-person groups beginning with verdict splits comparable (i.e., proportional) to the larger groups' had markedly different final verdict distributions; they were generally less likely to hang, were more likely to convict when the majority favored conviction, and were less likely to acquit when the majority favored acquittal. Altogether, these findings suggest genuine process differences between the 3-person groups and the larger groups (cf. Penrod & Hastie's 1980 analysis for nonunanimous juries). The following analyses also support this conclusion.

Deliberation Process: Transition Frequencies

The frequencies with which groups moved between adjacent "states" (i.e., distributions of verdict preferences) were tallied. In effect, this is an estimate of the applicable social transition scheme matrix, T (see Kerr, 1981, 1982). These data appear in Table 3. The rows of this table represent a group's verdict split before a member shifted positions, and the columns represent the two possible directions of movement. So, for example, there were 34 instances in which a member of a group with a 10-guilty-to-2-not-guilty (10G-2NG) split of opinion changed position. In 4 of those 34 instances, the shift served to reduce the number of jurors supporting conviction (G↓); that is, one of the members of the majority defected and the group went from 10G-2NG to 9G-3NG. In the other 30 instances, the shift served to increase the number supporting conviction (G↑); that is, one of the two minority-faction members joined the majority, and the group went from 10G-2NG to 11G-1NG.

One reasonable basis for comparison of the decision-making process in the different size groups is to examine the relative "attractiveness" (i.e., power to attract converts) of factions of the same relative size (i.e., relative to the opposing faction). In the present

TABLE 11.3
Observed Transition Frequencies

% for conviction	12-person jury			6-person jury			3-person jury		
	Pre-shift distribution	Shift G↓	Shift G↑	Pre-shift distribution	Shift G↓	Shift G↑	Pre-shift distribution	Shift G↓	Shift G↑
100	12–0	2	—	6–0	0	—	3–0	1	—
92	11–1	3	41						
83	10–2	4	30	5–1	4	41			
75	9–3	9	25						
67	8–4	15	16	4–2	22	16	2–1	11	43
58	7–5	21	15						
50	6–6	29	11	3–3	37	8			
42	5–7	40	8						
33	4–8	46	7	2–4	48	7	1–2	49	4
25	3–9	43	2						
17	2–10	41	1	1–5	63	0			
8	1–11	43	0						
0	0–12	—	0	0–6	—	1	0–3	—	0

Note: G↓ = shift of position reducing the number of guilty votes; G↑ = shift of position increasing the number of guilty votes. In the "Pre-shift distribution" columns, the first number in each pair = number of votes for conviction; the second number = number of votes for acquittal.

instance, there were two proportional splits that could be compared across all three group sizes, namely, the 2:1 and 1:2 ratios of guilty to not-guilty voters. The corresponding entries in Table 3 can be viewed as a Ratio (2:1 vs. 1:2) × Direction of Movement (G↑ vs. G↓) × Size (3-, 6-, and 12-person group) contingency table. Applying a log-linear analysis to this table resulted in a significant Size × Direction effect, $\chi^2(2, N = 284) = 6.7, p < .05, \tau = .08$, qualified by a significant three-way association effect, $\chi^2(2, N = 284) = 9.7, p < .01$, indicating that the likelihood of transitions to and from factions depends not only on their relative sizes but also on the overall group size. Inspection of Table 3 suggests that this effect was primarily attributable to the 3-person group with the 2:1 ratio. Additional log-linear analyses confirmed this. An analysis based on only the 2:1 row produced a significant Size × Direction effect, $\chi^2(2, N = 123) = 15.27, p < .01, = .12$; this effect vanished, $\chi^2(1, N = 69) = .6$, when one dropped the 3-person groups from the analysis. A similar analysis based on only the 1:2 row produced no Size × Direction effect, $\chi^2(2, N = 161) = 1.1, ns$.

In the 2:1 ratio row, the majority for conviction was much more successful in attracting a minority member in the 3-person groups than in either the 6- or 12-person groups. In fact, in these larger groups, the minority position was as or more likely to gain a convert as the majority position was. This pattern clearly did not hold in the 1:2 ratio row, in which—regardless of group size—the majority of acquitters exhibited much greater drawing power than the minority of convictors. (This asymmetry in the drawing power of proconviction vs. proacquittal factions has been repeatedly observed in jury research. It is most clearly evident here in the 50% row of Table 3. See Stasser, Kerr, & Bray, 1982, for a review and discussion of this leniency bias.)

As the preceding analyses show, the 6- and 12-person groups appear to satisfy the proportionality rule fairly well. We further substantiated this conclusion by comparing transition frequencies for all the comparable splits in 6- and 12-person groups. There are five such ratios: 5:1, 2:1, 1:1, 1:2, and 1:5. Analysis of the $5 \times 2 \times 2$ (Ratio $\times$ Direction of Movement $\times$ Size) contingency table resulted in no size effects: Size $\times$ Direction, $\chi^2(1, N = 446) = .83$, *ns.*, and Size $\times$ Direction $\times$ Ratio $\chi^2(4, N = 446) = 1.12$, *ns.* Altogether, these analyses indicate that a proportionality model that assumes equal attractiveness of equal ratios fits the 6- and 12-person groups, but breaks down when we include the smaller, 3-person groups, for which minorities are necessarily minorities of one.

A second reasonable basis for comparison—suggested by intuition, by Asch's conformity research, and by Godwin and Restle's (1974) study of decision-making groups—is between splits in which a minority of one is opposed by a unanimous majority. There has been some controversy about the nature of the functional relation between the size of a unanimous majority and yielding to that majority (Asch, 1951; Gerard et al., 1968; Latané & Wolf, 1981). In previous studies conformity paradigms have been used; this study permits examination of the same question in the context of an interacting, decision-making group. Therefore, the transition frequencies for the $(n - 1)$G-1NG (where n = group size) and the 1G-$(n-1)$NG splits were compared across group sizes. Analyses of the $2 \times 2 \times 3$ (Unanimous Majority for Conviction vs. Acquittal $\times$ Direction of Movement $\times$ 3 Group Size) contingency table resulted in a significant three-way association, $\chi^2(2, N = 302) = 13.1$, $p < .01$. As Table 3 indicates, the minority of one was more successful at attracting a convert from the unanimous majority in the 3-person group than in either of the larger groups. Again, comparisons of 6- with 12-person groups resulted in no such effect, $\chi^2(1, N = 195) = .004$, *ns.*

In summary, by comparison with similar factions in 6- and 12-person groups, a minority (necessarily of one) in a 3-person group is somewhat less able to win converts than minority factions of the same proportional size in the larger groups, but somewhat more able to win converts than minority factions of the same absolute size in the larger groups.

Deliberation Process: Time to Shift

A previous analysis suggested that larger groups took more time to deliberate. The question we address here is whether this was due to process differences in the rate of movement toward consensus. But first, it is of interest to reexamine total deliberation time. We have seen that small groups are more likely to be near or at unanimity at the outset of group deliberation. This could account for the shorter deliberation times of the smaller groups. To explore this possibility, we performed a regression analysis on the juries' deliberation times. The study's two main independent variables (group size and polling method) were dummy coded as predictor variables. In addition, two other predictor variables were defined. The first indexed how sharply divided the group was at the beginning of deliberation. It was defined as EXTDEV $= |(\#G)/(\#NG) - .5|$, where $\#G$ = the number of votes for a guilty verdict before deliberations, and $\#NG$ = the number of votes for a not-guilty verdict. The second predictor was closely related but conceptually distinct. It was the minimum number of verdict changes required for the group to achieve unanimity (termed NTU, or number to unanimity). These predictor variables and all possible interaction terms were entered into a standard regression analysis in order to predict deliberation times for each jury on each case. This analysis produced only one significant predictor, EXTDEV $F(1, 703) = 13.6, p <$ .001. The more even the initial split in the group, the longer the group deliberated. But when one controlled for group size differences in this variable, and in the related NTU variable, group size per se did not affect deliberation time.

More direct analyses of group process were then performed. As with the previous process analyses, we first compared groups with identical ratios of convictors to acquitters. In the earlier analyses we asked whether the direction of vote shifts varied with group size. Here we asked whether the speed of shifts varied with group size. The time required for the next shift was analyzed in a $2 \times 2 \times 2$ (Ratio, 2:1 vs. 1:2 $\times$ Size $\times$ Polling Method) least-squares ANOVA. Two effects were significant: size $F(2, 266) = 6.5, p < .01$; and ratio, $F(1, 26) = 7.1, p < .01$. Shifts were more rapid when the groups were larger (3-person = 162.7 s, 6-person = 154.1 s, and 12-person = 89.8 s) and when the majority favored acquittal (2:1 ratio = 167.7 s, 1:2 ratio = 114.7 s). These effects were spurious, however. Kerr (1981) showed that a group's first shift in opinion was slower than later shifts, all else being equal. In the present study, smaller groups tended to have had fewer shifts preceding the shift out of the 2:1 or 1:2 state (largely because, as we have already shown, smaller groups are more likely to *begin* deliberation with an

extreme split). Likewise, because of the leniency bias in jury deliberation, groups with nearly even initial splits were more likely to move
toward acquittal than conviction and, therefore, groups in a 1:2 ratio
were more likely to have had a previous shift than groups in a 2:1 ratio.
A simple way to remove these confounds was to examine groups' first
shift only. An ANOVA like the previous one was performed on this
subsample. It produced no significant effects. Thus in terms of the time
taken to produce a shift, a proportionality rule seemed to apply.

We performed a final analysis to see whether the time to shift out of
the minority of one split depended on the size of the unanimous
majority. A $2 \times 2 \times 3$ (Unanimous Majority for Conviction vs. Acquittal
$\times$ Polling Method $\times$ Size) ANOVA resulted in an affirmative answer,
even when only first shifts were examined ($p < .01$; 11-person majority
= 97.6 s, 5-person majority = 158.4 s, and 2-person majority = 175.2 s).

DISCUSSION

Products of Deliberation

The prediction that the rate of hung juries would increase with
mock jury size was confirmed. The effect was not entirely attributable
to a low rate of hung juries in the 3-person groups; the 6- and 12-
person groups also differed strongly and significantly. This is, to our
knowledge, the first of many field and experimental simulation studies
of jury size that has demonstrated a significant positive relation
between jury size and the rate of hung juries.

Of course, because this was only a simulation of the jury's task,
considerable caution must be exercised in generalizing these findings
to actual jury behavior. Like the majority of juror/jury studies, the
present simulation was artificial in many ways (see Bray & Kerr, 1982).
In order to have enough data to fairly test the models' prediction and
to undertake the process analyses of interest, it was essential that a very
large number of deliberations be observed at each group size. This
made it infeasible to present each group with a single case of realistic
length and detail and to impose no time limit on group deliberation.
An efficient alternative was to have each group deliberate several
different cases. This required that the case materials be brief and that
deliberation time be limited.

Of the several differences between actual juries and our laboratory
groups, the imposition of the 10-min time limit may raise the most
important ecological validity questions. Although the deliberation

time of actual juries is not limitless, it is rarely as short as (and is never restricted to) the interval imposed in the present experiment. Both intuition and research (Kerr, 1981) suggest that giving juries less time to deliberate makes it more difficult for them to reach consensus. So it seems probable that the overall rate of hung juries would have been lower had there been no time limits. Time limits also seem likely to create a greater impediment to unanimous agreement in larger groups. Any time limit leaves less time per member to speak in a larger group. With less speaking time per member, larger groups may have more trouble accumulating the preponderance of verbal support that has been linked to group consensus (Hoffman, 1979). Furthermore larger groups are likely to face greater problems of coordination (Steiner, 1972), such as managing speaking orders, avoiding interruptions, and so on, especially when time is limited. Such coordination problems would tend to make it harder for larger groups to complete the task of reaching agreement. All these considerations suggest that short time limits tend to make it particularly hard for larger groups to reach agreement.

We now know that larger groups are less likely to begin deliberation at or near unanimity. Or, as Roper (1980) puts it, larger groups are relatively more likely to have "viable minorities." We also know from a great deal of research on mock juries (e.g., Davis, 1980; Stasser et al., 1982) and actual juries (Kalven & Zeisel, 1966) that the further a jury is from unanimity, the more likely it is to hang. Together, these facts strongly imply that larger juries should hang more often, especially for very close cases. The present study confirms this prediction for mock juries with rather limited deliberation times. The unresolved question is whether this effect will also obtain in actual juries, who operate without effective time limit. (Of course, we should not forget that many if not most decision-making groups do operate under time pressures and time limits. The time limit of the present study poses less of an ecological validity concern for this large and interesting class of groups.)

The generalizability question is, of course, an empirical issue that cannot be resolved without additional research. Unfortunately, the crucial experiment is exorbitantly expensive (requiring many larger groups that deliberate without time limit). Two alternative approaches to the generalizability question may be noted. First, it should be possible to do more careful field research on the effects of jury size, particularly because the use of juries with fewer than 12 members is becoming more commonplace. Second, theory and research on the causes of jury hanging would help us to evaluate the relevance of deliberation time limits. For example, if juries hang largely out of fatigue, then very short time limits may strongly distort results. However, if hanging is largely due to the presence of intransigent, uncompromising jurors (cf. Tanford & Penrod, 1983), then larger groups should be more likely to hang whether or not deliberation time is limited.

Disregarding hung juries, group size had no effect on the relative likelihood of conviction or acquittal. It would be misleading to conclude from this finding that the use of smaller juries results in no net pro- or antidefendant bias. A hung jury is a relatively favorable outcome for a defendant (cf. Kerr et al., 1976; Lempert, 1975). It may prompt the dropping of charges, may lead to renewed plea bargaining, and always offers the possibility of acquittal upon retrial. Thus although the use of smaller juries may result in certain economies, by reducing the odds of a hung jury it may do so at the defendant's expense.

There were two other results of interest involving size and deliberation products. Smaller juries required shorter deliberation times, even when hung juries were excluded from the analysis. This replicates a finding of several earlier studies (e.g., Friedman & Shaver, 1975; Padawer-Singer et al., 1977). However, if one controls for size effects on initial splits, size did not affect deliberation time. Second, group polarization was not detectably stronger in the larger groups, as some formal models have predicted. However, the models also predict that this effect should be very small, particularly for very close cases, such as those used here.

Process of Deliberation

Examination of the deliberation process revealed no differences between 6- and 12-person groups. The estimated decision schemes and transition schemes (Tables 2 and 3, respectively) indicated that movement between states and to a final verdict were highly similar for those two conditions. For example, factions of the same relative size were equally able to attract converts and to ultimately prevail in 6- and 12-person groups. Also, the time required for a shift was the same for comparable 6- and 12-person groups. These findings reinforce the conclusion that the lower likelihood of a hung jury in the 6-person group did not stem from deliberation process differences between 6- and 12-person groups, but rather stemmed from the greater probability that the group was at or near unanimity at the outset of deliberations for the smaller groups (cf. Grofman, 1976; Padawer-Singer et al., 1977).

But as we consider still smaller groups, certain process differences did begin to emerge from the transition data. The proportionality model broke down for 3-person groups. For example, when there was a 2:1 ratio of convictors to acquitters, the majority faction was relatively more likely to attract a convert in the 3-person groups than in the two larger group sizes. In essence, a minority for acquittal had less influence in the 3-person group than in the larger groups. This can be most plausibly attributed to the lack of social support for minority members of 3-person groups. Asch (1951) has demonstrated the importance of social support for resisting a majority in a conformity situation; in this experiment we find a similar pattern within interacting decision-making groups.

We also observed in group decision-making context what Asch (1956) and Gerard et al. (1968) have observed in conformity paradigms: As the size of a unanimous majority increases, the likelihood of a minority-of-one yielding increases. Just as in Asch's experiments, yielding to a majority appeared to level off at higher group sizes. In our study, however, floor and ceiling effects may have had more to do with this leveling off than the psychological equivalence of unanimous majorities of three or more. In addition, we found that shifts occurred faster as the size of the majority faced by a minority of one increased.

We might note several implications of these findings. First, quite apart from other relevant concerns about jury size (e.g., representativeness), our results tend to support the Supreme Court's assumption of process equivalence between 6- and 12-person groups, although they are at odds with the Court's assumption of outcome equivalence (if we may consider a hung jury an outcome). They also tend to support the general conclusion of Ballew v. Georgia (1978) that juries may not continue to shrink in size much below 6 without somewhat different group dynamics coming into play. However, whether the effects reported here enhance or corrupt the jury's functioning is ultimately not an empirical question, but a matter of weighing competing sociolegal values. Finally, these results are of particular relevance for those attempting to develop formal models of the jury decision-making process (e.g., Davis, 1973, 1980; Grofman, 1976; Klevorick & Rothschild, 1979; Penrod & Hastie, 1979). Like Godwin and Restle's (1974), our results strongly suggest that a complete model must take both the relative and absolute size of a faction into account when attempting to estimate its power to attract converts, particularly in smaller groups. On the other hand, even though they were reliable, the size effects on deliberation process were fairly weak. This suggests that a model that assumed proportionality would not predict much more poorly than one that did not.

Method of Polling

The method used to poll the jury was also found to significantly affect the likelihood of hung juries for close cases. In a correlational study, Hawkins (1960) found that 12-person mock juries that used a secret ballot tended to hang more often than those that did not. However, in the present experimental study, exactly the opposite effect was found, at least for the 6-and 12-person groups considering close cases. Under these conditions, secret balloting significantly reduced the likelihood of hanging.

Hastie et al. (1984) have recently suggested that juries adopt one of two distinct styles of deliberation. In *verdict-driven* deliberations, jurors quickly align in factions and jurors become committed advocates of their positions. In *evidence-driven* juries, jurors tend to review and evaluate the trial evidence in a more impartial and accommodative fashion. Hastie et al. suggest that early public ballots tend to encourage verdict-driven deliberations. Their data also suggested that this style was more likely to produce a hung jury. Our results for the larger groups are entirely consistent with this analysis. Being publicly identified with a position may force early commitment to that position and make it difficult to change one's position without appearing inconsistent or irresolute. The result is a verdict-driven deliberation and, commonly, a hung jury. But if one can avoid making a clear public commitment to a position, it should be easier to switch sides and hence easier for the group to reach consensus. Whenever one is likely to be part of a small minority, it may be difficult to avoid public disclosure of one's preference regardless of the polling procedure, but when the opposing factions are both fairly large, a juror may be able to avoid commitment until the stronger position becomes evident. And one would expect two large opposing factions to result most often when the group is large and the case is close. Of course, these were exactly the conditions under which secret balloting discouraged hanging. These findings suggest that the correlation reported by Hawkins (1960) may have been spurious. Juries (or, perhaps, just forepersons) predisposed to avoid the open conflict necessary to achieve consensus may have preferred the secret ballot technique. Thus in Hawkins's study, secret balloting may have been an effect rather than a cause of an inability to reach agreement.

The only other effect of polling method was an effect like Hawkins's in the 3-person groups considering close cases. We have no compelling explanation of this effect.[7] Although the polling effect in the 3-person groups is theoretically intriguing, because most juries now have a minimum size of 6, it is the larger groups' polling effect that has greater practical significance for actual juries. It seems most relevant to foreperson behavior, because she or he would probably have the greatest influence on such procedural matters as polling. The present findings suggest that under the appropriate condition (viz., when the case is a very close one), the jury foreperson's choice of a secret balloting technique can help reduce the risk of a hung jury. Of course, the relevance of these polling effects, like the size effects, for actual jury behavior must still be demonstrated empirically in future research.

NOTES

1. As noted, the *Ballew v. Georgia* (1978) decision has barred reduction of jury size below 6 persons for criminal trials. However, states may still use juries with fewer than 6 persons for civil trials. Thus the study of 3-person groups is not only of theoretical interest, but also of some interest for jury applications.

2. At each group size our design called for over 250 verdicts to be reached. With an alpha of .05, Cohen (1977, chap. 6) suggests that a sample of this size would detect a "small" difference in proportions (viz., an effect size = h = .20) with a probability of .83. For purposes of comparison, Davis, Stasser, Spitzer, and Holt's (1976) model predicts that for perfectly balanced cases, the effect size for comparing 6- and 12-person juries would be approximately .75. (A comparison of 12- and 3-person groups would produce an even larger effect.) A sample of 250 observations would have power in excess of .99 to detect an effect of this magnitude. Thus the proposed design should have sufficient power to detect the predicted effect in hung jury rates, assuming the cases are very close ones.

3. In a preliminary analysis of rates of hanging and convicting, juror sex was also included as a factor. Sex entered into no significant interactions with the primary independent variables, jury size and polling method. In light of these results and Kerr's (1981) finding of no deliberation process differences between male and female mock juries, juror sex was not examined further.

4. In one study, Valenti and Downing (1975) reported that their 6-person groups were significantly more likely to convict than their 12-person groups when the case against the defendant was strong. However, it was later discovered (e.g., Saks, 1977) that random assignment had failed to equate conditions before deliberation and that, when allowance was made for this, the reported size effect was eliminated.

5. In this analysis the unit of analysis was the group verdict. In the following process analyses of shifts between states, the unit of analysis is a shift by a group member. Statistically, this means that we have assumed that each verdict (or shift) is an independent event. Of course, because each group considered several cases, the same group produced several verdicts. Likewise, the same kind of shift was sometimes made more than once by a single group (either on different cases or, infrequently, on the same case). The reason for making these assumptions was that parameter estimation and statistical inference would have effectively been impossible for several of the questions of interest had we followed the standard practice of using the group as the unit of analysis. If only one observation per group were permitted, it is clear that the reliable estimates of the applicable social decision schemes (Table 2) or social transaction schemes (Table 3) could not have been obtained. The only other alternative—obtaining

sufficiently many observations from each group to estimate the complete matrix for each group—was equally impractical. Because of such problems, the use of the shift as the unit of analysis has been standard practice in research of this type. Statistical analyses of all previous applications of similar stochastic process models (e.g., Davis et al., 1976; Godwin & Restle, 1974) have made such assumptions, either explicitly or implicitly.

6. See Bishop, Fienberg, and Holland (1975) for a description of the τ statistic, which indexes strength of association.

7. There should have been little difficulty identifying a minority member in these small groups; so there should have been little anonymity to be gained through secret balloting. On very close cases, every juror has only a weak preference of one alternative over the other. Perhaps under secret polling, the difficulty of choosing between the verdict alternatives, and the risk that one could become a minority of one, is made more salient as one personally debates how to mark one's ballot. Such considerations might temper the majority faction's determination to advocate their verdict preference, which would improve the probability of a hung jury. But under open polling, the lack of social support may make yielding to the other, narrowly rejected position an easy choice for a minority of one. The latter reasoning would also seem to suggest very low rates of hanging in the corresponding (i.e., 3-person, open-polling) clear-case condition; but there was no polling effect in this condition (see Table 1). Perhaps with fairly clear cases one is more likely to find oneself in the minority position as a result of carelessness (e.g., missing or misinterpreting significant facts) rather than as a result of careful reasoning (which recommends the majority position for a truly clear case). When being in the minority is a result of carelessness, it may be preferable to defend one's ill-advised choice rather than to reveal that one had failed to discern the "obvious" choice.

REFERENCES

Allen, V. (1965). Situational factors in conformity. In L. Berkowitz (Ed.), *Advances in experimental social psychology* (Vol. 2, pp. 133-176). New York: Academic Press.

Asch, S. E. (1951). Effects of group pressure upon the modification and distortion of judgments. In H. Guetzkow (Ed.), *Groups, leadership and men.* Pittsburgh: Carnegie Press.

Asch, S. E. (1956). Studies of independence and submission to group pressure: I. On minority of one against a unanimous majority. *Psychological Monographs, 70* (9, Whole No. 417).

Ballew v. Georgia 435 U.S. 223 (1978).

Beiser, E., & Varrin, R. (1975). Six-member juries in the federal courts. *Judicature, 58,* 423-433.

Bermant, G., & Coppock, R. (1973). Outcomes of six- and twelve-member jury trials: An analysis of 128 civil cases in the State of Washington. *Washington Law Review, 48,* 593-596.

Bishop, Y., Fienberg, S., & Holland, P. (1975). *Discrete multivariate analysis: Theory and practice.* Cambridge, MA: MIT Press.

Bray, R. M., & Kerr, N. L. (1982). Methodological considerations in the study of the psychology of the courtroom. In N. Kerr & R. Bray (Eds.), *The psychology of the courtroom* (pp. 287-323). New York: Academic Press.

Buckhout, R., Weg, S., Reilly, V., & Frohboese, R. (1977). Jury verdicts: Comparison of 6- and 12-person juries and unanimous vs. majority decision rule in a murder trial. *Bulletin of the Psychonomic Society, 10,* 175-178.

Cohen, J. (1977). *Statistical power analysis for the behavioral science* (rev. ed.). New York: Academic Press.

Davis, J. H. (1973). Group decision and social interaction: A theory of social decision schemes. *Psychological Review, 80,* 97-125.

Davis, J. H. (1980). Group decision and procedural justice. In M. Fishbein (Ed.), *Progress in social psychology* (pp. 157-229). Hillsdale, NJ: Erlbaum.

Davis, J. H., Kerr, N. L., Atkin, R. S., Holt, R., & Meek, D. (1975). The decision processes of 6-and 12-person juries assigned unanimous and two-thirds majority rules. *Journal of Personality and Social Psychology, 32,* 1-14.

Davis, J. H., & Nagao, D. (1980). Some implications of temporal drift in social parameters. *Journal of Experimental Social Psychology, 16,* 479-496.

Davis, J. H., Stasser, G., Spitzer, C. E., & Holt, R. W. (1976). Changes in group members' decision preferences during discussion: An illustration with mock juries. *Journal of Personality and Social Psychology, 34,* 1177-1187.

Friedman, H., & Shaver, K. (1975). *The effect of jury deliberations and decisions in mock criminal cases of 6- and 12-member juries and of unanimous and nonunanimous verdict requirements.* Unpublished manuscript, College of William and Mary, Williamsburg, VA.

Gerard, H., Wilhelmy, R., & Conolley, E. (1968). Conformity and group size. *Journal of Personality and Social Psychology, 8,* 79-82.

Godwin, F., & Restle, F. (1974). The road to agreement: Subgroup pressures in small group consensus processes. *Journal of Personality and Social Psychology, 30,* 500-509.

Grofman, B. (1976).Not necessarily twelve and not necessarily unanimous. In G. Bermant, C. Nemeth, & N. Vidmar (Eds.), *Psychology and the law* (pp. 149-168). Lexington, MA: D. C. Heath.

Hastie, R., Penrod, S., & Pennington, N. (1984). *Inside the jury.* Cambridge, MA: Harvard University Press.

Hawkins, C. H. (1960). *Interaction and coalition realignments in consensus seeking groups: A study of experimental jury deliberations.* Unpublished doctoral dissertation, Department of Sociology, University of Chicago.

Hoffman, L. R. (1979). *The group problem solving process: Studies of a valence model.* New York: Praeger.

Institute of Judicial Administration (1972). *A comparison of six- and twelve-member juries in New Jersey superior and county courts.* New York: Author.

Kalven, H., & Zeisel, H. (1966). *The American jury.* Boston: Little, Brown.

Kerr, N. L. (1981). Social transition schemes: Charting the group's road to agreement. *Journal of Personality and Social Psychology, 41,* 684-702.

Kerr, N. L. (1982). Social transition schemes: Model, method, and applications. In H. Bradstatter, J. H. Davis, & G. Stocker-Kreichgauer (Eds.), *Group decision making* (pp. 59-80). London: Academic Press.

Kerr, N. L., Atkin, R., Stasser, G., Meek, D., Holt, R., & Davis, J. H. (1976). Guilt beyond a reasonable doubt: Effects of concept definition and assigned decision rule on the judgments of mock jurors. *Journal of Personality and Social Psychology, 34,* 282-294.

Kerr, N. L., Stasser, G., & Davis, J. H. (1979). Model-testing, model-fitting, and social decision schemes. *Organizational Behavior and Human Performance, 23,* 339-410.

Kessler, J. B. (1973). An empirical study of six- and twelve-member jury decision-making processes. *University of Michigan Journal of Law Reform, 6,* 712-734.

Klevorick, A, & Rothschild, M. (1979). A model of the jury decision process. *Journal of Legal Studies, 8,* 141-161.

Latané, B. (1981). Psychology of social impact. *American Psychologist, 36,* 343-356.

Latané, B., & Wolf, S. (1981). The social impact of majorities and minorities. *Psychological Review, 88,* 438-453.

Lempert, R. O. (1975) Uncovering "nondiscernible" differences: Empirical research and the jury-size cases. *Michigan Law Review, 73,* 643-708.

Mills, L. R. (1973). Six-member and twelve-member juries: An empirical study of trial results. *University of Michigan Journal of Law Reform, 6,* 671-711.

Myers, D. G., & Lamm, H. (1976). The group polarization phenomenon. *Psychological Bulletin, 83,* 602-627.

Padawer-Singer, A. M., Singer, A. N., & Singer, R. (1977). An experimental study of twelve vs. six member juries under unanimous vs. nonunanimous decisions. In B. D. Sales (Ed.), *Psychology in the legal process.* New York: Spectrum.

Penrod, S. D., & Hastie, R. (1979). Models of jury decision making: A critical review, *Psychological Bulletin, 86,* 462-492.

Penrod, S., & Hastie, R. (1980). A computer simulation of jury decision making. *Psychological Review, 87,* 133-159.

Roper, R. T. (1980). Jury size and verdict consistency: "A line has to be drawn somewhere"? *Law & Society Review, 14,* 977-999.

Saks, M. (1977). *Jury verdicts: The role of group size and social decision rule.* Lexington, MA: Lexington Books.

Saks, M. (1982). Innovation and change in the courtroom. In N. Kerr & R. Bray (Eds.), *The psychology of the courtroom* (pp. 325-352). New York: Academic Press.

Stasser, G., Kerr, N. L., & Bray, R. M. (1982). The social psychology of jury deliberations: Structure, process, and product. In N. Kerr & R. Bray (Eds.), *The psychology of the courtroom* (pp. 221-256). New York: Academic Press.

Steiner, I. D. (1972). *Group process and productivity.* New York: Academic Press.

Tanford, S., & Penrod, S. (1983). Computer modeling of influence in the jury: The role of the consistent juror. *Social Psychology Quarterly, 46,* 200-212.

Tanford, S., & Penrod, S. (1984). Social influence model: A formal integration of research on majority and minority influence processes. *Psychological Bulletin, 95,* 189-225.

Williams v. Florida 399 U.S. 78C (1970).

Valenti, A. C., & Downing, L. L. (1975). Differential effects of jury size on verdicts following deliberations as a function of the apparent guilt of a defendant. *Journal of Personality and Social Psychology, 32,* 655-663.

Woodward, J. A., & Overall, J. E. (1976). Nonorthogonal analysis of variance in repeated measures experimental designs. *Educational and Psychological Measurement, 68,* 855-859.

Zeisel, H. (1971). . . . And then there were none: The diminution of the federal jury. *University of Chicago Law Review, 38,* 710-724.

12

INTERACTIONS BETWEEN JURORS AS A FUNCTION OF MAJORITY VS. UNANIMITY DECISION RULES

CHARLAN NEMETH[1,2]
University of California, Berkeley

Many Supreme Court decisions involve numerous psychological assumptions and judgments. And, empirical evidence lacking, the justices are forced to rely on their own judgment as to how people will behave and on the probable consequences of their rulings. A case in point is the recent Supreme Court ruling on less than unanimous juries. Two cases, *Johnson vs. Louisiana* and *Apodaca, Cooper, and Madden vs. Oregon,* were based on appellant's claims that their constitutional rights were violated since they were convicted by less

From *Journal of Applied Social Psychology* (1977) 7(1),38-56. Reprinted with permission of the publisher.

than unanimous juries.[3] Johnson, who was tried for robbery, was convicted by a 9-3 verdict. Apodaca, Cooper, and Madden were convicted respectively of assault with a deadly weapon, burglary in a dwelling, and grand larceny. All three convictions were by less than unanimous juries (11-1, 10-2, and 11-1, respectively). The Court ruled that provisions allowing for less than unanimous verdicts did not violate either due process or the equal protection clause of the Fourteenth Amendment.

In so ruling, the Court remained unconvinced that appellants' constitutional rights had been violated and implied that they were not convinced that the verdict would have been otherwise had the jury been required to deliberate to unanimity. But the issue was really larger than whether or not these specific cases would have been decided otherwise had unanimity been required. The questions were whether the defendants' constitutional rights had been violated, whether the concept of due process had been violated, and whether justice had been administered. In attempting to answer these questions, the justices considered whether or not all viewpoints of the jurors had been fully and justly considered and, specifically, whether minority opinion was, and would be, considered if their votes were not required for the verdict.

In arguing its position, the Court offered some hypotheses regarding social influence processes in jury deliberations and, in particular, the interactions between majority and minority members. Mr. Justice White, delivering the opinion of the Court in *Johnson vs. Louisiana*, argued that the majority would not impose its will on the minority as long as the minority had reasoned arguments.

> We have no grounds for believing that majority jurors, aware of their responsibility and power over the liberty of the defendant, would simply refuse to listen to arguments presented to them in favor of acquittal, terminate discussion, and render a verdict. On the contrary it is far more likely that a juror presenting reasoned argument in favor of acquittal could either have his arguments answered or would carry enough other jurors with him to prevent conviction. A majority will cease discussion and outvote a minority only after reasoned discussion has ceased to have persuasive effect or to serve any other purpose—when a minority, that is, continues to insist upon acquittal without having persuasive reasons in support of its position.[4]

And yet, one is struck by the fact that a majority of five justices concurring in the above psychological premises prevailed over four justices who appear to have persuasive reasons of their own. Mr.

Justice Douglas, with Mr. Justices Marshall and Brennan concurring, offers an alternative view of majority-minority interactions as a result of allowing less than unanimous verdicts.

> Non-unanimous juries need not debate and deliberate as fully as most unanimous juries. As soon as the requisite majority is attained, further consideration is not required either by Oregon or by Louisiana even though the dissident jurors might, if given the chance, be able to convince the majority . . . the collective effort to piece together the puzzle of historical truth . . . is cut short as soon as the requisite majority is reached in Oregon and Louisiana. . . . It is said that there is no evidence that majority jurors will refuse to listen to dissenters whose votes are unneeded for conviction. Yet human experience teaches that polite and academic conversation is no substitute for the earnest and robust argument necessary to reach unanimity.[5]

Thus the majority of justices (5) offer a view of reasonableness and fair-mindedness on the part of all jurors, the majority in particular. The minority of justices (4) maintain that juries can act unreasonably and even improperly. Therefore, safeguards have to be maintained in order to protect minority viewpoints and to promote full consideration of all positions. The justices agree that consideration should be given to all viewpoints. They differ in their assessment of whether consideration would be given to minority viewpoints if unanimity were not required. For Mr. Justice Powell, the "risk . . . . that a jury in a particular case will fail to meet its high responsibility is inherent in any system that commits decisions of guilt or innocence to untrained laymen drawn at random from the community."[6] He places emphasis on the fact that jurors still have the duty to consider minority viewpoints when they have sufficient votes for a verdict. And there is, of course, the reciprocal question of whether or not the minority jurors will defend their position as fully or present it as well when their votes are not needed for the verdict.

Most empirical evidence does not answer these questions directly. Kalven and Zeisel's (1966) classic work shows that verdicts tend to be the position that was initially held by a majority of the jurors. When the "guilty" position was held by a majority (7-11), 86% of their 105 cases went "guilty," 9% hung, and 5% went "not guilty." When the "not guilty" position was held by a majority (7-11), 91% of their 41 cases went "not guilty," 7% hung, and 2% went "guilty." Hence, some argue that verdict outcome would not be appreciably altered if some form of majority rule replaced the unanimity requirement. This type of assumption is further fostered by some experimental studies (e.g., Davis, 1975) which report that a model of 2/3 majority, otherwise hung, is the best fit of the deliberation process. This study as well as others (e.g., Broeder, 1958) find no significant differences in verdict distribution between majority and unanimity decision rules except for the finding that groups assigned the unanimity rule "hang" more often.

The questions that the justices are raising, however, deal more with the nature of the deliberation process and whether all viewpoints are fairly and justly considered than with verdict distribution per se. And they also concern themselves with the symbolic function of the jury, i.e., whether the jurors themselves and the community at large would have as much confidence in a verdict rendered by majority as they would in one rendered by unanimity. Mr. Justice Stewart, with Mr. Justices Brennan and Marshall concurring, raises the possibility that votes could be associated with membership in particular groups and that imposition by a majority would have serious consequences for community confidence.

> Community confidence in the administration of criminal justice cannot but be corroded under a system in which a defendant who is conspicuously identified with a particular group can be acquitted or convicted by a jury split along group lines. The requirements of unanimity and impartial selection thus complement each other in ensuring the fair performance of the vital functions of a criminal court jury.[7]

Thus there are more subtle questions being raised than simply verdict distribution. Will less than unanimity requirements lead to an imposition of will by a majority who has sufficient votes for a verdict? Will the deliberation, even if as long, be as "earnest and robust" under less than unanimity requirements? And will the confidence of the community, or even the confidence of the jurors themselves, in the administration of justice be affected by such changes in decision rule?

The best evidence to address these questions would come from actual court cases where two juries, one under unanimity and the other under majority rule, deliberated the same case or very comparable cases. But this is procedurally impossible and cases are never truly comparable in real life. As a result, we attempted to control that aspect by designing experimental studies. These are obviously limited in generalizability but they can often "put a microscope to details of the deliberation process that cannot be properly observed in an actual court" (Zeisel & Diamond, 1974). Further, experimental studies allow us to control the distribution of initial votes by jurors, thus allowing for an investigation of majority-minority interactions. A sequence of three studies investigating unanimity vs. 2/3 majority rule, are here reported.

For the first two studies, 753 persons were asked their judgment of "guilty" or "not guilty" on a mock case involving first degree murder. Several weeks later, groups of 6 were formed in such a way that 4 persons held the position of "guilty" and 2 persons held the position of "not guilty." There were 19 such groups. Other groups of 6 were formed so that 4 persons held the position of "not guilty" and 2 persons held the position of "guilty." There were 18 such groups. Half of each type of group was required to deliberate to a 2/3 majority. The other half was required to deliberate to unanimity.

In the third study, 84 persons in 7 groups of 12 were brought to a trial in an actual courtroom over which a circuit court judge of the state of Virginia presided. This was in conjunction with the trial court practice course at the University of Virginia Law School.[8]. Live witnesses testified and third-year law students served as prosecution and defense attorneys. Seven cases were used, four criminal and three civil. After viewing the 2-hour trial, the 12 people were returned to deliberation rooms in two groups of 6, randomly chosen. One group was required to deliberate to unanimity; the other was required to deliberate to a 2/3 majority. Deliberations of all three studies were videotaped and the interaction patterns were analyzed.

EXPERIMENTS I AND II[9]

Procedure

Seven hundred fifty-three undergraduates at the University of Virginia, 418 males and 335 females, were given an account of the testimony which presumably was offered at a trial involving first degree murder. The case, very briefly, involved the death of a woman whose husband was charged with first degree murder. The prosecution based its case on two main pieces of evidence. The murder weapon, a fireplace poker, was found to have only two sets of fingerprints on it, those of the wife and those of the husband. A neighbor testified that the wife received a male visitor on the night in question; the husband was seen staring into the windows; an argument ensued; the husband was then seen leaving the house. There was some question as to whether or not the light was sufficient for a positive identification, but the witness testified that she was positive. The defense contended that the husband was away on a business trip. This was confirmed by both his employer and a motel manager. However, the business trip was to a city 150 miles away from his home and the husband could only corroborate his presence at the motel up to 7:10 on the night in question and on the following morning. The wife died at 11:45 p.m.

After carefully reading the testimony, subjects were asked to indicate whether they would vote "guilty" or "not guilty" if they were a juror on the case and, second, whether they believed that the defendant was actually "guilty" or "not guilty" of the crime. Of this sample, 474 subjects (254 male and 220 female) indicated a clear position of either "guilty" or "not guilty," i.e., they both believed and would vote that way. There were 346 (or 73%) of the sample who took the position of "guilty" and 128 (or 27%) who took the position of "not guilty." It was from this population of 474 subjects that the sample for the experiments was drawn.

Persons were allowed to volunteer for the experiment in such a way that a 4 to 2 split initial position would be ensured. Half the groups were created so that, unknown to the individual jurors, 4 persons would vote "guilty" and 2 would vote "not guilty." The other half of the groups would split 4 for "not guilty" and 2 for "guilty." Thirty-seven such groups were created (222 subjects). Nineteen of these groups consisted of a majority (4 persons) taking a "guilty" position and a minority (2 persons) taking a "not guilty" position (Study I), and 18 groups consisted of a majority taking a "not guilty" position and a minority taking a "guilty" position (Study II).

When the 6 subjects for any given group arrived, they were told that they would be deliberating on the same case that they had read 3 weeks earlier. Each subject was given a copy of the case testimony to refresh his or her memory of the evidence. Each group was then given a maximum of 2 hours to come to a decision. Half of the groups were told that they would have to come to a unanimous decision, in other words, everyone had to agree to the verdict. The other half of the groups were told that they needed at least a majority agreement for a verdict, i.e., at least 4 of the 6 people would have to agree to the verdict.

In summary, groups of 6 individuals (composed of both males and females) deliberated on the same case involving a charge of first degree murder in which 4 persons favored one verdict and 2 persons favored the reverse. Subjects were required to come to either a unanimous or a 2/3 majority verdict. The deliberation process was videotaped without the knowledge of the subjects and the interactions were analyzed by various coding methods. When a group reached a verdict, subjects completed a questionnaire which entailed perceptions and impressions of the members of the groups, assessment of the deliberation process, and moods during the process of deliberation. After completion of the questionnaire, subjects were fully debriefed and then dismissed.

Results

The verdict distribution for the two studies can be found in Table 1. Groups required to deliberate to unanimity "hung" significantly more often than those required to reach a 2/3 majority (X^2_{2df} = 41.87, $p <$ .001). There were no differences between majority and unanimity groups in the frequency of "guilty" or "not guilty" verdicts (X^2_{1df} = .18, NS).

It is also clear from Table 1 that an initial majority holding a position of "not guilty" (Study II) is highly likely to prevail (X^2_{1df} = 20.25, $p <$ .001). Eight out of 9 deliberations ended in a "not guilty" verdict when 4 of the 6 jurors initially believed "not guilty." This finding held for both majority and unanimity instructions. When the original majority held the position of "guilty," however, the verdict was as likely to be "not guilty" as "guilty" (X^2_{1df} = .31, NS).

Considering the total amount of time spent in deliberation, an analysis of variance shows a significant main effect for the study ($F_{1,33}$ = 5.74, $p <$ .05). The deliberations in Study I (Majority G) were significantly longer than those in Study II (Majority NG).

There was also a significant study by instruction interaction ($F_{1,33}$ = 8.41, $p <$ .05). In Study I, where the majority favored guilty, groups under unanimity required more time to reach a verdict than did groups under majority instructions. In Study II, where the majority favored not guilty, there were no significant differences between unanimity and majority instructions on deliberation time.

A related dependent variable, termed functional deliberation time, is an indication of the point at which the verdict can be predicted.[10] An analysis of variance on this dependent variable shows a significant main effect for study ($F_{1,33}$ = 12.57, $p <$ .01). Study I had longer functional deliberation time than did Study II.

TABLE 12.1
Verdict Outcome

	Guilty	Not guilty	Hung
Study I (majority G; minority NG)			
Majority	4	5	0
Unanimity	3	2	5
Study II (majority NG; minority G)			
Majority	1	8	0
Unanimity	0	8	1

Note: G = guilty; NG = not guilty.

The videotaped deliberations of our 37 groups were also analyzed by means of a Bales Interaction Analysis. Each comment uttered was coded in terms of who initiated the comment, to whom it was addressed, and which of 12 Bales categories is represented. The Bales categories and a typical example of each category are as follows:

(1) Seems friendly (Ex. "I'm sorry"; "that's a good point")
(2) Dramatization (Ex. "The butler did it," joking; undue exaggeration)
(3) Agrees (Ex. nodding in agreement; "Yes, that's right")
(4) Gives suggestion (Ex. "Let's take a vote"; "let's look at the motel clerk")
(5) Gives opinion (Ex. "I think he's guilty")
(6) Gives information (Ex. "There was one eye witness")
(7) Asks for information (Ex. "Don't they usually give salesmen a special company credit card"; "what time did the guy leave")
(8) Asks for opinion (Ex. "What do you think now"; "what do you think of the fact that Mr. Smith's fingerprints were found on the poker")
(9) Asks for suggestion (Ex. "How shall we get started"; "what do you want to do")
(10) Disagrees (Ex. "You are wrong"; opinions in direct disagreement to a previous recent statement)
(11) Shows tension (Ex. laughter, stuttering, fiddling)
(12) Seems unfriendly (Ex. interruptions, "That's a stupid thing to say")

In this study, there were approximately 4.7 Bales categories coded per minute of deliberation. Two pairs of trained coders were used and

TABLE 12.2
Real and Functional Deliberation Time

	Study I (majority G; minority NG)		Study II (majority NG; minority G)	
	Majority	Unanimity	Majority	Unanimity
Real deliberation time	37.889_a	68.300_b	41.556_a	29.778_a
Functional deliberation time	16.889_c	25.550_c	8.000_d	9.778_d

Note: G = guilty; NG = not guilty. Subscripts in common indicate that the differences are not significant at the .05 level.

reliability checks showed a .95 correlation between pairs of coders. Analyses of variance on each of the 12 Bales categories showed main effects for instruction, i.e., majority vs. unanimity, on categories 1, 5, 6, 10, and 12, and on total number of comments ($p < .05$). In general, groups under unanimity instructions showed more friendliness, gave more opinions, gave more information, disagreed more, and showed more unfriendliness (this being mainly interruptions) than did groups under majority instructions ($p < .05$). With the exception of disagreement, these findings hold mainly for Study I, i.e., where the majority favored guilty and the minority favored not guilty. There are significant interactions between study and instruction on categories 1, 3, 4, 5, 6, 11, and 12 ($p < .05$). As with the deliberation times, the differences between unanimity and majority decision rules are particularly great for Study I. It is when the minority favors the "not guilty" position that the unanimity deliberations are characterized by more friendliness and unfriendliness, by more agreement, by giving more suggestions, more opinions, and more information relative to the majority decision rule. With regard to disagreement, however, the groups under unanimity instructions disagreed more than did groups under majority instructions regardless of the position of the minority.

There were no main effects for the initiator, i.e., whether the majority or the minority initiated more comments. In general, the majority and the minority members uttered approximately the same number of total comments and initiated approximately the same number of comments per Bales category. However, there were a number of main effects for the target of a comment. A minority member was significantly more likely to be the object of comments that are coded as agreement, suggestions, opinions, information, disagreement, and tension release. These are categories 3, 4, 5, 6, 10, and 11, respectively ($p < .05$). The group as a whole tended to be addressed for dramatization; it was most asked for information and suggestions; and it was least likely to be interrupted (categories 2, 7, 9, and 12, respectively). All the above reported findings are significant at the .05 level.

In considering public and private consensus, analyses were first completed on the final ballot. As shown in Table 3, the groups required to deliberate to unanimity followed that instruction. In all 13 groups under unanimity instructions which did not "hang," the voice vote on the final ballot was 6-0. Under majority requirements, only 5 out of 18 deliberations reached full consensus. Thus even of those 5 groups in Study I under majority decision rule where the minority prevailed, i.e., the verdict went "not guilty," none was characterized by a unanimous voice vote. In these groups, a majority of 4 prevailed in 3 of the groups and a majority of 5 prevailed in 2 of the groups. In other words, the minority swayed just enough votes to constitute a majority and then imposed their decision on the remaining individuals.

Private opinions which were assessed by individual responses on a questionnaire were also more effectively changed under unanimity than under majority instructions. As one might expect from the voice votes, private opinion was less likely to coincide with the verdict under majority decision rule than under unanimity ($X^2_{3df} = 7.5$, $p < .06$).

While the above private opinions were taken from the individual juror's belief of "guilty" or "not guilty" on a postexperimental questionnaire, individuals were also asked their subjective agreement with the verdict on a 7-point scale. Analysis of their responses shows the same results as above. Subjects who deliberated under the unanimity requirement indicated that they agreed more with the group verdict than did subjects who deliberated under a 2/3 majority rule ($F_{1,196} = 4.74$, $p < .05$). Individuals under unanimity requirements also tended more to agree that justice had been administered than individuals required to deliberate to 2/3 majority ($F_{1,214} = 2.13$, $p < .15$), and they reported feeling more uncomfortable during the deliberation ($F_{1,214} = 4.00$, $p < .05$).

There were also some significant findings between majority and minority members of these experimental groups. Members of the initial majority, be that "guilty" or "not guilty," were more likely to say that they agreed with the verdict, that the deliberation was fair, that the group was open to differing views, and that justice had been

TABLE 12.3
Public and Private Consensus

	Majority				Unanimity			
	6–0	5–1	4–2	3–3	6–0	5–1	4–2	3–3
Voice vote	5	9	4	0	13	0	0	0 [6 "hung"]
Private opinion	3	3	8	4	4	6	3	0 [6 "hung"]

administered than were the members of the initial minority ($p < .05$). This, of course, attests to the difficult status of minority members and the fact that the group verdicts, by and large, went in the direction held by the majority.

EXPERIMENT III

In an attempt to generalize the preceding findings regarding majority vs. unanimity requirements to trial proceedings, a third experiment was conducted in conjunction with the Law School of the University of Virginia. Third-year law students at the University of Virginia participate in a trial court practice course in which trials are heard in an actual courtroom before a judge.

Scripts are used for the testimony of live witnesses. Attorneys for the plaintiff and the defense give opening and closing arguments; objections are made and ruled upon; live witnesses appear and are cross-examined; and instructions are given by the judge to the jury.

For this experiment, 102 subjects, volunteers from the under-graduate student population at the University of Virginia, were brought to the courtroom. Approximately 15 were brought to each trial. Twelve were chosen at random to sit in the jury box and as many as three challenges were allowed. Each group of 12 viewed one of 7 cases, 3 of which were criminal and 4 were civil. There were thus 84 subjects. The cases consisted of the following:

Commonwealth vs. Snodgrass: first degree murder
Commonwealth vs. Wright: arson
Commonwealth vs. Adams: first degree murder
Malinsky vs. Shifflett: slander
Allen vs. Starr Construction Co.: personal injury

TABLE 12.4
Perceptions of Due Process

	Majority	Unanimity	F
Agreement with verdict	3.231	2.552	4.74
Justice administered	3.509	3.219	2.13
Felt comfortable	2.833	3.386	4.00

Note: The lower the number, the higher the perception of agreement, justice administered, and comfort.

Mason vs. Prudential Life Insurance Co.: suicide; payment of insurance
Foster vs. Herkimer: contract default

Each trial lasted approximately 2 hours. Upon completion of the
trial, the 12 jurors were returned to the Psychology Building for
deliberation. They were randomly assigned to one of two groups, one
being required to deliberate to unanimity and the other required to
deliberate to at least a 2/3 majority. Deliberations were videotaped
without the knowledge of the subjects involved.

Results

As can be seen in Table 5, there were no significant differences in
verdict as a result of the instructional requirements. Statistical tests
comparing verdicts for the plaintiff vs. the defense as a function of
unanimity vs. majority rule were nonsignificant ($X^2 = 1.17$, *NS*). In fact,
there were only two (out of the 7) cases where the majority and
unanimity instructions differed in verdict (Snodgrass and Allen). In
both of these cases, the initial vote of the jury differed in the unanimity
and majority rule groups by chance. Both unanimity groups initially
had a 3 to 3 split, whereas their counterpart, given majority instructions, had a 4 to 2 split in which the majority prevailed. Thus the
differences between the two instructional sets are quite likely due to
the initial vote distribution differences. It is also clear that this
tendency for the majority to prevail was found in every group studied.
Of the 7 groups that initially had a majority/minority split in vote, all
seven reached a verdict in agreement with the initial majority ($X^2_{1df} =
7.0$ $p < .01$).

TABLE 12.5
Initial Votes and Group Verdicts

Case	Majority		Unanimity	
	Initial vote	Final verdict	Verdict vote	Final verdict
Snodgrass	2 G; 4 NG	NG	3 G; 3 NG	G (voluntary manslaughter
Wright	6 NG	NG	6 NG	NG
Adams	1 G; 5 NG	NG	6NG	NG
Malinsky	4 Pl.; 2 Def.	Pl.	4 Pl.; 2 Def.	Pl.
Allen	2 Pl.; 4 Def.	Def.	3 Pl.; 3 Def.	Pl.
Mason	3 Pl.; 3 Def.	Pl.	4 Pl.; 2 Def.	Pl.
Foster	3 Pl.; 3 Def.	Def.	2 Pl.; 4 Def.	Def

Note: G = guilty; NG = not guilty; Pl. = plaintiff; Def. = defendant.

In terms of the amount of the time spent in deliberation, Table 6 shows that there was no statistically significant difference between the groups assigned unanimity and those assigned majority rule ($F_{1,33}$ = 1.64, NS). The direction, however, is that groups required to deliberate to unanimity deliberated longer than those assigned a 2/3 majority rule. For the four cases where we had complete tapes of both majority and unanimity deliberations, the mean deliberation time for majority groups was 29.25, whereas the mean deliberation time for groups under unanimity was 35 min.

Functional deliberation time, though, differed significantly on the basis of instruction (t_6 = 2.29, $p < .01$). Groups under 2/3 majority instructions had a shorter functional deliberation time (4.5 min.) than those under unanimity requirements (10 min). Further, the functional deliberation time was higher for unanimity groups than for majority groups in every one of these four cases.

As with the previous studies, influence was measured by voice vote at the end of the deliberation, private opinion, subjective agreement with the verdict, and perceptions of the influence processes that occurred. Voice vote was significantly affected by the instructional set. As instructed, groups under unanimity instructions reached public agreement. All groups had voice votes of 6 to 0. Groups required to deliberate to at least 2/3 majority, however, rarely reached full verbal consensus. This difference is statistically significant (X^2_{2df} = 7.32, $p < .05$).

TABLE 12.6
Real (and Functional) Deliberation Time

Case	Majority	Unanimity
Snodgrass	1(1)	20(3)
Starr	18(2)	36(3)
Foster	52(8)	18(16)
Mason	46(7)	66(18)
Mean time	29.25(4.5)	35(10)
Adams	13(4)	— *
Malinsky	— *	19(3)
Wright	— *	12(1)

*Due to equipment failures, these three tapes were incomplete and are excluded from the analyses.

The number of persons who changed their opinion in the direction of the group verdict was also found to be affected by instructional set. The mean number of changes in the direction of the group verdict was .429 for groups deliberating under 2/3 majority rule, whereas it was 1.429 for groups deliberating to unanimity. Considering the number of changes relative to the number of possible changes, the mean for the 2/3 majority groups was .500 and the mean for the unanimity groups was 2.00. The difference between these means is statistically significant (X^2_{1df} = 3.77, $p < .06$). Hence, more influence was occurring in the unanimity groups than in the majority groups.

This finding of greater influence in the unanimity groups is further corroborated by the individuals' subjective judgments of agreement with the verdict. Individuals required to deliberate to unanimity reported more agreement with the verdict than did individuals required to deliberate to 2/3 majority ($F_{1,36}$ = 11.9, $p < .01$).

Further, individuals perceived the process of influence in their deliberation differently, depending on the instructional set. Asked to characterize the influence process in their group deliberation (the choices being compromise, majority influence, minority influence, polarization, and no influence), individuals deliberating to a 2/3 majority perceived the process to be one of "no influence," whereas those deliberating to unanimity were more likely to characterize the process as one of "majority influence." The difference in perceptions as a function of instructional set is statistically significant (X^2_{4df} = 17.5, $p < .01$).

TABLE 12.7
Voice Vote

Case	Majority	Unanimity
Snodgrass	2 G; 4 NG	6 G
Wright	—*	6 NG
Adams	6 NG	—*
Malinsky	—*	6 Pl.
Allen	2 Pl.; 4 Def.	6 Pl.
Mason	4 Pl.; 2 Def.	6 Pl.
Foster	2 Pl.; 4 Def.	6 Def.

Note: G = guilty; NG = not guilty; Pl. = plaintiff; Def. = defendant.
*Due to equipment failures, these three tapes were incomplete and therefore excluded from analysis.

In analyzing the deliberation process, we again coded every comment in terms of who uttered the comment, to whom it was addressed, and which of the 12 Bales categories it represented. None of the Bales categories was found to differ significantly on the basis of unanimity vs. majority instructions. The small sample size, of course, makes it difficult to reach statistical significance, particularly given the high variability between cases.

On the questionnaire following the deliberation, individuals who were required to deliberate to unanimity reported that they felt less comfortable during the deliberation than those required to deliberate to 2/3 majority ($F_{1,36}$ = 4.1, $p < .05$). And, again, those required to deliberate to unanimity had a tendency to feel that "justice had been administered" relative to those under 2/3 majority rule ($F_{1,36}$ = 3.4, $p < .10$).

DISCUSSION

In these studies, we attempted to ascertain the effects of allowing less than unanimous juries on both the verdict distribution and on the deliberation process itself. In one set of studies, we conducted controlled experiments. This allowed for an analysis of unanimity vs. 2/3 majority requirements with essentially all other things being equal. The initial vote split was controlled (being 4 to 2 for these studies). The same case was used and the information was presented in the same

TABLE 12.8
Number of Persons Who Changed Their Opinions
in the Direction of the Verdict

Case	Majority	Unanimity
Snodgrass	0 (of 2 possible)	3 (of 3 possible)
Wright	0 (of none possible)	0 (of none possible)
Adams	1 (of 1 possible)	0 (of none possible)
Shifflett	0 (of 2 possible)	2 (of 2 possible)
Allen	0 (of 2 possible)	2 (of 3 possible)
Mason	1 (of 3 possible)	1 (of 2 possible)
Foster	1 (of 3 possible)	2 (of 2 possible)

way. While such studies allow for the control that is needed to make particular kinds of assessments, we also attempted to see if the results could be generalized to different kinds of cases and to situations which are closer to an actual trial situation. Therefore, we also manipulated instructions set in a courtroom setting using civil as well as criminal cases. Both the similarities and the differences between these two sets of studies will be examined.

Neither set of studies demonstrated any significant effect of instruction (unanimity vs. 2/3 majority) on verdict distribution, i.e., the tendency to convict or acquit. However, the experimental studies demonstrated that groups required to deliberate to unanimity "hung" significantly more often than those required to deliberate to 2/3 majority. These findings confirm previous results by other researchers. Our trial simulation study, however, resulted in no "hung" juries. So, it appears that if the jury does hang, this is likely to occur more frequently under unanimity requirements.

While the actual verdict was not seen to be significantly affected by instructional set, both sets of studies indicate some major differences in terms of the influence processes that occur. Groups required to deliberate to unanimity do in fact reach verbal consensus on a verdict. Those deliberating under the requirement of 2/3 majority rarely deliberate until all individuals assent to the verdict. A number of them stopped the deliberation when the required number was reached.

This tendency to stop short of full consensus when nonunanimity is allowed has several consequences. One is that both real and functional deliberation time appear to be shortened. This consequence of unanimity was particularly apparent when the majority favored "guilty" and the minority favored "not guilty." Here, the minority prevailed in a number of groups. And it was in this situation that unanimity led to longer deliberation times as well as tended to lengthen functional deliberation times, i.e., the time before the verdict could be predicted. In the reverse situation—i.e., where the majority favored "not guilty" and the minority favored "guilty"—the majority almost always prevailed. Here, there were no significant differences between majority and unanimity requirements on deliberation times. In the trial court study, unanimity led to longer functional deliberation times. The pattern, therefore, is that unanimity fosters the type of deliberation that prolongs the decision. In this sense, it may encourage the "robust argument" that Mr. Justice Douglas sought in jury deliberations.

Another consequence of the lack of verbal consensus in groups that are not required to deliberate to unanimity is that the individual jurors are less convinced of the final verdict. Fewer opinions were changed during the course of deliberation and individuals indicated less agreement with the group verdict when nonunanimity was allowed. Further, individuals were less likely to feel that justice had been administered under nonunanimity requirements.

While the above conclusions were corroborated by both sets of studies—i.e., the controlled experimental studies and the simulated trial study—there were also some differences between the studies. The two experimental studies indicated that groups under unanimity requirements gave more agreement and disagreement, gave more opinions and information, and were both more friendly and unfriendly toward each other. These findings were not corroborated by the simulated trial study. This is in part due to the small sample size and to the high variability between cases. It may also be partly due to the initial vote distribution in the groups. The increase in giving opinions and information, agreeing, being friendly and unfriendly in unanimity groups held mainly for the situation where a 2/3 majority favored "guilty" and a 1/3 minority favored "not guilty." It was in this situation that the instructions for 2/3 majority vs. unanimity had the most significant effect. To the extent that our courtroom trials rarely had this type of initial vote split, it is possible that the heightened interaction stimulated by a requirement of unanimity holds mainly for the situation where a significant minority favors "not guilty."

Another major difference between the studies concerns the role of the minority in effecting influence. The experimental studies demonstrated a fairly high tendency for the minority to prevail. However, this occurred only when the minority took the position of "not guilty." It is likely that the position of "not guilty" may be easier to defend, all other things being equal, since it is easier to raise a "reasonable doubt" than to convince a person beyond such doubt. However, the reader must also be cautioned that this subject population might orient to a "not guilty" position more easily than the general population.[11]

In contrast to the effectiveness of the minority (when taking the "not guilty" position) in the experimental studies, however, the simulated trials showed no such tendency. In all of those trials, the initial majority prevailed if such a majority existed. This is consistent with findings previously reported by Kalven and Zeisel (1966).

While such differences have implications both for the methodologies used in research on jury behavior as well as practical applications thereof, the findings that were consistent across these different procedures should be reemphasized. There appears to be a tendency for at least these mock juries to not deliberate to unanimity unless they are required to do so. They do not reach consensus; they are less effective in convincing all members of the appropriateness of the verdict; they do not deliberate as long or as "robust"; and they leave members with the feeling that justice has not been administered.

If we remember the Supreme Court decisions, the importance of reasoned discussion, lack of imposition of opinion, and the symbolic function of the jury were not overlooked by either the affirming or the dissenting justices in *Johnson vs. Louisiana* and *Apodaca et al. vs. Oregon*. The justices differed in terms of their assumptions regarding how nonunanimity would affect these processes. The affirming justices assumed that a majority would not outvote a minority that it did not need for a verdict without first exhausting reasoned discussion, whereas the dissenting justices feared that the minority would be outvoted if unanimity were not required. And the dissenting justices feared that "polite and academic conversation" might take the place of "earnest and robust argument" once the requisite majority was achieved. The affirming justices believed that community confidence would not be greatly affected by the allowance of nonunanimity, whereas the dissenting justices feared it might be "corroded."

The present studies tend to corroborate the fears of the dissenting justices. The majority appears to outvote the minority, not necessarily as soon as the requisite majority is reached, but sooner than would be the case under unanimity requirements. The groups allowed nonunanimity tended to stop short of achieving even verbal consensus among their members. And groups required to deliberate to unanimity were more effective in actually persuading their members that the final verdict was the appropriate one. Unanimity also seemed to lead to more robust argument and less polite conversation if one can assume that our measure of functional deliberation time comes close to making that distinction. Groups under unanimity requirements tended to take longer to reach a point where the verdict could be predicted than did groups allowed to deliberate to 2/3 majority. And the jurors' own confidence that justice had been administered (if not that of the community at large) was greater when unanimity was required.

Thus there is some suggestion that allowing nonunanimity may decrease the robustness of the arguments and the conflict engendered. It may also hamper the ability of the minority to persuade the majority, particularly since even verbal consensus is rarely achieved. However, one should also not overlook the importance of the symbolic function of the jury. As Tribe (1971) has pointed out,

> rules of trial procedure in particular have importance largely as expressive entities and only in part as means of influencing independently significant conduct and outcomes. . . . [They] can serve a vital role as . . . a reminder to the community of the principles it holds important. The presumption of innocence, the rights to counsel . . . matter not only as devices for achieving or avoiding certain kinds of trial outcomes, but also as affirmations of respect for the accused as a human being— affirmations that remind him and the public about the sort of society we want to become and, indeed, about the sort of society we are.

Thus the considerations involved in unanimity vs. nonunanimity in jury deliberation are not simply whether or not the actual verdicts are significantly altered. This appears not to occur, at least on a large scale. What may well be altered is the belief on the part of the jurors that they have deliberated until all persons have agreed, that they feel that the verdict was appropriate, and that they have a sense that justice has been administered. If the jurors themselves feel that these values have not been implemented, the very important symbolic function of the trial by jury may suffer, not only for the jurors themselves, but for the community at large.

NOTES

1. Preparation of this manuscript was completed while the author was a Visiting Fellow at Battelle Seattle Research Center. The studies were supported by National Institutes of Mental Health Grants 1 R01 MH 25374-01 and 1 R01 MH 25374-02.

2. Requests for reprints should be sent to Charlan Nemeth, Department of Psychology, University of California Berkeley, CA 94720.

3. In Louisiana, cases in which the punishment may be at hard labor are tried by a jury of 5 persons who must be unanimous in their verdict; cases in which the punishment is necessarily at hard labor are tried by 12 persons, 9 of whom must concur in the verdict; cases where the punishment may be capital are tried by 12 persons who must be unanimous. In Oregon, criminal cases require 10 of the 12 persons in agreement to render a verdict (except for first degree murder, where unanimity is required).

4. *Johnson vs. Louisiana* 92 S. Ct. at 1624. These are assumptions that would not be shared by many social scientists. See, for example, Schachter, S., and Moscovici, S. and Nemeth, C., 1974.

5. *Johnson vs. Louisiana* 92 S. Ct. at 1647, 1648.

6. *Johnson vs. Louisiana* 92 S. Ct. at 1642.

7. *Johnson vs. Louisiana* 92 S. Ct. at 1627.

8. Appreciation is extended to H. Lane Kneedler of the University of Virginia Law School and to the Honorable Joshua Robinson for their cooperation.

9. Gratitude is expressed to Jeffrey Endicott, Joel Wachtler, Edward Hodge, Patrick Huyghe, David Doggett, and John Sullivan for their help in conducting these studies and analyzing the results.

10. Some researchers, e.g., L. Richard Hoffman (personal communication), have utilized an analysis known as valence where each comment is coded in terms of which position is favored and a tabulation is kept over time. If one cumulates the comments for "guilty" and "not guilty," respectively, regardless of who utters the comments, one finds in the present study that, when the difference between such sums exceeds 7, all but one of the 37 group verdicts can be predicted. Since, at this point, the group verdict is essentially a fait accompli, we considered the amount of time to reach this difference of 7 to be the functional deliberation time.

11. The University of Virginia student population, however, does not describe itself as "liberal". Given four categories (radical, liberal, moderate, and conservative), half described themselves as "moderate," one-third described themselves as "liberal," and one-sixth described themselves as "conservative."

REFERENCES

Broeder, D. W. The University of Chicago jury project. *Nebraska Law Review,* 1958, *38,* 744-761.

Davis, J. H., Kerr, N. L., Atkin, R. S., Holt, R. & Meek, D. The decision process of 6- and 12-person mock juries assigned unanimous and 2/3 majority rules. *Journal of Personality and Social Psychology,* 1975, *32,* 1-14.

Hoffman, L. R. Personal communication, 1900?

Kalven, H. & Zeisel, H. *The American jury.* Boston: Little, Brown, 1966.

Moscovici, S., & Nemeth, C. Social influence: II. Minority influence. In C. Nemeth (Ed.), *Social psychology: Classic and contemporary integrations.* Chicago: Rand McNally, 1974.

Schachter, S. Deviation, rejection and communication. *Journal of Abnormal and Social Psychology,* 1951, *46,* 190-207.

Tribe, L. Trial by mathematics: Precision and ritual in the legal process. *Harvard Law Review*, 1971, *84*, 1391-1392.

Zeisel, H., & Diamond, S. S. Convincing empirical evidence on the six-member jury. *University of Chicago Law Review*, 1974, *41*, 281-295.

SECTION IV

SUMMARY

Why a 12-person jury, as opposed to some other number? The traditional reliance on 12 people may be based on Christ's 12 apostles; we are not sure. We do know that the requirement of a unanimous majority was established in Great Britain in the fourteenth century. Both regulations were extended to North America as a part of British colonization.

These procedures were never really challenged or modified until 1966, when Great Britain changed its jury decision rule so that only a majority of 10 out of 12 was required. In response to a challenge from a losing defendant in the state of Florida, the Supreme Court established its ruling that juries numbering as few as six were constitutionally acceptable.

If six is acceptable, what about an even smaller jury? Claude Ballew, manager of an adult theater in Atlanta, had been convicted of obscenity by a five-person Georgia jury. (His theater had been showing the X-rated film *Behind the Green Door*.) Ballew appealed his conviction, claiming that five people was too small a number to be representative. In its *Ballew v. Georgia* (1978) decision, the Court agreed; it would permit no reductions in size below six. This decision is also noteworthy on other grounds; as Saks (1982) observes, "This opinion is, in fact, by far the Supreme Court's most thoroughgoing consideration and discussion of social science research to date" (p. 335). Ironically, the empirical studies on which the Court's decision was based were comparisons of juries composed of 12 people versus those composed of 6, much like some of those described in chapter 11.

No one had done studies comparing 6-person and 5-person juries, the real issue in the *Ballew* case.

The Court's decision about the acceptability of a nonunanimous decision rule is disturbing for other reasons. As chapter 12 and other empirical studies indicate, the fundamental process of deliberating is altered when the rules are changed and unanimity is not required. Jurors in the minority feel, justifiably, that their opinions are not given fair treatment. The Court's justification of a nonunanimous decision rule is disturbing for another reason, too; it misinterpreted a basic social science finding. In the *Williams* decision the Court invoked Solomon Asch's (1956) conformity experiment as *support* for its conclusion that the minority juror in a 6-to-1 split was under no more pressure to change than was a minority juror in a 10-to-2 split (McConahay, 1978). Surely a label of "law and psychology in conflict" seems appropriate when a legal decision is partly based on a misreading of research results.

In summary, we believe that in their desire to increase efficiency and reduce costs, the courts have tampered with the deliberative process. Maintenance of a requirement of a unanimous verdict would force further resolution of disagreements, and leave the original minority more satisfied. It would also lead to a binding together of all opinions within the jury.

The courts have also neglected to consider the interaction of these two reforms. Consider the three-level system in operation in Louisiana. Capital crimes are tried before 12-person juries in which unanimity is required, but serious crimes are tried before 12-person juries with a requirement that only 9 must concur, and lesser crimes are tried before 5-person unanimous juries. The appellant in the *Johnson v. Louisiana* (1972) case argued that by having been tried under a 9-of-12 decision rule, he had received less protection from conviction than did defendants with 12-of-12 or 5-of-5 decision rules. The Court chose to ignore the possible interactive effects of group size and decision rule, but social scientists have not. For example, Saks and Ostrom (1975) developed a model that permits the computation of the probability that a verdict will be reached for any level of certainty of defendant's guilt in a jury of any size, operating under any decision rule. According to their model, the 12-of-12 jury is least likely to reach a verdict, the 5-of-5 more likely, and the 9-of-12 most likely. Thus the appellant, Johnson, was apparently correct; it would have been less likely that the jury would have convicted him, had he had a 12-of-12 or 5-of-5 decision rule.

REFERENCES

Asch, S. E. (1956). Studies of independence and submission to group pressure: I. A minority of one against a unanimous majority. *Psychological Monographs, 70* (Whole No. 417).

Ballew v. Georgia, 435 U.S. 233 (1978).

Johnson v. Louisiana, 32 L. Ed. 2d 152 (1972).

McConahay, J. B. (1978). Jury size, decision rule, and the null hypothesis. *Contemporary Psychology, 23,* 171-172.

Saks, M. J. (1982). Innovation and change in the courtroom. In N. L. Kerr & R. M. Bray (Eds.), *The psychology of the courtroom* (pp. 325-352). New York: Academic Press.

Saks, M. J., & Ostrom, T. M. (1975). Jury size and consensus requirements: The laws of probability v. the laws of the land. *Journal of Contemporary Law, 1,* 163.

About the Editors

Lawrence S. Wrightsman is Professor of Psychology at the University of Kansas, where he served as department chairperson from 1976 to 1981. For the academic year 1981-1982 he was Intra-University Visiting Professor at the University of Kansas School of Law. He received a B.A. and an M.A. from Southern Methodist University and a Ph.D. in social psychology from the University of Minnesota. The author or editor of 10 books (including, with Saul M. Kassin, *The Psychology of Evidence and Trial Procedure,* Sage, 1985) and numerous journal articles, he has also served as President of the Society for the Psychological Study of Social Issues (SPSSI) and the Society of Personality and Social Psychology (Division 8 of the American Psychological Association). He currently directs the Kansas Jury Research Project and teaches a course on jury decision making to law students there.

Saul M. Kassin is Associate Professor of Psychology at Williams College. He received his Ph.D. in personality and social psychology at the University of Connecticut after which he served as a postdoctoral research fellow at the University of Kansas and on the faculty at Purdue University. He is the author of numerous journal articles and book chapters, and has coedited three other books, including *The Psychology of Evidence and Trial Procedure* (Sage, 1985). Interested in various aspects of jury decision making and trial procedures, he has recently held a Judicial Fellowship at the U.S. Supreme Court (1984-1985) and an NIMH Postdoctoral Research position at Stanford University (1985-1986).

Cynthia E. Willis is currently a doctoral student in the Department of Psychology at the University of Kansas. She holds a B.A. degree from Washburn University and an M.A. degree from the University of

Kansas. She has prepared affidavits for appeals to the Kansas Supreme Court and has taught a psychology-and-the-law course at the U.S. Penitentiary in Leavenworth, Kansas. Her interests concentrate on jury decision making, especially jurors' reactions to the testimony of eyewitnesses.

NOTES

NOTES

NOTES

NOTES

DATE DUE		
JUL 0 8 1992		
JUN 0 3 1994		
NOV 3 0 1996		
OCT 1 7 1998		
NOV 2 9 1998		
MAR 2 2 1999		